Rachel Hill-Brown

CW01083574

Intergenera **ion**

Intergenerational Religious Education

MODELS, THEORY, AND PRESCRIPTION FOR INTERAGE LIFE AND LEARNING IN THE FAITH COMMUNITY

JAMES W. WHITE

Religious Education Press
Birmingham, Alabama

Copyright © 1988 by Religious Education Press
All rights reserved

No part of this publication may be reproduced, stored in a retrieval system, or transmitted, in any form or by any means, electronic, photocopying, recording, or otherwise, without the prior written permission of the publisher.

Library of Congress Cataloging-in-Publication Data

White, James W.
Intergenerational religious education: models, theory, and prescription for interage life and learning in the faith community/James W. White.
Includes index.
ISBN 0-89135-067-5
1. Intergenerational Christian education. 2. Intergenerational religious education. I. Title.
BV1579.W45 1988 88-23310
268'.4—dc19 CIP

Acknowledgment: "Developmental Periods in Early and Middle Adulthood" table is from *The Seasons of a Man's Life* by Daniel J. Levinson et al. Copyright © 1978 by Daniel J. Levinson. Reprinted by permission Alfred A Knopf, Inc.

Religious Education Press, Inc.
5316 Meadow Brook Road
Birmingham, Alabama 35243
10 9 8 7 6 5 4 3

Religious Education Press publishes books exclusively in religious education and in areas closely related to religious education. It is committed to enhancing and professionalizing religious education through the publication of serious, significant, and scholarly works.

PUBLISHER TO THE PROFESSION

DEDICATION

For the worker and the warrior
The lover and the liar
For the native
And the wanderer in time
For the maker and the user
The mother and her son
I am looking for my family
And all of you are mine
—John Denver, "I Want to Live."

Abby, Adrienne, Alex, Alice, Alison, Amanda, Amber, Amy, Andy, Anita, Ann(e,ie), Barb(ara), Barbara Lee, Ben, Beth, Betsy, Betty, Bev(erly), Bill, Blythe, Bob, Bobbi(e,ye,yi), Bonner. Bonnie, Boyd, Brenda, Brian, Brownie, Bruce, Bryan, Carl(a), Carol(e), Cary, Catherine, Cathi(y), Ceil, Charlotte, Charles(ie,ey), Cheril(lynne), Cheryl, Chris(ti,tine,topher), Courtney, Chuck, Cindi(y), Clara(ence), Cora, Craig, Dalyce, Dan(iel,ny), Dannika, Dave(id), Debbi(ie,y), Devon, Diane, Dick, Don, Dora, Dorothy, Doug, Ed, Edith, Eileen, Elaine, Eleanor, Ellen, Emma Kathryn, Emma Mae, Eric(k), Ernie, Estie, Evelyn, Fernando, Fran, Frank, Fred, Freia, Gale(yle), Galen, Gary, Gaye, Gene, George, Gertrude, Gib, Gil, Graham, Gretchen, Hal, Hank, Harold, Harry, Hart, Heidi, Helen, Herb, Howie, Ilona, Inga, Irene, Jack, Jan(ne,ie), Jeannette, Jen(mie,my), Joan(ie,ne,y), di(y), Juli(a), June, Kahla, Kathi(y,leen), Karl, **to for WITH** (n,et), Jan(ice,yce), Jeanni(e,fer,y), Jerry, Jill, Jim-John(ny), Jon, Judith, Ju-Kara, Karen, Kat, Kate, Kay(e), Kelley(i), Ken(t),

Kim(berly), Kirk, Kirsten, Kitten, Kurt, Larry, Laurie, Lee, LeeAnne, Leigh, Lenora, Les(lie), Linda, Lisa, Lois, Lola, Loree, Lorna, Lori, Lou(ise), Lu(cille,cretia), Lyn(n,ne), Marci, Maren, Marsha, Margaret, Mark, Marlys, Marnie, Martha, Marti, Matt (hew), Mary, Mary Joyce, Mary Lee, Meg, Mel(anie), Melissa, Merle, Michael, Mike, Miki, Milton, Mim, Mitzi, Molly, Nancy, Nini, Norm, O.L., Opal, Oren, Oz, Pam(ela), Paul, Pat(ti,ty,tricia), Peg, Penny, Pete(r), Phil, Pinkie, Polly, Ralph, Ray, Reid, Reina, Richard, Rob(ert,i), Robin, Rochelle, Roddy, Roger, Roy, Ruth, Sally, Sandi(y), Sandra Jean, Sara(h), Satone, Scott, Sevier, Sheila, Sherri(y), Sidney, Stacy, Stan, Steve(n,phen), Stu, Sue(zi, san,sanne), Sunny, Tim, Todd, Tom, Trish, Tula, Vi, Virginia, Walker, Wes, Win(i), and YOU who blessed me and I did not remember.

Contents

Preface

By the shores of Lake Dillon, where the Blue River comes in, we were fishing when my friend asked, "Well, what would a book on this look like?" A few hours later, the first outline of the present volume was down on a yellow legal pad. Ten years later the book is finished.

This book describes what religious institutions of America are and can be doing in the way of programed *intergenerational* (IG) life and learning. After providing an analysis of our isolating social situation and a descriptive review of the field of *intergenerational religious education* (IGRE), these pages lay out theoretical bases for cross-generational action and programs. This occurs in Parts I and II. In Part III, I present a comprehensive Total Parish Paradigm for IGRE with chapters for further developing the same in the religious communities. Some readers may want to start with the Appendix.

There are many, many people to thank for help and assistance along the way to completion. I acknowledge most of them—but all too slightly—in the dedication. I just know I am extremely grateful for understandably impatient family and friends who kept asking, in Pope Julius II's words to Michelangelo regarding work on the Sistine Chapel: "When will you make an end?"

Well, it now ends . . . sort of (as the work of IGRE goes on). And here is a serious book based on a lot of very enjoyable "being with" which, I trust, will enable more good togetherness across the generations in the years to come.

JAMES W. WHITE
Denver, Colorado

PART I
Models

Chapter 1

Separation and Congregation

If rightly responsive to the opening of the twenty-first century, faith communities will more and more be engaged in intergenerational religious education. "*Inter*Generational *R*eligious *E*ducation" (IGRE) is the descriptive phrase for what churches and synagogues have done for a long time, whether they called it by this name or something else. It is what we need to continue to do—and better—in the years ahead.

The reason IGRE seems mandated is because of a need which can be told of in two social analyses. One is on the changing family, underscoring the context in which individuals and families now live. The second analysis is of institutions and structures which create and maintain separation-by-age-group, with growing isolation and insulation of persons, a major contemporary problem. Following these analyses I will argue that faith communities are uniquely positioned to take steps to draw people together across the generations for the well-being of individuals, families, and the larger society.

SOCIAL ANALYSIS I: THE CHANGING FAMILY

Religious institutions with attendant intergenerational (IG) relationships do not exist in a vacuum. The life of any given congregation needs to be placed in the context of its wider social/cultural matrix. Understanding this matrix may help religious leaders in developing creative and helpful responses to meet the faith development needs of people.

As a general diagnosis of what is transpiring in our time, I argue that *segregation, isolation, and insulation of persons are prevailing conditions.* We are not so much talking about racial segregation (real as that is) as speaking of compartmentalization by age group and speaking of

1

the atomization of individuals within those groups. In our time the "ties that bind" generations one to another are too few and everywhere tenuous. Let us consider some of the changes that have occurred.

Changes in "Family"

Family units today, first of all, are smaller in size than in previous decades. In 1950 the average number of children in a family with children was four. By 1980, 1.89 children had become the norm for families with children. The size of family ("family" being two or more persons living together who are related by marriage, blood, or adoption) decreased from 3.67 per family in 1960 to 3.23 per family in 1985. The average number of persons per household ("household" includes persons living alone as well as in families) in the 1980s was 2.74 people per household, down from 3.14 per household where it had been in 1970. The big change in household type is in single person households going from 13 percent of all households in 1960 to 24 percent of all households in 1985. The trend toward more single-family households and fewer offspring per family (in families with children) seems to be continuing. The point to be made is simply that there are not as many people today in families and households, and, so, fewer people are available to be related and interactive in extended multigenerational family life.[1]

Mobility

Second, families—especially middle- and upper-middle-class families—tend toward geographical mobility. Statistics indicate that every year 25 percent of the families in the United States move beyond the borders of the county in which they formerly lived. Many move thousands of miles. This mobility is possible, in part, precisely because families are smaller. As a usual consequence of such moves, it is no longer possible to see and be with grandparents, uncles, cousins, and so on, to the extent such was possible in less transient days. In 1950 one of every two homes had a live-in grandparent. Today only 2 percent of the homes have a grandparent present in the home. With the separation by miles it is harder for kinsfolk to become "significant others" in a child's world—or in an adult's. In an earlier age of familial proximity, relatives served more easily as a source of information, support, and ventilation for individuals. A child when bored or frustrated could walk over to his or her nearby aunt's home for interested attention. These things do not work quite so well by phone. In terms of social skills, youngsters may not have liked an Aunt Gussie or Cousin Dizzy whom they saw regularly, but at least they knew what such relatives were like—and how to get around them. The latter is no mean social skill. Life-pilgrimage observer, James Fowler, notes that geographical and social mobility "represent the disruption of systems of interaction that formed and maintained societal consensus regarding worthy lifestyles and aspirations."[2] If such is the case, we are the poorer for it.

Divorce

Marital separation and divorce is a third factor attenuating family ties. Fifty percent of first marriages today end in divorce. The percentage is higher for second marriages. One effect of husband-wife breakups is on children. Twenty percent of the children who are under five today live in one-parent households. More than a third of the children born in the 1970s will spend part of their childhood living with a single parent. During critical formative years, then, they are often cut off from developing multiple primary bonds. Children, parents, and related others in a divorce are all inhibited from developing significant cross-generational interpersonal relationships.

Couple Families

In the late 1940s and for a decade or so thereafter, the American family may have been described rightly as "nuclear." It was "Mummy'n-Daddy'n-Kids," a pretty tight grouping. The mid-century nuclear family was distinct from the family of earlier decades which was "extended" to include a larger number of relatives in the grouping. Some people think that today we are moving toward a family condition which sociologist Eugene Litwak describes as "weak or dissolving."[3] That could be true, but I think Edward Shorter's notion of the family is more accurate. He claims the "couple family" is the prevailing pattern.[4] Certainly the statistics show that in the 1980 population census of persons fifteen years of age and older, six of ten are married. Most of the couples are *without* children at home, as many are either young working, empty-nest, or retired. The couple phenomenon creates a further factor loosening generational bonds, for couple families typically are made up by partners near the same age. Cross-generational transactions are not going to occur in such households.

Family—of whatever composition—let us be clear, is not unimportant or devalued. A 1987 survey of Americans taken by *U.S.A. Today* found that "making the family work is still our No. 1 priority."[5] We value family and we value being married. Though divorce is high, more people in the United States are marrying than ever before. Of the persons who divorce, 75 percent remarry and 50 percent within three years. Hence, couple families are the prevailing norm. In 1890 only 63.1 percent of the population were, had been, or would ever be married. In

1980, however, 94.5 percent are, have been, or will be married. Such data hardly reflect a diminution of the value of being married. Then too, though divorce is more common today, children are not being orphaned. In fact, more children live with one or both their parents now than at any time in the past. That is undoubtedly a plus.

It is erroneous, then, to suggest that families are devalued or necessarily declining, as compared with some former golden age. Clarissa Atkinson notes that "the notion of the steady unchanging American family may be true as myth, but it is false as history."[6] It is more nearly true what Talcott Parsons says: The family has become "a more specialized agency than ever before."[7]

Individualism

The specialization of the family's work has much to do with providing individual persons, young and old, with emotional support and a sense of value and worth. It is no mean responsibility. Social ethicist James Nelson puts it this way: "There is one thing central to the family which no other institution can offer: emotional and physical intimacy, nurture, and support. And that is a need which will never go out of style. It is absolutely vital for genuinely human life."[8] That need goes on, but families are changing. John Scanzoni rightly observes why: *"The changes result from the erosion of ancient traditions—traditions that favored the family as an institution over its individual members. During past eras, the institution of the family had priority over the individual; and for the sake of the family the individual was called upon to sacrifice."*[9] This pattern of individual sacrifice for the collective family, Scanzoni notes, has changed: personal individual rights and needs have taken greater ascendancy. Now, however, the individual may find him or herself increasingly isolated and the family not able to do its best sustaining work for individuals, itself, or others.

SOCIAL ANALYSIS II: INSTITUTIONS FOSTERING SEPARATION

The ability of the institution of the family to fulfill its specialized function is restricted in part because so many other institutions in which family members are involved actually pull them apart. Evelyn Mills Duvall says, "There was time when family members spent most of their time together. They worked side by side on the old home place. They played together or with their closest neighbors from nearby farms. Today family members are scattered."[10] They are scattered, I submit, by and through numerous prevailing social patterns and institutions. It is almost a conspiracy.

Work

As first example of a primary agency in on the compartmentalizing action to segregate, isolate, and insulate, consider employment arrangement. Industrialization and urbanization brought about work locations which are distinct and distant from where people live. Spouse and children now know very little about what bread-winning family members "do for a living" or the place where they do it.

Let me share a personal illustration to the point: When I took a position as executive director (interpreter and fund-raiser) for three theological schools in the midwest—Chicago, United (in Minneapolis), and Eden (in St. Louis) Theological Seminaries—my working office initially was in Milwaukee. I moved there to work, but my family stayed in Denver so our eldest daughter could finish high school. The next fall she went to college. She told me at Christmas that, when asked what her father did, she said, "He's assistant dean of the Wisconsin Divinity School." There is no such position or school!

In truth, children's perceptions of adults at work were different "back in the olden days" on the family farm or in the family store. Then people tended to live on the work premises—or vice versa. Lawyers, dentists, blacksmiths, and so on, regularly had their businesses in their homes. Closeness of barn/shop/office/study to domicile meant several important things. One was that children got a clearer picture of adults going about everyday life. Especially they learned what "working" was. In fact, they usually worked right alongside their father/mother/sister/uncle. Moreover, children working alongside generational others got a sense of making an essential contribution to the welfare of the family. They knew themselves to be a part of a unit of production rather than a unit for consumption.

Besides doing vital work together, family members could engage in significant conversation. Psychologist and family educator Stephen Glenn claims that in 1930 a child spent three to four hours a day in interaction with various adult members of his or her family. Today, Glenn says, the time is reduced to "fourteen and one-half minutes, of which twelve and one-half minutes are spent with parents issuing warnings or correcting things that have gone wrong."[11]

Besides talking with parents and others while working alongside, children witnessed how others go about planning. They participated in decision making. They experienced how espoused values are and are not put into practice. They had better opportunity to learn firsthand what it means to be a responsible adult. Likewise, adults learned from children in important ways. Children, for one thing, have a heuristically helpful three-letter word for their elders: "Why?"

By close contact with real children, adults kept better touch with their own "child" self. They observed children closeup, interacted with them and reflected upon the interactions. Children were seldom out of mind because they were seldom out of sight. Such interage transmittals are not possible in most of today's work worlds. Work and home life are separated by miles and by, at least, a third of the day.

Schools

Schools are a second illustration of how institutions create generational separation. Long gone are the days of the one room interage school house. Now we put children into grades-by-age. Frequently they are placed on narrow ability tracks: "You, Cindy, are a sky bird; and you, Danny, you go with the bulldozers."

Even as work today pulls parents out of a residential setting, schools do the same for children. Bussing in city schools—as bussing in rural areas—makes the home-school distance even greater. Little or no contact with parents or nonteacher elders is possible during the day.

In addition to distance, there is time separation. Schooling today, as compared with schooling at the turn of the century, involves more hours per day (a compulsory seven to nine as opposed to a loose three to four hours). Schooling involves more days per year (a state mandated 180 vs. post harvest/preplanting "good weather" days). Schooling involves more years per lifetime (on average thirteen total years, and going up, rather than six).[12] The meaning of this increase in the number of hours/ days/years of schooling is that children simply have less overall time available to talk with nonteacher older or younger people—assuming, of course that those others were around. The latch-key child comes home to an empty house, watches television alone or talks on the phone to a same-age peer. Sociologist Phillipe Aries says that "family and school together removed the child from adult society."[13]

Regarding conversation in school, the basic message most heard is "DON'T!": "Don't talk to your neighbor" . . . "Don't make a fuss" . . . "Don't touch one another" . . . "Hush now" . . . "Be quiet!" Such statements are delivered every hour/day/year when one is in school. When students do manage to talk—and, of course, they do—it is with someone their own age. Youth are increasingly out of communication with anyone except peer-group others. When I was in campus ministry, a co-ed once acknowledged that she had not spoken face-to-face with anyone under-eighteen or over-twenty-three in three weeks! Such is part of the problem which contemporary schooling creates and aggravates.

Early in this century there was hope that the public schools might promote community cohesiveness, relating to and relating *all* members of society. It was thought that the schools could put people of various classes, races, and ages into democratic conversation. That hope has fallen so short of realization that is hardly worth trying to resuscitate.

There are several reasons for the failure. One is that we had not anticipated what "compulsory attendance" does to people's feeling about an institution. Schools have become "buildings of dread" for many. Former attendees scrupulously avoid the places to which in childhood they were mandatorily sent. With a widespread feeling of fear about them, schools cannot do much to attract multiple generations to their halls for civil or edifying discourse.

The advent of the large, monolithic public school system brought with it impersonality, incomprehensible bureaucracy, computer processing, authoritarianism, drivenness, alienation, and more. "Small is beautiful," but small is not what our schools are. I think they are best imaged as large factories where raw materials, stacked in bundles of thirty, are 1) processed by a worker for fifty minutes, 2) conveyed to another landing for an additional treatment till six such movements/treatments are completed, and the products are 3) rendered out in the afternoon. They will be reprocessed the next day. Understandably, schools and schooling are not attractive to students, parents, the taxpaying public, or even to teachers. Schools are institutions not facilitating the kinds of interhuman meetings needed. (What exceptions there are to this bleak picture of the schools are noted in the last major section of this chapter.)

Residence

A third institution contributing to generational separation is housing. There was a time in America's small-town past when rich and poor, as well as young and old, lived in relative proximity to one another. A retired Mr. Wilson living next door to a preschool Dennis the Menace was fairly common. Today, however, housing developments and covenants being what they are, most folk never see other than "their own kind" in terms of economics, skin color, educational level, and age. A drive through city neighborhoods on a warm spring Saturday afternoon will reveal distinct median ages for people in each development tract.

Moreover, during the week, our youngest societal members are housed in day-care and, often, evening-care centers. Our eldest societal members are located all week and every week in nondescript nursing homes, out of sight/mind/way. In between those age extremes, single young adults live in downtown apartments and in no-children/no-pet condominiums. Widowed older adults live in efficiency retirement complexes. And so on. As deplorable as mobile home "parks" may be in terms of space and safety, they could be the widest age-range human communities in America today and, as such, among the healthiest.

Government

A fourth institution capable of facilitating multigenerational life is government(s). That governments do so is seldom the reality. Colonial

New England town meetings and Norman Rockwell paintings notwithstanding, our political institutions characteristically are not sources for significant intergenerational activity. In small town America it may be that governments still do create projects and parades that involve a wide spectrum of the ages, but that opportunity is not an option for the vast majority of urban/suburban people. Exceptions to note regarding government are two programs of the Volunteers of America (formerly VISTA) where 1) volunteer seniors tell of their "lived history" to school children and 2) over-sixty poor people are paid to perform foster grandparenting roles for disabled and institutionalized children.[14] Most often, though, government programs are age-focused as in youth job corps, ADC, or senior citizen centers. So far as I know, no political party in the United States ever had a plank in its platform endorsing intergenerational programs. Even more regrettably, there is no National Support Policy for families. Ad hoc responses are all we have.

Clubs and Organizations

Constituting a fifth category of age-separating institutions are various voluntary associations and orders. They too pull generations apart. Grandma has her bridge group, dad his fraternal meetings, mom P.E.O., Bud his Led Zeppelin devotee group, and Sally, Blue Birds. The clubs and organizations of America tend to be rather age-specific, that is, narrow. Exceptions—or activities within organizations which do make exceptions—are noted below.

Sports

Though they do not have to be restrictive, sports separate by age too. Retired people do conscientious walking and shuffle-board playing. Middle-aged men are on the golf links during the day while younger men bang the racquetball before and after work. Middle-aged women are into aerobic dance. Teenagers tend to monopolize lacrosse. For children there is little league soccer—the leagues determined by the birth date (and sex). While the "sports" category has some exceptions making for positive multi-age mixing, all too regularly recreational pursuits are defined for restricted peer group age ranges.

The Media

Irony of ironies, not the least of the contributors to generational separation is the *communications* industry. Television may be the worst divider. A visitor from outer space could observe human beings watching television. The space visitor might think people were doing something together. The set's real effect, though, is to promote atomization. Americans, on average, watch five hours of television every day. They sit transfixed and silent. In this one-way communication viewers receive input, but their own responses do not directly influence the programing. More significantly for this analysis, viewers seldom relate to others beside them. In discussing TV-in-the-home with people, one finds that the set is seldom turned off—even for meals. The norm seems to be that the "tube" is the center of each eater's attention.

With television's advent, traditional parlor activities, board games, and card playing have been woefully undercut. These had been mainstay fare for intergenerational life in earlier decades. Grandad, mom, and Junior could all play dominoes together. Today's Junior likely has not heard of the game and would misunderstand the XX's on the scratch pad.

Still considering the communications industry, we note that modern living environments are usually noise-filled. Radios, tape decks, and the stereo typically are all on at once. Each person is hearing his or her own age-tailored audio. Richard Blake describes our situation as follows: "Radio listening has become an essentially private experience. No longer do people gather round the radio, but each person creates a private acoustical shell. Finally, lightweight headphones isolate the individual from his surrounding environment completely. Watch a group of new-wired listeners standing elbow-to-elbow on the corner waiting for the light to change, each following the beat of his own drummer, with street noise and fellow listeners effectively filtered out."[15] Humans trying to voice or hear something of cognitive, interpersonal, or lifestyle significance are almost unable to do so.

The things which we do communicate are too often trivial, only occasionally informative. People may have a conversation, for example, about football. Such a conversation is worth having, but so what "if the Jets get into the semifinals . . ."? Contrast such talk with the conversations taking place in the last century around the family dinner table of William and Henry James. As reported, the James family meals were characterized by lively and informative exchanges precipitated by the stimulating guests whom their father regularly brought home. The listening, probing, sharing, arguing, and learning were intensive. The meal often lasted well into the evening.[16] By comparison, today's around-the-barbeque-grill-banter, which is usually age divided, pales into banality. Moreover, our homes do not have the "boarders, lodgers, servants, hired hands, apprentices, and other employees" found in many homes of the last century.[17]

Entertainment Industry

In 1900 Americans were still experiencing quite widely the Chautauqua Movement. It sent all kinds of speakers, musicians, acts, and talent into the hinterlands of North America. Entertainment predominated in the Chautauqua assemblies, but there were also things of intellectual substance. The content and quality of these mobile assemblies doubtless varied, but it is not difficult to imagine that the offerings surpassed much of today's "Weekend World of Entertainment." More importantly, one would find in the Chautauqua assemblies several generations of people. Afterward the assembly-goers would be able to consider and evaluate in mutual exchange what they had seen and heard. Whether it had been an orchestral concert or a maudlin "Hearth and Heaven" lecture, that offering would be discussed on the ride back home.

Such post-event, shared reflections are not so likely to happen in response to today's entertainment fare. Why? Because most of our entertainment is age-specific, as suggested by the G/PG/R/X ratings for movies. The movies and other entertainments, such as rock concerts for youth and nostalgic Big Band Era dances for older adults divide more than they unite generations.

Social Events

One last consideration: Everywhere we look modern-day social activities tend toward age exclusiveness. Play at the infant care center, a fifth grader's attic slumber party, teenage "cruising," a college kegger, adult male poker parties, Beyond Divorce socials, couples' marathon bridge groups, Senior Citizen Bingo Nights, and all the rest give multiple generations little to do in common or talk about. Week-long camp meetings, county fairs, box supper-square dance evenings where such occurred in the past are almost gone from the face of the land.

> A glance at the diverse cultures and experiential worlds of the age groups (e.g., the young's discos and bars, subcultural movements like the Teds, Mods, Punks, etc., and the senior citizens' culture and old-age homes of the elderly) underscores the impression of effective separation and alienation tendencies. Advertising, marketing, and the manufacture of age-specific consumer goods (from toys and textiles to furniture, food, hobby and sporting goods, music, etc.) encourage these tendencies and contribute to a consolidation of age-specific world experience. And this consolidation in turn implies the formation of age-specific spaces . . . as, for example, children's playgrounds, which find their counterparts in youth centers for adolescents and leisure centers for the elderly. Due to the relatively monofunctional specialization of these spaces . . . they reinforce the tendency towards age-specific segregation. Thus the conditions are created for such phenomena as speechlessness and estrangement in the interaction between age and generational groups.[18]

The institutions of earlier eras which facilitated significant interpersonal sharing and meaningful cross-age learning do not do so today. We are segregated, atomized, insulated, and often ignorant. Something is needed to turn our social/cultural situation in a new interrelated direction.

AN INSTITUTION TO BRING PEOPLE TOGETHER: THE CHURCH/SYNAGOGUE

Our social and cultural condition may not be quite as dismal as the analyses above sound. The "social animal" which *Homo sapiens* is finds a way to bridge individual isolation. Consider the following generational connections: Many "modified extended families" still exist and flourish. Grandparents get taught Atari "Pac Man" games. Nieces learn how to sew. Family businesses continue. Long distance calls are placed to parents. Some schools are community centers. People live next door to quite older or quite younger others. In today's expensive housing market more single young adults reenter their parents's empty nest. Mothers and daughters play tennis. At holidays the airports are jammed by family travelers. And so forth. There are many exceptions to the previously described picture. The National Opinion Poll Research Center concluded from a survey that "more American children knew their grandparents and visit them regularly than in the past," though what "past" was not specified. The survey takers say, "The three-generation family may never have been stronger or closer than it is today," which actually supports earlier studies (predating 1970) which show that three generations are in "almost weekly interkin visiting, and in a vast nexus of help exchange of mutual aid."[19]

So, intergenerational relations have by no means disappeared.

Connections ongoing and existing notwithstanding, the general characterization of society as segregated by age still stands. Insulation/isolation are too real as the previous testimony and studies indicate. Such may be especially so for more mobile, middle-, and upper-middle class persons.

The question to ask is, "Who or what will deliver us from this bond to isolation?"

The answer proposed in this book is the church/synagogue. The faith community which is intergenerational in its life will promote lifestyle growth in individuals which affirms human connectedness.

What institution other than the church/synagogue is there to take on the task? So far we have said and seen—with exceptions to be noted below—that housing, employment, schools, government, social clubs, athletics, communications, entertainment, and social activities do not foster generational connectedness. In looking around at still other institutions of major significance in our society, no relief will be forthcoming from labor unions, the military, medicine, advertising, transportation,

high-tech industry, or business. There really are not many modern institutions which hold generations together in helpful ways . . . but, there
are some.

Age-Binding Institutions

On a societal-wide basis it may be that the institution of *sports* comes
the closest of any to facilitating multiple generational association. Participatory sports is activity which young and old do together. In a fanciful
vein, consider: "The family that golfs together rolfs together" or "The
folks who play ball go to the wall together" or "Those who ski stones
mend bones together." In truth, people of various ages can cross-country
ski, fish, swim, play croquet or golf, knock the volleyball, snowmobile,
and so forth together. They often do.

Spectator sports are not to be excluded from the plus category either.
Going to see the Broncos, Bucs, or Braves play is doing something open
to all ages together and positive. The main problem, though, is that
spectator sports are about matters quite transitory. Often they are diver-
sionary from genuine human tasks.

Closely related to sports, *leisure activities* are frequently cross-generational. "Shopping" is the number one pastime of women in America.
Such activity can be and often is intergenerational. Grandmothers,
mothers, and daughters can do it together and have fun doing it. There
is sharing of values. That the values primarily revolve around consu-
merism and appearance, however, is no cause for general rejoicing.

In recent years, some *education-related programs* of an IG nature
have been generated. They have positive portents. In reviewing the
literature on secular IG development, Kaye Parnell notes, "A number
of programs exist at the national, state, and local levels that bring young
and old together."[20] Besides the previously noted governmental Foster
Grandparent Program, she highlights the "Generations Together Program" at the University of Pittsburgh. There Sally Newman and colleagues have launched, among other things, a Senior Citizen School
Volunteer Program and a Senior Citizen Artists Resource program.
They have put older people in over seventy schools in western Pennsyl-
vania. Generations Together also initiated a "Youth in Service to Elders" program. Similar activity is replicated in other places, such as the
University of Georgia where students in social work and other fields are
assigned to work with and learn from the elderly.[21] Elsewhere, a ten
million dollar private foundation grant enabled seven major school
systems in the United States to start IG educational programs. Sally
Newman in 1983 said, "There are an estimated 300,000 people over 60
years volunteering in schools throughout the U. S. and working directly
with several million children and youth between five and eighteen years

of age."[22] Across the nation there is also a growing Elderhostel program which enables older citizens to return to campuses, take courses, and mix with younger people.

So, some good starts have been made in the wider society. Sadly, most of these efforts do not involve persons from the middle years of life.

In addition to sports, leisure activities, and school programs, there are *voluntary associations* operational today. In them significant interage life and learning may also occur. Y-Indian Guides for fathers and sons, mother-daughter dinners of Blue Birds, women's clubs which integrate several ages of women, and even Veterans' Halls where men from "differing wars of life" meet are illustrative examples of voluntary associations which bring people of different ages together. Sometimes a sewing group of Job's Daughters or, to repeat Wood Allen's description, a "Divorced Fathers and Sons Annual Baseball Game" or a trip to the seashore or eating out or vacation camping or a lake cruise will bring more than two generations of people together for positive exchange. These associations are not unerringly ideal (e.g., the Veterans' Hall), but they are better than many other collectivities. They are the secular matrices which make and keep life human.

Religious Institutions

Now enter the church/synagogue. It too is a voluntary organization. *The faith community is, I suggest, the institution best suited to facilitate significant cross-generational life and learning.* Many people belong to religious institutions. In fact, over 60 percent of the population in the United States is formally affiliated. Moreover, people tend to join for a lifetime. Most importantly they draw meaning and find significant satisfaction from that affiliation. Stephen Cutler, for example, found that among the dozens of voluntary associations in which older persons participate, only membership in religiously affiliated groups emerges as a significant predictor of life satisfaction.[23]

John Scanzoni, among others, makes the case for the faith community being positioned to be most helpful when he writes: "The church may be the one institution in our society uniquely suited to raise aspirations aimed at new family traditions, and to provide a framework for their attainment."[24] Family Clusters educator, Margaret Sawin, says much the same thing—and powerfully: "The Church is the only agency in Western civilization which has all the members of the family as part of its clientele. It is the only organized group which reaches persons through the complete life cycle from birth to death."[25] Susan Lidums echoes Sawin: "The church is the one institution in society that touches people at all the significant stages in the life cycle—from birth to death, and all the touchstones in between."[26] The church/synagogue then, is "unique" (as still another observer notes)[27] in that people of all ages are drawn together on a regular basis.

With all its potential, unfortunately, the church/synagogue has a less than glorious track record in bringing people of multiple ages together, enabling them to learn something worthwhile with and from each other.

Why so inept?

Because faith communities too often have followed rather than led.

If the public schools, for example, put people in narrow age-range classes, then so have churches and synagogues. From "Crib Room" to "Golden Age Class" we have organized religious education by age group—and, just as often, by sex. Witness: the "Senior Men's Bible Class." We design and implement graded religious curriculum in ways similar to that of the public schools. We build our "religious education wings" on the model of the schools, which built theirs a la the model of the factory.

There is some value in graded and traditionally structured learning. I will indicate what, when, and where later. By and large, though, we have aped the model of public education in religious education. Persons are thus less made "in the image of God" because of it.

Beyond educational structures per se, there are still other church/synagogue groups which are overly age-specific. Young "Sarah's Circle" and the Older "Homemakers' Circle" do not go around together. The former is busy unisexing God and the latter making cancer bandages for *H*im. Elsewhere, there are music programs with choirs organized by age: Cherubs, Children's, Youth, Men's, Women's, Adult, and so on. In sum, religious institutions often foster generational separation.

The church/synagogue, to state the obvious, is *not* a very good institution for fostering generational cohesiveness. BUT, just like democracy, it is "better than whatever is in second place." Even at its worst our earthen vessel institution is doing a better job than any other of contemporary society in bringing non- and family-related persons of different ages together for worship, fellowship, life, and learning. At least, congregations *want* to be inclusive. Regularly we define ourselves as family-oriented places. One church sign said it rather blatantly: "WELCOME TO THE HAPPY FAMILY CHURCH WITH FRIENDLY FATHER BOB!" Many more congregations try to convey the same idea more subtly. It is certainly true that the one place to which all family members together can come and leave is the religious meeting house. Since attendance is normally voluntary, people usually develop a more positive mind-set about the institution. In the long run, the faith community's voluntary status creates a people favorably disposed toward helping one another grow.

A church/synagogue may not *do* anything which is intentionally intergenerational in its life. Even so, on Sabbat/Sunday people of different generations may be *seen*—and seen by each other—going to worship. In itself that is good. Frequently these generational others are *acknowledged* in a get-acquainted moment in the worship service. In a post-service refreshments time there can be *conversation,* pedantic or profound. In short, the faith communities are already involved in the intergenerational existence. Often there is sharing and learning from and with one another.

I believe—and this is the main contention of this book—*we can do a much better job in facilitating intergenerational life and learning, leading to faith lifestyle that creates wholeness in persons and the world.* If we did IGRE better, it would be a boon both to the church/synagogue and to individual persons in our fragmented, isolating, and "dumbing" society. As an example, consider the possibility of including "older alienated young adults" into wider corporate life. Sociologist Barbara Hargrove says in this regard:

> Ideally. . . the churches are the institutions of modern society most capable of bringing the dislocated generation back into contact with the rest of society and of making that contact fruitful in a mutual acceptance of the task of adapting our culture to its times. In the intergenerational community of the church it is possible to put a human face on our understanding of where we have been and where we seem to be heading. . . .
>
> It may be the churches, at this point in history, have a unique ability to save these generations for a society that cannot be maintained without them.[28]

This is true for other generations as well. One of the ways the faith community can effectively "save," minister to, teach the world—even the on-looking unaffiliated is through intentional programs of IGRE.

There are, of course, millions of people who are unaffiliated with religious institutions. I have but few ideas on which secular institutions, other than the few matrices mentioned earlier, can facilitate intergenerational meetings for them. Effective IGRE programs in faith communities, though, might attract some of these extramural persons. On this score educationist Gabriel Moran argues that the church should "demonstrate" IGRE for the society.[29] Equally important, congregations may stimulate their own members to begin building intergenerational structures in other arenas of societal life. That would be a wonderful lifestyle outcome, well worth prescribing and filling!

Notes

1. Statistical Information from the U. S. Department of Commerce, Bureau of Census, *Household and Family Characteristics: March, 1980* (Washington, D. C.: U. S. Government Printing Office, 1981), pp. 1 and 7; and from

"America's Changing Families," *EHS Today* (Oakbrook, Ill.: Evangelical Health Systems, Fall, 1986), p. 15.

2. James W. Fowler, *Becoming Adult, Becoming Christian: Adult Development and Christian Faith* (San Francisco: Harper & Row, 1984), p. 5.

3. Eugene Litwak, "Extended Kin Relations in an Industrial Society," in *Social Structure and the Family: Generational Relations*, ed. Ethel Shanas and Gordon F. Streibe (Englewood Cliffs, N.J.: Prentice Hall, 1965), p. 308.

4. Edward Shorter, "Changing from Nuclear Nest to Intimate Couple: A Response to Amitai Etzioni," *Journal of Current Social Issues*, ed. Paul Sherry 14:1 (Winter, 1977), p. 10.

5. Julia Lawler, Denise Kelette, and Mei-Mei Chan, "Family Ties in U. S. A. Know No Bounds," *U. S. A. Today*, April 13, 1987, p. 1.

6. See Clarissa Atkinson, "The Myth of the American Family," *A. D. 1982* 11:5 (May, 1982), p. 16.

7. Talcott Parsons, "The Stability of the American Family System," in *The Individual, Marriage, and the Family: Current Perspectives*, ed. Lloyd Saxton (Belmont, Calif.: Wadsworth, 1970), p. 367.

8. James B. Nelson, "The Future of the Family: An Address," *Theological Markings* (A United Theological Seminary Journal), (Spring, 1982), pp. 5-6.

9. John Scanzoni, "Family: Crisis or Change?" *The Christian Century* (August 12-19, 1981), p. 796.

10. Evelyn Mills Duvall, "Families Reflect Social Change," in *The Individual, Marriage and the Family*, p. 358.

11. H. Stephen Glenn, *Strengthening the Family* (Washington, D. C.: Potomac Press, 1981), p. 5. (I have personally asked and twice written Glenn for the research documentation on these statistics but have received no reply. His data, then, may be more impressionistic than verified.)

12. H. Stephen Glenn and Joel W. Warner say, regarding earlier eras, "Parents formed groups, pooled resources, and 'invented' schools. But school was two to three hours a day once or twice a week because no more time away from work could be afforded by the family." See their "The Developmental Approach to Preventing Problem Dependencies" (Washington, D. C.: Family Development Institute, 1982), p. 149 (mimeographed). Wildred E. Woolridge, in an article entitled "The Barefoot School," printed in *The Ozarks Mountaineer* (November-December, 1984), says that in Missouri at the turn of the century, the school year "started on Monday after the Fourth of July and usually finished by Christmas," p. 40.

13. Phillipe Aries, "The Family" in *Readings in the Sociology of the Family*, ed. Bert N. Adams and Thomas Weirath (Chicago: Markham, 1971), p. 10.

14. See the publications, "Loving, Caring, Sharing, Living" (Washington, D.C.: U. S. Government Printing Office, October, 1976, No. 4500.7) and "FGP—Foster Grandparent Program" (Washington, D. C.: U. S. Government Printing Office, April, 1979, No. 4400.1). In Denver, Colorado, with a population of one and a half million people, in 1985 there were 113 foster grandparents. So reported Linda Dee, Project Director, Foster Grandparent Program, Denver, Colorado, via personal telephone conversation, January 15, 1985.

15. Richard A. Blake, "Condominiums in the Global Village," *America* 146:22 (June 5, 1982), pp. 433-436.

16. F. O. Matthiessen, *The James Family: Including Selections from the Writ-

ings of Henry James, Senior, William, Henry & Alice James (New York: Knopf, 1961), p. 71.
17. Michael Dahlin, "Perspectives in Family Life in 1900," *Gerontologist* 20:1 (1980), p. 99.
18. Vjenka Garms-Homolova, Erika M. Hoerning, and Doris Schaeffer, eds., *Intergenerational Relationships* (Lewiston, N.Y.: Hogrefe, 1984), p. 154.
19. "American Family Closer Than Ever," *The Denver Post,* September 26, 1985, p. 1. And, Reuben Hill and others, *Family Development in Three Generations: A Longitudinal Study of Changing Family Patterns of Planning and Achievement* (Cambridge, Mass.: Schenkman, 1970), p. 78. Sometimes these attributional and survey data are hard to reconcile with other studies. Michael Dahlin, writing on the elderly, says, "Old people probably spent considerable more time with their grandchildren in 1900 than they do today." See his "Perspectives on the Family Life of Elderly in 1900," *The Gerontologist* 20:1 (1980), p. 104. Certainly Social Security provisions and pension plans have facilitated movement away from multigenerational living and toward solitary living.
20. Kaye Parnell, "Young and Old Together: A Literature Review," *Childhood Education* 53:3 (January, 1980), p. 185.
21. See Martha Baum, Sally Newman, and Barbara K. Shore, "Learning About Aging Through Intergenerational Experiences," *Gerontology and Geriatrics Education* 2:4 (Summer, 1982), p. 314.
22. Sally Newman, "Intergenerational Programs: Their Role in American Society" (Pittsburgh: Generations Together, May, 1983), p. 4 (mimeographed).
23. Stephen J. Cutler, "Membership in Different Types of Voluntary Associations and Psychological Well-Being," *Gerontologist* 14:4 (1976), p. 336.
24. Scanzoni, "Family," *Christian Century,* p. 799.
25. Margaret M. Sawin, *Family Enrichment with Family Clusters* (Valley Forge, Pa.: Judson, 1979), p. 22.
26. Susan B. Lidums, *Church Family Ministry: Changing Loneliness to Fellowship in the Church* (St. Louis: Concordia, 1985), p. 9.
27. "Unique" is Carol A. Wehrheim's word in "The Extended Family," *The Family Album: Resources for Family Life Ministry* (New York: United Church Board for Homeland Ministries, 1983), p. C-3.
28. Barbara Hargrove, "Religion for a Dislocated Generation," *The Iliff Review* 37:2 (Spring, 1980), pp. 21-22.
29. Gabriel Moran, *Interplay: A Theory of Religion and Education* (Winona, Minn.: Saint Mary's College Press, 1981), p. 117.

Chapter 2

IGRE Is . . .
(an Exposition of Terms)

In the first chapter "intergenerational religious education" (IGRE) was spoken of but without definition. This chapter provides it.

INTERGENERATIONAL RELIGIOUS EDUCATION IS TWO OR MORE DIFFERENT AGE GROUPS OF PEOPLE IN A RELIGIOUS COMMUNITY TOGETHER LEARNING/GROWING/ LIVING IN FAITH THROUGH IN-COMMON-EXPERIENCES, PARALLEL-LEARNING, CONTRIBUTIVE-OCCASIONS, AND INTERACTIVE-SHARING.

This definition can be displayed almost as a sentence diagramed or a mathematical formula. See Figure 1.

*I*NTER		=TWO OR MORE
*G*ENERATIONAL		=DIFFERENT AGE GROUPS OF PEOPLE
*R*ELIGIOUS	is	=IN A RELIGIOUS COMMUNITY TOGETHER
*E*DUCATION		=LEARNING/GROWING/LIVING IN FAITH

through

In-Common-Experiences
Parallel-Learning
Contributive-Occasions and
Interactive-Sharing

Figure 1. "IGRE" Definition Diagramed.

The major equations in the figure's definition of IGRE are enfleshed in this chapter. Supplementary words, concepts, and phrases are provided to make clear what I, G, R, and E mean. We will begin with discussion about the meaning of "generation," then move to explain "inter" in "intergenerational," go on to commentary on "education," and end with treatment of "religious."

First, though, a word about alternative definitions of IGRE.

Definitions of "Intergenerational Religious Education"

Though widely practiced, by no means is "intergenerational religious education" a well-known term. In the 1984 *Dictionary of Religious Education,* the concept is not even mentioned. Nothing resembling it is offered.[1] Such an omission is passing strange in that "intergenerational education" as a concept is centuries old, and it has been spoken of in the religious education literature for a score of years.

Even so, there are a few definitions of IGRE per se (or of similar concepts) available in the literature. They are worth reviewing as insightful variations and alternative definitions. Their presentation will clarify, broadly speaking, what is talked about in this volume.

In speaking of an "intergenerational experience," the editors of the *Quarterly Intergenerational Guide* say, "An 'intergenerational experience' is one in which two or more generations come together intentionally for an occasion of worship, fellowship, study, decision making, mission, or any combination of these functions."[2] George Koehler, who has done extensive work in the field, says a "setting for intergenerational education" is "a planned opportunity for teaching-learning as a faith community in which a major purpose is to engage persons of two or more generations in shared experiences/interaction, caring, and mutual responsibility for learning."[3] In speaking in their guidebook about "Intergenerational Education," Don and Pat Griggs simply talk about "involving mixed groups in common learning experiences"[4] as the essence of generations learning together. Educationalist Charles Foster in reviewing the field says, "Intergenerational education gathers people from at least two and preferably three or more age groups or generations into a teaching-learning process in which all members give and receive from the experience."[5]

Obviously there is common phraseology in these several definitions. Together with the definition offered in this book, they point to a similar approach to faith and learning. The definition offered in these pages, though, may be more adequate in that it is both descriptive of the field and prescriptive for ways to proceed in the further development of IGRE.

We begin with explication of "generation."

G . . . GENERATIONAL . . .
DIFFERENT AGE GROUPS OF PEOPLE

To gain understanding of "generation," the first consideration is that of years-involved-to-constitute-a-generation. In common conversation people seem to assume that a generation is the interval between the age of parents and the birth of offspring, roughly a quarter of century. Such lay thinking suggests a threefold categorization of generations which include Children . . . Parents . . . Grandparents. It is the simplest understanding of generation.

When Daniel Levinson discusses generations a slightly shorter time frame is used. He thinks twenty year blocks encompass a "season" of a person's life before another generation is on the scene.[6] At the opposite pole of these twenty-five and twenty year categories, the case for *three years* constituting a generation can be made. Many a religious educator comes to such a conclusion after working with confirmation classes over time. A popular cultural referent (e.g., to the rock group "U2") which the teacher found to communicate with ninth graders three years ago, when used now draws a blank look. A few years make a big difference with youth. As vividly recent as the conflict in Vietnam may seem to be for some, to talk to youth of it is tantamount to speaking of the Peloponnesian War. Beatles records are definitely "oldies," and no one under fifty ever heard of Johnny Ray. Determinative experience with attendant memory is relatively short, even among older persons. A few short years make a major difference in a generation's perception of the world, as suggested by those raised *before, during,* and *after* the Depression of the 1930s. Likewise, life is different for parents having young people at home than for those whose children are "on their own."

So, a definition of "generation" which suggests only a few years is preferred over one involving a score.

Another way to say this is to suggest that generation is linked more to "cohort" than to "biological lineage." Following the lead of social scientist Karl Mannheim, who in the 1920s first spoke of "cohort" in description of generation, other observers now use his term, saying it "refers to a group of individuals who were born at approximately the same time (generally within a five to ten year period) and who therefore share some similar characteristics or experiences."[7] The idea of cohort is that at a given, formative time, usually in youth, persons are shaped and influenced by historical events and situations which color the way they perceive and act thereafter. Their unique experience helps to constitute them as a distinct generational group. In thinking of depression babies, flower children, and baby boomers, we get a sense of what a cohort may be.

In practical consideration of written curriculum material and the organization of educational programs, some compromise age-span grouping for generations is needed. Two helpful classifications on "generation" used by publishers may be considered. The Joint Educational Development publishers use an age classification format with six categories, as follows: 1) younger children . . . pre-readers, 2) older children . . . readers to junior high, 3) youth . . . junior to senior highs, 4) young adults . . . ages 18-30, 5) middle adults . . . ages 30-55, and 6) older adults . . . starting at age 55.[8] From the United Methodists, a curriculum schema with five categories for the generations is suggested: 1) children (birth through sixth grade, generally), 2) youth (roughly seventh through twelfth grades), 3) young adults (high school graduation till about age 30), 4) middle adults (roughly 30-35 to 65 or retirement), and 5) older adults (beyond age 65).[9]

However one chooses to define generation, the point is that there are important differences in people brought about by years lived and social/cultural/historical events in these years. Those differences in lineage and cohort generation are what have to be accounted for in working with people together in IGRE.

I . . . INTER(GENERATIONAL) . . . TWO OR MORE

The above fills out some of the meaning of "generation," but "inter" in "*inter*generational needs elaboration. Beginning strictly from the previous discussion regarding a relatively short span of years between generations, one might then understand the following illustrative programs to be *inter*generational: junior high youth joining with high school students to see a movie and discuss it; teachers working out a nature trip for first and fourth graders; employed and retired persons participating in a workshop on planned giving.

Characteristically *inter*generational is meant to involve adults-with-children. Two such generations in relationship are quite enough to fit the definition, but in most congregational IGRE programs more than two are present.

Within the meaning of intergenerational there are a host of similar words, phrases, and terms to describe the ways persons of differing ages relate. In the display below I have put these many expressions in an order to show connectedness. They are arrayed from individual-to-universal and grouped accordingly.

In this book we are primarily referring to the terms in the Number II grouping when saying "intergenerational." The terms in categories I and III, though, are never totally out of sight. They are current and in use (if in different context). They all need to be understood in relation to the middle group.

R	I.	INTRA-INDIVIDUAL	R
E		ONE-TO-ONE	E
L		FAMILIAL	L
A		CLASSROOM	A
T		COMBINED GROUPS	T
I	II.	INTERAGE (Age Inclusive)	I
O		INTERGENERATIONAL	O
N		MULTIGENERATIONAL	N
S			S
H	III.	ALL-AGE HOMOGENEOUS	H
I		SOCIETAL/CULTURAL	I
P		BIOLOGICAL	P
		HUMANKIND	

Please also consult Figure 2 which is a presentation of these same terms in a "rainbow spectrum."

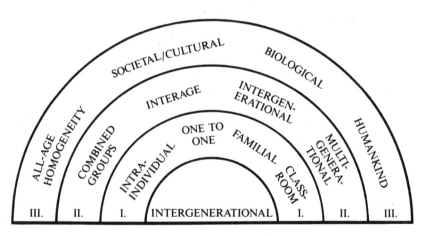

Figure 2. SPECTRUM OF TERMS RELATED TO
"INTERGENERATIONAL"

Starting from the left and inside on Figure 2, the first term to consider is *Intra-individual.* Intra-individual suggests that though individual persons are discrete entities, there is yet operative *within* each man or woman a generational relationship. There are inner psychological states which are generational, such as "the parent, adult, and child" in each of us.[10] Such states are interacting. Considered in yet another intra-individual way, even in solitude a person can be learning from past, present, or future generations through relation with a physical object such as a book. In reading Studs Terkel's *Working* or Alvin Toffler's *Third Wave,* the reader in solitude is connecting up with past or future generations— generations of thought, anyway, and these relate to each other and the present. Also, a solitary individual out observing the "generations of nature" may make internal appropriations of dynamic generational relationships too. Even so, such intra-individual generational learnings are not what we are talking about in most discussions of IGRE.

Neither is IGRE proper being discussed when most ONE-TO-ONE relationships are considered, even when dyads involve persons of distinctly different ages. Witness, for example, one-to-one relationships in counseling, tutoring, friendship, mentoring, and love. Occasions of President Mark Hopkins of Williams College on one end of a log and a student on the other must happen—and they do in most every IGRE program—but one-to-one learning is not the main focus.

Familial relationships certainly have determinative IG dynamics to them. Improving such relations is a concern in many faith communities. It should be. In this book, however, the nuclear or extended, biological or melded family per se is not the primary concern. One exception to this rule would be when family units are basic building blocks by which particular but more inclusive IGRE programs are built.

In the spectrum of terms, the *Classroom* context for IGRE is shown next. Though familial relationships are generationally more complex than the typical classroom setting, the classroom is displayed here as a fuller IGRE expression. The reason is because the typical IG classroom includes persons mostly *not* related by blood. Thus, it has greater similarity to the next set of IGRE classifications. The classroom category is further along on the spectrum too because the purpose of people coming together in IGRE is explicitly for faith lifestyle growth. The relational flow of the traditional classroom is, however, usually too much older-to-younger and one-to-many in structure to be considered as rightly intergenerational.

In the spectrum of terms, the first expression which approaches the usual and intended meaning of IGRE in church/synagogue programs is that of *Combined Groups.* Illustrations of this would be when a fourth-grade class meets with a class of ninth graders to make musical instruments for Purim or when an adult group goes with high-school seniors on an "employment world" trip. Here one senses that two distinct generations of near equal numbers are involved in learning with and from each other.

A step toward greater inclusiveness in learning is suggested by the term *Interage* (and age inclusive). Interage is less school-grade connotative. It acknowledges that people are at different chronological ages. (They also may be at different stages of physical growth, development, and interest.) Yet, they can come together for life and learning. A hint of indiscriminate "age mixing"—which is another possible synonym for interage learning—is present here. Illustrative of this term would be an interage M.A.D.D. [music, art, drama, and dance] camp where junior high, high school, college, and young adults persons assemble, or when people in mid-life with those in retirement go on a bus trip to visit denominational service agencies. Even an Altar Guild with a wide range of ages represented may be classified as interage.

The term *Intergenerational* (which is also the inclusive expression for this spectrum's total description) is similar to interage. In the literature on IGRE, "intergenerational" in most cases involves *three* generations—children, youth, and adults—in a faithing dynamic. Even if only two generations are involved, such as children with adults learning together, that too is intergenerational.

If more than three generations are included in an IGRE activity, the more expansive title of *Multigenerational* is in order. In its fullest implementation, the term suggests that preschoolers, grade-school children, young adults, mid-life adults, and senior-age community members would all be in a learning environment together.

All-age Homogeneous is a term on the spectrum in the third major grouping of words. It is not what IGRE usually or finally means to suggest. "All-age" and "Age Inclusive" may be appropriate at times, but homogeneity is not what is wanted. In "homogeneous" relationship there is too much suggestion that differences among people are obliterated. Some people might think such obliteration a religious ideal in that people would be "as little children" or "grown into adult maturity." In some ways that is an attractive ideal. Insofar as a congregation, family, or community becomes homogenous in thought/acts/looks, that institution has become dangerously ingrown. In actuality such a homogeneous body needs a distinct and different collectivity with which to relate.

Societal structures constitute a larger-than-church/synagogue IG matrix. Every person is part of some such collectivities and learns in them. Generally speaking, these also are beyond the consideration of IGRE proper. "Societal" is here, though, to underscore the fact that people live in neighborhoods, relate to social groups, belong to an economic class, operate in political structures, and so on. All of these have people of varying ages in them. More broadly yet, persons of different ages relate in a *Cultural* context. In the United States people learn from each other "on the street" in an English speaking, scientifically oriented, technological, relatively affluent Western culture. In Peru, education for Indians takes place in the *communidad indigena* (native community) of the

Montana jungles, in the Quechua language, according to prescribed primitive custom, within a barter economy. Cultural transmission *and* transition are going on all the time in terms of language, symbols, and values, whether it be in Boston or along the Urubamba River. A primary component of any culture, of course, is religion, and IGRE is involved in cultural-level transmission/transition. Nevertheless, societal and cultural exchange is more nearly a background dynamic to interage learning in the faith community models of IGRE.

Toward the far end of the spectrum is *Biological* relationship. Generational connections will be found in color of hair, skin pigmentation, shape of nose, blood type, and so on, in family, ethnic, and racial heritage. Part of people's ability to learn may be genetically determined. Perceptual, cognitive, physical determinations are related to ancestry. This is part of a broad understanding of IG too, but it is more of a given than a focused-upon aspect.

Finally and most broadly, we learn intergenerationally as part of *Humankind*. The *Homo sapiens* of today is part of a larger multimillennial procession of generations. We are persons becoming, related to Cro-Magnon men and women, *and* to the Omega Human Beings of the future. Humankind across the generational eons may even share a collective unconscious which dynamically shapes learning. Again, though, unearthing or mollifying the collective generational unconscious is not the direct concern of IGRE programs. The term or thought will remain in the spectrum, however, because such constitutes a way of describing generational relations in contemporary language.

The key words from the spectrum of terms, then, are *Combined Group, Interage, Intergenerational* and *Multigenerational*. These four words are the center of consideration in this book. At times they (along with "age-inclusive") are used interchangeably. The other terms in the total spectrum—from "intra-individual" to "humankind"—are not to be totally forgotten, as they are operative at some level in IGRE activities.

E . . . EDUCATION . . .
LEARNING/GROWING/LIVING IN FAITH

With the above exposition, we are now better positioned to define EDUCATION. This noun needs to come before the adjective "religious," even as "generation" went before "inter."

Education (from the Latin *educare*—"to lead out") is understood in these pages primarily as a leading in terms of the *"Patterns of Relationship"* to be described below. People lead one another to Truth/Life/Love/Faith by the ways they are together.

In the definition of IGR*E* I indicate that the "E" has to do with

Learning/Growing/Living. These near-synonym words are three and together by design. Each word needs the other because "learning" alone too often suggests strictly the cognitive acquisition of information. Such learning is involved and important but not that only. "Growing" conveys a fuller development of persons, especially in terms of one's inner or subjective side, having to do with the affections but also to do with the psycho-motor or physical aspects of the self. Together "learning" and "growing" have to do with life "living" which in this book relates to faith *life*style development. In discussing lifestyle, James Michael Lee says, "Religion is a lifestyle which embraces many molar contents and fuses them into a pattern of life. To be a pilgrim is to walk in the valley of life, to walk in The Way. The religious instruction act is a pilgrimage. And we are all pilgrims. Pilgrims of religion."[11] Part of the good news in IGRE is that one's pilgrimage is not alone but done in company with those who help learning/growing/living.

Cognitive, affective, and lifestyle developments occur in IGRE through four Patterns of Relationship. In the definition of IGRE, I say that "E . . . *Education . . . Learning/Growing/Living in Faith*" takes place "through 1) In-Common-Experiences, 2) Parallel-Learning, 3) Contributive-Occasions, and 4) Interactive-Sharing." We turn to consider each.

In-Common-Experiences

In the literature describing specific IGRE programs, all-age in-common-experiences are described regularly. There are times, for example, when eight-year-old children and octogenarians are together, seeing or doing something in a similar way at the same time. They share the identical moment or ground or event, such as watching a film, hearing a story, eating the bitter herb, reciting a common litany, fast-walking in musical chairs, or raking leaves together. Participants have an experience in-common. In-common-experiences of generations are usually less verbal and more observatory than in some of the other pattern relationships. In this pattern there is something "out there" or "over there" for us to see or do. Taking in that something equalizes the ages, so that hearing a flutist, making a symbol banner, witnessing a bat mitzvah, singing a camp song, and so on, are things that different-aged people do at the same time and place in a similar way. In-common-experiences for the most part remain at what Jean Piaget calls the "concrete operational" level.[12] Learning is thus kept at a level where all may do it together.

At one time I described in-common-experiences as "identical experiences." But that is wrong. People of two different ages may take in the same out-there thing, but each experiences it differently. They may see the same play, but they have unique appropriations. The common moment may mean different things internally. Bread and wine when lifted up in the celebration of the eucharist, for example, are viewed similarly by young and old. The meaning of the lifting up, though, may be interpreted in radically varying ways. So we need to exercise some caution, not claiming too much for in-common-experiences.

Nevertheless, shared experiences are absolutely critical for building IGRE. They are the stuff by which other patterns of relationship are built. To the point, Fred Rogers of television's "Mr. Rogers' Neighborhood" makes the case for what is prescribed here when he asks rhetorically, "How can older and younger people respond to each other if they have no experiences together?"[13]

Parallel-Learning

Parallel-learning is the second major IG relational pattern. With it the generations are separated in order to work on the same topic or project but in different ways at a "best fit" development, interest, or skill level. Some of the developmental levels we are talking about are cognitive, psychological, physical, moral, valuational, and so on—all the ways that make people different and special.

Though age groups may be separated, each one is focusing on the same learning task or topic. If such a separation of ages does not occur in IGRE programing at times, instruction will often be below some people's ability to reason, thus insulting them. Likewise instruction could be above others' ability, thus frustrating them. One of the major criticisms of IGRE is "the tendency to view equality of persons across the age spectrum with uniformity of experience,"[14] with that experience only from the vantage point of the child. By engaging in parallel learning, however, this IGRE short-coming is avoided.

Certainly there are some things all people can appropriate simultaneously, but for further elaboration of learning, participants need to progress at their own optimum speed in their own way. Adherents to uniform lesson curricula will recognize in parallel-learning a long-observed practice. The key is to have learning on the same subject. In one IGRE program, for example, children may leave their elders to do a lawn dramatization of the Ruth/Naomi/Boaz story (Ruth 1-4), while the adults remain in the sanctuary to hear a same-subject sermon on "Wherefore Art Thou, Boaz?" Both groups learn together, "in tandem," but differently. It might be argued that paralleling defeats the purpose of IGRE by separating the generations. I argue that without doing so, faith lifestyle growth is unduly minimized. Illustration of the problem is in order. The New Testament Pauline conflict between "Law and Gospel" is at the very heart of the Christian religion. It is an abstract issue, difficult even for adults to grasp. This vital faith issue needs to be dealt with by young and old—but in different ways. Adults may handle the subject verbally and intellectually, as a starter. Children will do better with a game which simulates to them "binding law" and "freeing love" in a physical way. The children may come to grasp the distinction more concretely, the adults more abstractly; hopefully, both existentially. The illustrations of the problem could go on, but the point is that we do learn at different levels and in different ways. Hence: parallel-learning.

Contributive-Occasions

The third pattern of learning is that of contributive-occasions. These occasions are often the step after parallel-learning. What is involved is a coming together of different-age groups or classes for purposes of sharing what has been learned or created previously. The joining or rejoining becomes a contributive-occasion where separated pieces to a whole are added together for everyone's benefit. Adults, youth, and children in separate or mixed age groups, for example, might work out portions of a worship service in which they will all later participate. Various age groups could contribute skits or musical numbers to an evening program. A CCD program sometimes enacts this pattern when participants have a closing celebration to which all the classes of all the ages contribute separate learnings.

Contributive-occasions are less observatory of something "over there" (as in in-common-experiences) and more participatory in something "right here between us." If the contributions come from a previous period of parallel-learning, the last part of that parallel-learning would have been concerned with how to communicate acquired insights or behaviors to other age groups. By engaging "in mutual contribution" to one another, IG learners discover that the educational whole is greater than the sum of its parts.

Interactive-Sharing

Interactive-sharing is the fourth major pattern in IGRE relationships. It is a distinctive style or way for learning. Instead of various-age people 1) together looking at something or 2) working on the same thing in parallel settings or 3) building something in the middle by contributing pieces, here 4) persons are sent toward each other for purposes of interpersonal exchange. There may be an exchange of experiences or thoughts or feelings or actions. At its best, interactive sharing facilitates a "crossing over" to get another's perspective.

Interactive-sharing is present in an among-families session on handling conflict, in a workshop where Christmases past are remembered mutually, and even in worship services when the congregants are encouraged to say to others, "It seems to me . . ." The appropriate rejoinder to such a statement begins with the Rogerian counselor's words: "What I hear you saying is . . ." When that happens people are giving and receiving in a reciprocal way, engaged in interactive-sharing.

Obviously interactive-sharing, which is significant communication back and forth across generations, does not occur in all things labeled IGRE. This level of interchange is what some persons think is happening when "intergenerational education" is discussed. In truth, interactive-sharing is quite difficult to facilitate. Its enactment serves almost as a goal as much as a realized practice. Nevertheless, illustrations of interactive-sharing are available. When children in one church made "Good News Reports" on Jesus and shared them with adults who likewise added their own understanding of "The Gospel," that was interactive-sharing. On an all-congregation weekend the facilitator led multiage attendees on a fantasy trip (an in-common-experience—experienced uniquely) and afterward invited "trippers" to share their imaginings with one another. In a "Walk in My Moccasins" lifestyle learning project, folks crossed over one another's literal residential thresholds, there to eat, talk, and recreate for an evening. Later the visit was exchanged. The project put members into rest homes, condos, dormitories, basement apartments, and mansions. In an IG setting where interactive-sharing occurs people may even reveal thoughts about the "five forbidden topics"—politics, religion(!), sex, money, and death—or, at least about some issues that are more personal, familial, societal, and cultural. Interactive-sharing is IGRE at its best.

Patterns of Relationship Summarized

In an *ideal* IGRE program or event, all four of the patterns of relationship will be enacted. People come together and have an in-common-experience. Then they break to separately investigate the common subject at a level appropriate for their highest learning abilities. They come back together to present their insights and works in a shared program. Then different generations might finally interact with one another, giving and receiving in the exchanges. In the latter case the participants are

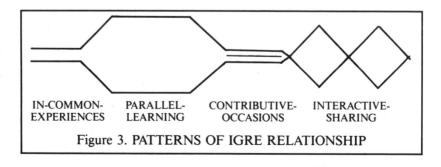

IN-COMMON-   PARALLEL-   CONTRIBUTIVE-   INTERACTIVE-
EXPERIENCES   LEARNING   OCCASIONS   SHARING

Figure 3. PATTERNS OF IGRE RELATIONSHIP

sharing, reflecting, debating, and dreaming from the side of the other but for their own edification. Figure 3 suggests in dynamic line form what the four patterns of IGRE relationship look like.

This book includes all four patterns of learning relationship when IGRE is discussed.

R . . . RELIGIOUS . . .
IN A RELIGIOUS COMMUNITY TOGETHER

As far as words go, there are no words harder to pin down than the words "religious" or "religion." In everyday parlance people operate comfortably with the word "religion," folks having a working understanding that "it has something to do with God and prayer and church, you know." Most attempts at precision with the word though, lead to difficulty and to the pouring over of a lot of literature on the topic.

Broadly understood, religion is human concern for "*m*eaning and *m*otivation" in life. It also has to do with "*m*ovement" or behavior in the world in response to an ultimate environment. Alan Richardson says that from an anthropological and sociological perspective, religion can be described as a person's "response to the exigency of the human condition, in which he is driven to seek security, status, and permanence by identifying himself with a reality greater, more worthy and more durable than himself."[15] While this broad definition of religion is helpful, in this book we can be more specific about the religion under consideration and even specify the content and character of *religious* education. The learning/growing/living which was spoken of under the word "education," according to definition takes place *"In A Religious Community Together."* By this community I mean to suggest the Christian church and/or the Jewish synagogue or temple. In this volume those two major Western religions are shown simply as "church/synagogue," one institution. By "religion," then, I am talking primarily about the Judaeo-Christian faith tradition related to the institutions of church and synagogue.

What is written here likely is germane to persons in other traditions, such as Islam, Buddhism, and so on, as every major religion with every new generation of people always has an educating task just for self-perpetuation. Characteristically that task is fulfilled in "community." To speak authoritatively for these many worldwide religions, however, would be too presumptuous on my part. It is difficult enough for a mainline Protestant to be inclusive of Catholics, Jews, Fundamentalist Protestants, or Orthodox believers, as I shall try to be. It is, then, the faith of the Judaeo-Christian tradition which gives specificity to "religion" and "religious" when spoken of in these pages. In truth, illustrations of IGRE herein are drawn most heavily from Reformed, Anglican-

Methodist, and Baptist-Congregational-type Protestant sources. These are the groups who most often have reported on IGRE programs.

Religion and religious, then, have not to do with "just anything" but specific things. The religious community's belief and practices have to do with Christian or Jewish faith . . . the things we believe about God . . . the scriptures and historic documents . . . the traditions handed down by the Fathers, Rabbis, and Reformers . . . the community of believers who care for one another . . . the world to which God's love is extended . . . the quality of relationships among people and working for peace and justice . . . and much more. It is about a congregation's ways in worship, behavior, observance, piety, and belief. IGRE engages people in a community which has an ultimate commitment to God, called by some "Yahweh," by others "Creator-Redeemer-Illuminator." The people in these communities are concerned that their loyalties and their lives are in keeping with the tradition *and* are relevant to the now *and* bode well for a fulfilling future.

I indicate in the definition for IGRE that the faith community is "together," simply making the case that no one is a Christian or a Jew alone. It is possible, I suppose, to be a "religious" person and not belong to a community. Such, though, is quite impossible in Judaism and Christianity. It would be a contradiction in basic terms. "To be a Christian," for example, *ipso facto* means "to belong to the Body of Christ" which is the church, and church is only lived in community. So with this religious tradition one belongs to people of The Way. "Together" with the people—of all ages—one learns/grows/lives.

Toward the close of this book, in the chapter on "Goals for IGRE," I talk in detail about "Purpose" in religious institutions. I say the purpose of the faith community is "to facilitate the movement of persons in holistic lifestyle toward the fulfillment of God, the world, and themselves."[16] My definition receives some of its focus from the well-known statement by H. Richard Niebuhr who said that the purpose of the church and its ministry is "the increase in the love of God and neighbor" among people.[17]

These forward-pointing statements underscore why intergenerational life and learning are so important. The purpose statements declare that the avowed religion is about fulfillment and love—especially *living one's love* so that new becoming and fruition are possible. Love and living one's love is interpersonal leading *(educare)* for the self, others, the world, God.

In this interperson dynamic some people are just starting on their faith pilgrimage. Others are close to the end of theirs. For some the journey has grown stale. For others there is current vitality and strength. For all persons in all situations, intergenerational religious education can forward learning/growing/living in faith.

Notes

1. See John M. Sutliff, ed., *Dictionary of Religious Education* (London: SCM Press, 1984).
2. Christian Education: Shared Approaches, *Quarterly Intergenerational Guide: Living the Word* (New York: United Church Press, 1979), p. 2.
3. George E. Koehler, "Foundations for Intergenerational Education, A Study Guide for use with *Foundations for Teaching and Learning in the United Methodist Church*" (Nashville, Discipleship Resources, August, 1979), p. 1. This definition grew out of a National Consultation on Intergenerational Education of the United Methodist Church, February 19-21, 1979. See the United Methodist Board of Discipleship Publication, "Recommendations for Intergenerational Education" p. 3. The definition given here replaces an older one in George E. Koehler's *Learning Together: A Guide for Intergenerational Education in the Church* (Nashville: The United Methodist Church, 1976), p. 14.
4. Donald Griggs and Patricia Griggs, *Generations Learning Together: Learning Activites for Intergenerational Groups in the Church* (Livermore, Calif.: Griggs Educational Service, 1976), Preface.
5. Charles R. Foster, "Intergenerational Religious Education" in *Changing Patterns of Religious Education,* ed. Marvin J. Taylor (Nashville: Abingdon, 1984), p. 282. Foster's is the only definition of "IGRE" as IGRE that I have seen.
6. Daniel J. Levinson et al., *Seasons of a Man's Life* (New York: Knopf, 1978), p. 27.
7. Charlotte Chorn Dunham and Vern L. Bengtson, "Conceptual and Theoretical Perspectives in Generational Relations" in *Life-Span Developmental Psychology: Intergenerational Relations,* ed. Nancy Datan, Anita Green, and Hayne Reese (Hillsdale, N.J.: Lawrence Erlbaum Associates, 1986), p. 5. Also see p. 23 for further definition of cohort and lineage.
8. Marguerite R. Beissert, *Intergenerational Manual for Christian Education: Shared Approaches* (New York: United Church Press), p. 7.
9. Koehler, *Learning Together,* p. 8.
10. See Thomas A. Harris, *I'm OK—You're OK* (New York: Avon Books, 1973), pp. 38-59.
11. James Michael Lee, *The Content of Religious Instruction: A Social Science Approach* (Birmingham, Ala.: Religious Education Press, 1985), p. xvi.
12. Jean Piaget, *Six Psychological Studies* (New York: Vintage Books, 1968), p. 48.
13. "An Interview with Fred Rogers," *Generations Together Exchange,* 1:2 (November, 1986), p. 3.
14. Foster, "Intergenerational," in *Changing Patterns,* p. 287.
15. Alan Richardson, ed., *A Dictionary of Christian Thought* (Philadelphia: Westminster, 1969), p. 289.
16. See chapter 9.
17. H. Richard Niebuhr, *The Purpose of the Church and Its Ministry: Reflections on the Aims of Theological Education* (New York: Harper & Brothers, 1956), p. 27.

Chapter 3

Basic IGRE Models

Intergenerational religious education regularly is a homegrown "do it yourself" enterprise for faith communities. Often enough, that is right and good. Program implementation in this field has not waited for published curricula to come down from ecclesiastical print shops. Local creativity in IGRE happens quite naturally because faith communities historically and structurally are almost innately positioned to engage in multi-age life and learning. It is their postured way of being in the world.

If somehow a religious community forgets that such life and learning is what it naturally does best, the basic notion of ages learning together is simple enough to reawaken—almost by dropping a phrase about "the whole people of God" or just offering a partial definition of "intergenerational." People can pick up on the idea and put it into operation *on* and *in* their own congregation.

Whether from recognized historic tradition or from recent creativity, there have been increased reports on IGRE programs. In hearing and reading about these many interage engagements, one may ask, "Are basic types of IGRE programs discernible? Can a comprehensive classification schema be drawn?"

Yes. The answer is yes.

In this chapter, six basic intergenerational religious education paradigms are described. They are the

1. FAMILY GROUP
2. WEEKLY CLASS
3. WORKSHOP OR EVENT
4. WORSHIP SERVICE
5. WORSHIP-EDUCATION PROGRAM
6. ALL-CONGREGATION CAMP

The thousands of individual IGRE programs enacted in congregations may be classified within this sixfold schema. The models are intrinsically related to one another, and yet each category is distinguishable, discrete.

Following an introductory discussion on IGRE classification systems generally, the bulk of what I say in this chapter is given to describing each of the six just-mentioned basic models for interage learning. The characteristics of the models, something of the breadth or variety of programs within each class, and an assessment of the relative strengths and weaknesses of each are provided.

In the notes I indicate principle resources regarding IGRE programs by type. These notes are tantamount to an annotated bibliography. Many references point beyond themselves to hundreds of additional IGRE resources, programs, and ideas which have been tried and described.

Concerning IGRE Classification Models

In developing an intergenerational religious education classification schema, certain criteria must be employed to order what otherwise might appear as disparate data. In the sixfold schema of this book, the primary criteria have been *time* and *intensity* for *church/synagogue-related* programs—that is, how much time commitment and how much depth of interpersonal sharing are involved with various kinds of IGRE programs connected with religious institutions.

Other criteria involving *place* of occurrence, *ages* involved, curricular *materials* used, *content* to be covered, *groups* targeted, and *method* or *style* of the programs figure more prominently in IGRE classification schemes which other analysts have developed. I want to outline some of these other schema quickly before elaborating on the sixfold classification of this book.

In describing "Six Learning Models," George Koehler uses a classification arrangement which relies more on "style" of learning. His models are the 1) experience-reflection model; 2) individualized model; 3) dialogue model; 4) presentation-reflection model; 5) workshop model; and 6) action model.[1] In a more recent categorization of IGRE programs Koehler uses "settings" to describe the field. The nine-category settings include 1) IG seasonal units; 2) IG vacation church schools; 3) one-unit IG church school classes; 4) IG elective study; 5) IG confirmation education; 6) IG overnight learning adventures; 7) family education programs; 8) IG fellowship-learning evenings; and 9) one-session IG learning events.[2] Just a little differently this schema echoes his earlier classification and, we shall see, that of this book. The ninefold schema is quite inclusive but may have some unnecessary categories.

A much simpler system to describe the program field is put forward by Marguerite Beissert. She talks about "patterns" or "options" in intergenerational learning. They are 1) a workshop on a common topic with a presentation to all participants, followed by small-group work with the option of reconvening for a final sharing; 2) cross-age-group sharing that is the culmination of previous peer work on a theme by various groups in the church; and 3) the learning-center approach.[3] With this schema one senses that Beissert is rather intentionally limiting the options to what may transpire in a church building in rather limited time—one or so hours on a Sunday morning.

A more exhaustive classification is presented by Margaret Sawin. She draws up a fourfold schema to describe some twenty-nine identified programs in family "enrichment." The categories are 1) Family Growth Groups (eight programs described); 2) Family Skill Models (nine programs); 3) Family-Based Models for Religious Indoctrination (also with nine programs); and 4) Family-Based Models for Recreation and Socializing (three programs).[4] While comprehensive of most of the field, this schema obviously stresses "family" gatherings for enrichment more than "congregational" life for education and/or worship. Even so, there is much overlap with all the other classifications.

Working more congregationally—and in the Catholic-Episcopal tradition, specifically—Jeanette Benson and Jack Hilyard speak of 1) Contract Groups; 2) Family Camps or Family Weekends; 3) Sacramental Preparation; 4) Family Days; and 5) Shepherd Groups as the primary categories for the field.[5]

Koehler's schemata, the Beissert, Sawin, and Benson-Hilyard classifications, and the sixfold structure presented in this book all describe ways of learning where generations are relating rather than segregated. The hundreds of specific IGRE programs are classifiable within most of the schema categories. These various schema help place specific programs in some context for the observer's understanding.

Now let us turn to a presentation of the six classification models of this present volume. Through the discourse I note the variety of programs that are included in each basic model and the resources which illustrate both the basic model and specific programs. At the end of each section an assessment of the relative merits of the model is made with an eye toward that model's viability for adoption into a congregation's life.

1. THE FAMILY GROUP

Many IGRE programs in faith communities are built around family units and concerns. Families join with families for purposes of fellowship, recreation, worship, social-psychological growth, and explicit religious education. I call these various collectivities the "family group" model. By including persons beyond immediate family members in one's nuclear family life, something of a vicarious extended family is created. The groupings expand possibilities for interage sharing and learning. By natural happenstance or conscious design most congregations have family, interfamily, and vicarious extended-family-learning groups of one kind or another.

The best-known program of intentional intergenerational family enrichment is called "Family Clusters." The family clustering idea is mentioned first in the book because, interpersonally, it is the most active and significant way of doing IGRE. It is also the most difficult to do well as, for one thing, it demands a somewhat higher level of skilled leadership than do most other models.

The basic concept of family clustering was developed by Margaret Sawin. Sawin is a widely traveled educational consultant and lecturer with a background in religious education and family psychology. Initially working with congregations in Rochester, New York, she began calling families together to explore new and more productive ways of learning and interacting. The program now has been expanded successfully all over the United States, Canada, and several other countries. Here is how she describes it: "A Family Cluster is a group of four or five complete family units which contract to meet together periodically over an extended period of time for shared educational experiences related to their living in relationship with their families."[6] The family unit of which Sawin speaks may be a mother/father/children nuclear family, a one-parent family, a single person (never married, divorced, widowed), an older couple, and so forth. Usually these families make up a group of twenty to twenty-five persons who deliberately "contract" to meet together for ten to twelve weeks. Many groups recontract and have gone on meeting for several years.

Meetings may take place in a home, but most often they are held in a church or synagogue. Characteristically an evening begins with a meal. After the meal there is an activity of an intergenerational nature. A filmstrip might be shown and discussed or a craft project done together. Some cluster groups concentrate on a subject matter, such as a book of the Bible.[7] Most frequently, though, cluster meetings are designed to deal with group-identified needs for interpersonal growth in families. Improving family communication is one topic dealt with early and regularly in family cluster groups.[8] When a topic is picked the cluster stays with it for six or so weeks until some real progress is made. Though not advertised as formally therapeutic, the family cluster programs certainly help family members deal with their emotions and look at interpersonal relationships and issues, including conflict.

Leadership, good leadership, is definitely needed for running a family cluster group. Usually it is a two-person team that provides this leadership. The facilitators are *not*, characteristically, in the group with their own family. While these leaders are not therapists, they have skills in group dynamic work developed through family cluster training workshops. Such special training enables them to maintain the most helpful environment for family enrichment. Additional support comes from the growing literature around the family cluster movement.[9]

There are other family groups somewhat similar in concern to family clusters. The type of program which family sociologist Herbert Otto put together is one. It also goes by the name "Family Cluster." It concentrates on enhancing positive attributes and strengths of families. Episcopal priest, Jack Hilyard, and Catholic sister, Jeannette Benson, describe a second cluster-like program of ten to twelve weeks in their book *Becoming Family.* The book has many ideas for structured IGRE activities. Yet another grouping is presented in *Learning Together: A Sourcebook on Jewish Family Education.* In that volume one writer describes a "Synagogue Havurah Program" constituted by a congregational group of fifteen to twenty people: "*Havurah* derives from the Hebrew word for friend. The *havurah* is composed of 'families' who have agreed to meet together in each other's homes to study, to socialize, celebrate Jewish life, and hopefully to form some surrogate for the extended family." These are but a few of the possible family learning programs which congregations have adopted and/or adapted.[10]

Along lines similar to the programs described above, faith communities on their own will enlist or employ someone with group process skills to lead an intergenerational families group. When the leader is a psychiatrist, psychologist, social worker, or the like—not excluding clergy with group counseling skills—the groups tend to be therapeutic in intent. Still, general enrichment, growth, and learning are every bit a part of the outcome as is treatment of family dynamics. The line between therapy and education is hard to draw. In their book, *The Family Crucible,* Whitaker and Napier say that some therapists interested in family systems will have four to five families in a group session, forming a "therapeutic community" that meets for many years.[11] Such a community sounds like it also has a strong "educational" as well as "psychological" dimension to it. The difference is hard to maintain clearly.

There is also a hard-to-draw line between education which is *family-oriented* and that which is *intergenerational*. In this book I am trying, difficult though that may be, to stay with the latter. What needs to be seen is that "family education" is primarily concerned with the facilitation of growth, communication, and learning *within* a nuclear family. In "intergenerational religious education," as considered here, the emphasis is on expanding the concept and interaction of family to include 1) a broader constituency of persons related to the faith community and 2)

learning dimensions which are more explicitly religious. Family education is usually two-generational and tends toward affective-domain
learning. Intergenerational learning is three-or-more generations and is
especially concerned about faith lifestyle learning, which has a strong
cognitive component. There is an immense amount of literature published on the subject of "The Family" and family education. This literature should be consulted by persons interested in the subject.[12] In these
pages we shall stay with the more inclusive topic of "intergenerational"
education and life in the church/synagogue.[13]

Most of the family groups which we have considered so far have a
psychological and interpersonal learning orientation. There are additional family groups focused on other concerns, such as sociological
inclusiveness. One such is the simulated extended family. Illustrative of
such an extended family are congregations promoting an Adopt-A-
Grandparent program among child-present families. Across the "Sun
Belt" of the United States, but also in northerly climes, a number of
congregations have established programs to bring nonrelated older
members into closer social relation with younger parish families. Very
often relations of significance are created—to the benefit of all involved. Other kinds of family extensions occur which include foreign
students, military personnel, institutionalized children, single working
people, and college students. The occasions for gathering of enlarged
families may be a holiday festival, a sabbath supper, an outing to the
country, a concert evening, bowling night, and so forth. Some Jewish
congregations have a series of IG family evenings based around Hanu-
kah observance. Such expanded family events reach out more toward a
human fellowship pole than toward a psychological enrichment or educational learning pole, but neither of the latter are ever far away.

Sometimes people of various ages in the faith community get together
in small family-like units just to play together. They might focus on
physical activities or game table recreational things. They may read
plays or poetry together. They might enjoy a gourmet potluck dinner or
go out to the countryside for some sight-seeing in the Fall. In all cases
they are informally developing interpersonal knowledge and skills much
like extended blood-related families did in previous eras.

Yet another variation in congregational life which facilitates IG learning is the parish-within-a-parish concept. Parish subdividing is rather
widely instituted in American churches. This may be simply for administrative purposes, but neighborhood groups also are formed to carry on
a support ministry, fellowship, worship, and education. They are almost
ipso facto intergenerational. Such a structuring is different from Sawin's
family clustering program in that people do not necessarily choose to
belong to their parish sub-group nor do they contract to participate.

The level and depth of interactive learning, therefore, is not so high, but seldom is it insignificant.

The neighborhood-based or interest-gathered groups often are forms of "house church" for intergenerational life and learning.[14] Such collectivities within church/synagogues exist as extant structures within which fuller IGRE programing can be implaced. Many Catholic parishes are being organized into Family Learning Teams (FLTs) of approximately fifteen households or family units living in geographical proximity. The FLTs assume material responsibility for the catechesis of their households. Joseph and Mercedes Iannone describe the goal of the FLTs as "to have all members interacting both catechetically with their peer level and also intergenerationally within their own family dynamic and other households."[15]

In sum, many faith communities build intergenerational education programs closely and intentionally around families. The purposes of each grouping may be anything from better information networking . . . to fun and socializing . . . to maintaining community . . . to receiving religious indoctrination . . . to revitalizing worship . . . to improving interfamily communication skills . . . to conducting formal therapy. Broadly considered, *all* these family-oriented groups are also for intergenerational learning.

Assessment. The family learning group model for doing interage education is most excellent. It is a program which offers help and growth for persons in what is usually a structured multiple-age group of limited members. This model, especially in the "family clustering" form, is one of the hardest to do of all the models because it requires a level of skilled leadership which not every congregation can put in place. If, though, the kind of leadership needed for the group is available and trained, the model can be effectively adopted and used in a congregation to the real benefit of persons involved.

While this model can—and does at times—involve participants in cognitive learning and worship, its primary strength is found in what it enables in the interpersonal or social-psychological realm. Characteristically, it has affective-domain objectives more than a cognitive focus. That is a plus. Not everyone, however, would be of a similar mind. Some religious people involved in the "sensitivity groups" which were so popular in the sixties recall that a number of folk got "burned" by such groups. So today people may be more than just a little leery when something is proposed sounding like those kinds of groups.

The program expressions which we examined above do not seem to have the problems of becoming overly therapeutic. On the whole they provide significant group experiences that often involve eating, working, playing, and worshiping together. The groups, however, do not involve the larger numbers of people, which some of the other models below can draw in. That is a disadvantage in this model. For those who do get involved, though, it is a quality interage experience.

The amount of time involved is adequate, too, as the groups usually meet for a set number of weeks and for two or three hours each session. Those are all plusses.

Emphasis in this model is characteristically given to learning for the nuclear family. Attention is paid to developing parenting skills, getting along with siblings, communicating in families, and so on. There is no question but that such learnings are sorely needed. Even so, *family* learning is not necessarily *religious* education. Concerns for faith life-style development, learning the Bible, exploring the wider mission of the church, and so on, might be slighted in domestic-centered programing. Moreover, since the learning groups usually focus on family dynamics, they may not include extra-family others of the church quite as well. If a psychologist is engaged to facilitate the group, that person will use his/her professional expertise which is not necessarily either pedagogical or theological.

These, then, are some of the potentialities and problems with the family group model. The model is viable. Congregations that adopt it will find it significant for the participants individually and for the faith community.

2. THE WEEKLY CLASS

More and better written curricular material for IGRE classes is coming off the denominational and independent religious publishing house presses.[16] With such materials educators will find it easier to move in the direction of the second major model of IGRE—that of the weekly or regularly scheduled longer-term class. The model finds IGRE activities occurring on a regular once-a-week basis with the sessions conducted most frequently in the context of the church/synagogue. A United Methodist Church survey of local congregations found that the weekly class was by far the most popular form of all forms of IGRE programing being done among its member churches.[17] This is especially so with congregations having smaller memberships. With neither enough pupils or teachers to maintain a fully graded church school, smaller congregations find it makes sense to teach and learn intergenerationally. On the other hand, many congregations with large membership rosters have gone toward weekly IGRE classes too. Such classes provide them with a significant learning option, a way to be experimental and a means to revitalize educational interest. More importantly, though, educational leaders sense that there is something inherently worthwhile in having generations learn together.

At least two major positive features about the regularly scheduled IGRE class should be highlighted. One is simply the tradition/convenience factor. If an IGRE class is offered at the time regular religious education has been done, *more people are likely to participate in it* than at any other time. The second positive feature of having a regularly scheduled IG class is *the benefit of extended calendar time.* The IGRE class is more nearly a long-term enterprise. There is value in continuity. People see one another consistently, get to know each other on a first-name basis, begin to trust, share, and often to care.

Congregations which conduct regular weekly IG classes use a variety of organizational patterns. Often twenty-five or so people of "reading age" (grade three and above)[18] are involved. A convener may get a class going by facilitating the group's decisions about learning goals, procedures, curriculum, and so on. A teacher may be chosen or appointed. If teachers—plural—are designated, frequently they are an IG team, as that of a teenager and an adult. Just as often, though, a family will take charge of a program or series of programs and then pass the responsibility for another month to another family. IGRE classes often employ a learning center approach in program design more than a teacher-pupil/presentation-discussion format. In such classes members try to stay, work, and interact together as much as possible. The curriculum used may be subscribed, but, just as often, it is devised by the participants.

One of the best single curricular resources for a weekly intergenerational class is that produced by the multidenominational Joint Education Development (JED) group. The previously mentioned *Intergenerational Manual* by Beissert is the place to begin. It is a guide first written to use with Christian Education: Shared Approaches (CE:SA) materials. The manual indicates that there are four primary curricula in the CE:SA program: Knowing the Word, Interpreting the Word, Living the Word, and Doing the Word. Intergenerational class materials are found by tapping into and adapting one of the four curricula. The tapping guide is called *Quarterly Intergenerational Guide.* What the guide does is tell the teacher how to adapt the regular graded church school material—usually in the Living the Word series—for an intergenerational class setting. The basic resource of grade level five, for example, might be expanded and worked out for a multi-age group. Additional specific suggestions for age-inclusive activities are given in the quarterly guide.

Though the United Methodist Church has done, by far, the most spade work in the field of IGRE, the Nashville educational offices and publishers have yet to develop a specific week-by-week curriculum. Instead, what they are saying to their constituents is 1) use resources which others have already prepared for IG groups, 2) adapt a one-age (e.g., middle-elementary) level curriculum, 3) adapt more than one-age level, or 4) combine resources.[19] As a starting place into Methodist IGRE resources, Koehler's *Learning Together* should be consulted. From Koehler, one should go to the previously listed publications, *Learning Together: Resources* and *Intergenerational Learning Experiences.* These are collections of the reports of United Methodist IGRE activities, many of which are descriptive of successful classes. Two magazines of the Methodists which carry class-resource ideas are 1) *The Church School Today,* which has occasional articles on the subject, and 2) *The Adult Leader,* which includes a four-session IGRE class guide in each quarterly publication. In addition to these resources, the UMC also offers laboratories for teacher training in IG classes.

The Catholic Church in the United States, through various independent publishers, also has materials available for use in IG classes. Most of it goes under the general heading of "family" education, thus having for this present volume some of the limitations mentioned previously. Even so, the materials are applicable to teaching-learning with multiple family households in a church-class context. The impetus-for-the-emphasis on family education comes in part from the National Conference of Catholic Bishops. In 1978 the bishops designated the 1980s as "The Decade of the Family." Catholic parishes everywhere were urged to develop programs aimed at strengthening families. Prior and subsequent to the bishops' statement, several Catholic-related publishing houses came out with curricular resources on family education.[20]

Jewish IGRE class materials are described in various publishing house catalogues. One finds there such listings as *Do It Yourself Shabbat, Shabbat Can Be,* and the story *The Narrowest Bar Mitzvah,* which can be adapted for IG use. For study by persons in grade seven and up, Sherry Bissell's *God: The Eternal Challenge* is highly recommended for the IG classroom.[21]

Other denominations have educational materials and other individual congregations have IGRE classes more or less like those described in the paragraphs above.[22]

Assessment. A chief advantage to doing intergenerational religious education in a weekly class is the fact that such a class (for Protestant Christians especially) takes place "at the right time to do church"—namely, Sunday morning. For that reason weekly IGRE classes offer the possibility of involving a larger number of people. Moreover, the Sunday morning class is clearly perceived as one of the church's basic programs more than as enrichment addendum. It may, then, involve both larger numbers of people and a wider age span.

The weekly class also has the distinct advantage of providing for quality interaction of people over substantial calendar time. It will meet for many months and, in some communities, for years. Such continuity has maturing/enduring worth for people as they grow. One-shot events and short-term programs, which characterize several of the other models, cannot offer this distinct feature.

Characteristically the IGRE class focuses on cognitive faith education—more than on interpersonal growth, lifestyle shaping, fellowship, recreation, worship enrichment, or any of the major features of the other models. Classes are clearly for acquisition of educational *knowledge.*

The disadvantages to the weekly class are twofold. One is that an hour's time does not allow for much in-depth sharing. Some of the other models provide such depth with their larger blocks of clock time.

Second, the available curriculum for IGRE classes is neither well-developed nor necessarily easy to enact. In addition, teachers are not accustomed to teaching intergenerationally. IG classroom instruction requires some special skills. To ask persons to lead such class for a year and, possibly, to create their own curriculum is no mean request. Such obstacles are reasons why some congregations do not have weekly IG classes or fail to continue with those they started.

Even so, as practiced, the weekly class will be found in place more often than any of the other forms of IGRE.

3. THE WORKSHOP OR EVENT

A quality learning experience which a number of faith communities have tried is that of a workshop or event with multiple ages involved. This constitutes a third basic model in IGRE programing. A strong plurality of the write-ups of IGRE programs appearing in the literature are, in effect, reports on workshops and one-time-only events.

A "workshop" typically takes place in a single day and usually is four or more hours in duration. The longer block of time enables important social happenings and learnings to transpire. The workshop is a distinguishable and popular way of doing intergenerational education. For the conduct of IGRE workshops, there are multiple resources available.[23]

An IGRE workshop is characterized by its focus on a specific theme, problem, or project. The focus enables mixed-age participants to relate in multiple ways. The ways include such things as a meal, worship, an audio-visual presentation, the doing of a craft project, conversational sharing, artistic expressions, and others. There is time in a workshop structure to stay with a chosen theme and deal with it at a depth level which a one-hour class—or a month of classes—would not allow.

In the literature on workshops the topics focused upon are many: Bible books/characters/events, how to worship more inclusively, interacting with the arts, planning a future series of IG outings, dealing with issues of peace, to name a few.

The most popular and oft-repeated IGRE workshops are those done relative to major holidays of the religious calendar year. Considerable resource material is available for such.[24] Some Christian congregations, for example, have three intergenerational workshops: one for Advent, another during Lent, and a third near Pentecost. The JED curriculum has workshop guides for such holy season events, as well as on other more topically focused concerns. Jewish congregations may do IG holiday workshops on and for Shabbat, Chanukuh, Purim, and Pesach. Often enough, educational leaders in the church will borrow from holiday workshop guides and then build in their own creative ideas for structuring the faithing event.

The ideal workshop is specifically focused yet with multiple ways of treating a topic. It brings people of various ages into contact with one another, learning together. All the "Patterns of Relationship" can be enacted during a good workshop, including in-common-experiences (e.g., seeing/hearing a filmstrip on Amos), parallel learning (e.g., studying a social problem at one's own level of societal understanding), contributive moments (e.g., doing playlets for one another on social injustice), and interactive sharing (e.g., discussing perceived and felt discrimination). If all that can happen in a one-day workshop—and it can—the educator may be sure that a quality event has transpired.

In the same general classification with workshops, yet a small step away, are gatherings which I call "events." Events are characterized by people of several ages getting together to experience or learn something in a single unbroken block of time, usually three or fewer hours. The classic example of this in most congregations is the family night potluck supper. *If* the attendees do not segregate themselves immediately by peer group (or even by isolated nuclear family) and *if* the children are not too soon shoveled off to see a library-loaned movie, *then* the family-night supper by structure is identifiable as a "natural" intergenerational event.[25] The "ifs" are big factors, of course, so even "natural" IGRE church life activities benefit from conscious attempts to make them intergenerationally significant. Natural events in the faith community which can be so shaped include: annual picnics, a Patron Saint's dance, Easter sunrise services, Senior Citizens' Nights, a congregation's anniversary celebration, and life-marker events such as baptism, circumcision, confirmation, a wedding, and even a funeral. Here are three other specially planned IGRE events described in the literature (and to which I have added ideas for possible expansion): first, preschoolers with their parents and older siblings have a valentines-making party together (what would it be like if they held the party in a college dormitory?); second, elementary school-age children holding a money-making square dance with many ages invited (especially, maybe, single people in the

congregation); and, third, high-school youth organizing an evening for
family role-playing on "conflict" (and could "empty nest" couples be
invited to contribute?). The opportunities are manifold. One group of
post-college young adults arranged for a meeting with residents in a
retirement home. They said to their elders, "Help us appreciate what it
is like to become old." When the young adults arrived, the seniors
1) affixed golf balls under the arms of their guests, 2) taped tongue
depressors over the young adults' knee joints, and 3) put hard alumi-
num foil balls in their shoes. After that the two groups began to socialize. Disco dancing began, taught to the seniors by the visitors-still-
encumbered. A new appreciation of age was engendered for all.[26]

One time, as part of its annual meeting, a Protestant church had an
IGRE song-fest. Each of three generations present—youth, middle age,
adults, and seniors—remembered and described "songs of faith I sang
when growing up." Sample songs identified by the three groups, respectively, were: "Stand Up, Stand Up for Jesus" by the seniors; "Tell Me
Why" by persons in mid-life; and "Hey, Hey, Anybody Listening?" by
the children. In singing their songs—with the help of a versatile pia-
nist—each generation also described what these growing-up songs
"meant" as part of their own faithing process. No one left the annual
meeting without greater appreciation of where others were or had been
in their pilgrimage. The meeting concluded that evening by singing
Avery and Marsh's "We Are The Church."

The possibilities for intergenerational single-block events are great
indeed. Such events and somewhat longer workshops provide a basic
model which is replicable. With a little imagination, planning, and
work, a committee can pick a workshop or event theme, develop a
program, and create a vital IGRE experience. The learning and social
interchange are consistently of high quality.

Assessment. This third model is clearly the easiest route to the IGRE
field. By it people get a good exposure to the possibilities inherent in
generations learning together. The demands on time and leadership are
not as great as in the first two models—or as in any of the other models.
With lots of resource materials available, to say nothing of the reservoir
of resources in most people's imagination, a one-time or two-to-three-
programs-a-year schedule is clearly within the reach of almost every
congregation. Whether known by the name "intergenerational religious
education" or not, variations on this model are what almost every faith
community does almost unconsciously at times during the course of its
yearly program. Witness, for example, the Purim Celebration, the
Shrove Tuesday Family Pancake Supper, or an all-congregation talent
show.

A major learning that most workshops and special events provide is in the province of social interaction. Good fellowship among people of various ages is usually effected. The enjoyable experience of togetherness occurs easily because there is an activity that can be completed or because there is something worth celebrating. In a workshop, for example, the learning is typically focused on something which is faith-related, such as learning about Pentecost. It may lead to the celebration of Pentecost, or, in one special reported event, the burning of the congregation's mortgage on Pentecost.

For the persons who participate in the workshop there is not "too much time involved," as might be the case with a weekend retreat. Nor is there "too much of a commitment" as to a nine-month class.

Because of the one-time nature of the event or the time elapsing between seasonal workshops, there may not be as much significant sharing among generations as can happen in the other models. So the event runs the risk of being a "flash in the pan," too soon forgotten. On the other hand, for many congregations it is a "foretaste" of what might be and, as such, has led them into deeper and longer term programing for IGRE.

4. THE WORSHIP SERVICE

Worship—which is an end in itself—is also an occasion for intergenerational learning. For many churches and synagogues, age-inclusive worship is an ongoing, unself-conscious practice. These faith communities have never considered doing anything else. For them worship life is *the* educational structure of the congregation, as there may be no formal educational program per se. Other faith communities are more self-conscious about designing IG worship. Intentionally they plan services which (a) actively include people of all ages and (b) have an obvious educational thrust. In both unself-conscious and intentional worship situations, the service is intergenerational religious education. It constitutes a distinct model.

John Westerhoff and William Willimon, in writing on the relatedness of liturgy and learning, say, "We learn what we do. We act our way into new ways of thinking and feeling. We make believe so that we can believe. We make love in order to fall in love. That is why it can be said that we can understand people by observing their rituals. The Sunday liturgy of the church and in particular the actions persons perform during the ritual express and shape their perceptions, understandings and ways of life."[27] With the worship service model of IGRE, Sunday morning (or Friday evening for Jews) is the usual time and the sanctuary is the usual place for generations to be together, praise God together, and learn together.

Some congregations actively encourage IG worship. By contrast, others seemingly train young people—almost systematically—*not* to worship, *not* to learn in and from sacred services, *not* to break bread with people of different ages. Many duly dedicated infants grow up with little familiarity with their born-into faith community's sacred practices. This can easily happen when the hour for religious education is the same as that of the worship service. "Convenience scheduling" to "do church in sixty minutes" prevents students—as well as teachers—from attending worship. A teenager may have a Sunday School Perfect Attendance Pin with year-bars dangling down to the belt and yet know nothing about liturgical life. It is reported that some graduate theological seminaries have to do remedial "Basic Worship" courses to prepare divinity students for the worship work of parish ministry![28]

The congregations who do IG worship services, however, suggest that it makes no sense to separate members of a family into different rooms the minute they cross the meeting house threshold. Better that children and parents enter the narthex together, shaking the "Welcome" hand of a nonfamily, different-age other. Thus religious education begins in a special connectional way.

The denominations having the most success in holding people of all ages together in worship and making it educational also seem to be the most liturgical. Catholics, Lutherans, and Episcopalians, for example, stress age-inclusive worship and have been increasingly diligent in saying how to be so.[29] Persons in these denominations—but others too—have a wealth of multi-age worship experience collected and recorded.[30] One basic lesson which the high-liturgy churches suggest from their experience is this: "More than ears" needs to be engaged in worship. IG services are aided by involving the full range of the human senses. The services are more active, participatory, visual, tactile, and literally "tastefull."

IG worship services show awareness of the varieties of ages involved in the rites and make some concessions to older worship forms. James White, Professor of Christian Worship at Notre Dame says, "Our worship must be constructed around a healthy respect for the varieties of people who will be worshiping either in homogeneous or heterogeneous groups. What is appropriate worship for children may not be so for teenagers or their parents. No longer can we afford to offer a menu with only one dinner on it. For years we have, in effect said: 'This is it and you can take it or leave it.' "[31] How and where it is done, worship for all ages must have faith-shaping purpose: "Worship is a multifaceted, multimedia, multimeaningful human activity. When we worship, many things are happening. . . . The most basic thing which happens in worship, the purpose of our gathering as Christians, is the meeting and praise of God by the people of God. But while this meeting and praise is occurring people are formed by their worship. We form our rites but they also form and reform us in fundamental ways."[32]

In many Protestant churches children are present in the sanctuary for the opening fifteen to twenty minutes of the service. For the time that children are present, IGRE-sensitive worship planners include litanies in which younger people can participate. Planners do songs which all can sing. Even if no age-inclusive concessions are made in the opening of worship, clergy usually preach a children's sermon or someone shares a story. If clergy will really work on the children's message, they can generate a high faith-learning experience for *all* participants.[33] Following the sermon or story, the students and teachers involved in religious education classes usually are dismissed.

One reason for having children participate in all or part of formal worship may be just to familiarize them with the order of service, the liturgical responses and standard hymns which their generational fore-parents in the faith handed down. There is "wisdom from the ages" to be communicated. More than that, children witness their parents and others enacting the role of "worshiper." A great deal is communicated nonverbally. And it goes the other way too! Adults learn from observing youngsters, as when a child gets up on tip-toe to see a baptism—thus suggesting to nearby adults that "something wonderful" *is* happening, causing those adults to look again.

As vital and important as IG services are, all the worship life of a church/synagogue need not—perhaps should not—be completely age-inclusive. There are important cognitive, aesthetic, experiential, histori-cal, and so on, differences between and among people of various ages. These differences suggest that some services rightfully should be age-tailored. Still, there are more times, places, and ways for people of varying ages and developmental stages to come together for prayer and praise, Word and Sacrament than is usually considered. The model of intergenerational worship is viable and commends itself as an appropriate response to the sound of the Shofar or the pealing of steeple bells.

Assessment. All ages together need to share the central weekly act of the faith community. For Christians that is the Mass or Sunday service. For Jews it is the Sabbath service but, especially, the high holy day celebrations when all should be in attendance. The worship of God is the bedrock activity of the faith communities, and IGRE can help in grounding persons therein. By being together and worshiping together, people learn together. The learning helps young and old focus on "right relationship" with God and with one another. In addition, worship helps connect people with generations hundreds and thousands of years re-moved. The historic rites, readings, and responses from the centuries are being enacted in the now for people's participation and ownership.

Insofar as worship services are age-inclusive, involving, and educational, the learning is nonpareil. We learn the faith best by worshiping God together.

There are limitations, though, to centering IGRE in worship, especially as worship is usually constituted. Many services are spiritually dull. There is not much aliveness between priest and people, between people and people, and too often between people and God. Services can be uninspiring and uninstructive. Which is just to say that lively and inclusive worship is something which has to be well conceived and enacted. On the whole, intentional IG worship is not bad because one key "person"—the "parson"—wants it to be relevant and faithful. Clergy participation in planning worship is one of the decided pluses with this model, for that professional's participation cannot always be guaranteed in the other models.

An unavoidable difficulty in doing IG worship is that services do not easily meet all people at each individual's highest and/or most appropriate level of cognitive, social, spiritual, and so on, development. Judaeo-Christian worship, evolving as it has through the centuries, has been the response to God by theologically mature adults. It is not always comprehended by or relevant to children. Protestant worship, which relies so heavily on the spoken abstract word, is especially remiss in accounting for the important differences in the way people of different ages appropriate the faith. There is need, then, to work on age-inclusiveness in services.

If IGRE is placed exclusively in worship, it should be noted that other liabilities are present. One is that this makes the IG experience very short. Moreover, the traditional service is usually hard-pressed to offer "variety of religious experience." Stretching in interpersonal and psychomotor directions, for example, is quite difficult to effect in screwed down pews that position the worshiper to look in only one direction and where "Be Still" is the opening instruction. Worship as a model for IGRE runs the risk, then, of omitting other important aspects of learning. The communion table, while absolutely essential in Christian worship, for example, needs to be supplemented by life around other tables—tables found in the classroom, the fellowship hall, the kitchen, and the campsite. Lest Christians and Jews forget, the ministry of the rabbis (Jesus included) was not fulfilled exclusively in the temple.

5. THE WORSHIP-EDUCATION PROGRAM

Among the models of IGRE there is one which intentionally integrates worship and education. As much or more than the other models seen so far, the worship-education program model facilitates a wide variety of IG growth experiences in a relatively short period of time.

Basically what this model does is 1) bring all ages together for worship and learning, 2) separate younger learners from adults for activities in different settings, and finally 3) bring them back together for celebration or sharing. The best written treatment of this particular way of working worship and education together is William Abernethy's *A New Look for Sunday Morning*. Abernethy describes the working out of a distinct new Sunday schedule for a New England church he served. In his structure there are forty-five minutes of worship, sixty-five minutes of education, and twenty minutes for a closing celebration. He describes Sunday morning in the church as "one service in three acts."[34] In the book Abernethy does not talk about "intergenerational integration" per se, but of necessity it is there.

My own introduction to IGRE was in and through a similar worship-education Sunday morning program at All Saints Church which brought various ages together.[35] At All Saints Church the worship-education integration model was developed for summer programing. Over time the influence of this annual two-month program went on to shape the whole church in multiple dimensions throughout the entire calendar year. The basic program model involved: 1) selection of a worship-education theme for a ten-week program; 2) choice of a unit topic or session for each week consistent with the overall theme; 3) beginning each Sunday morning with a time for all ages to pray, sing, and learn together in worship; 4) effecting a parallel learning time when children (*not* divided by age) have education in the fellowship hall while adults learn about the same topic in the context of the sanctuary; and then at morning's end 5) reuniting all ages either in the sanctuary, fellowship hall, the courtyard (with coffee and punch), or elsewhere for mutual sharing. The summer programs at All Saints Church kept worship services and religious education in a complementary teaching-learning posture.

Maureen Gallagher, a Catholic educator, developed an education-with-worship curriculum which is similar to the two discussed above. Her comprehensive curriculum is called *Family: Parish Religious Education*.[36] It is a five-year-cycle curriculum resource. In each year's packet are leadership guides, 35mm slides, cassette tapes, ditto spirit masters, transparencies, and more, making the packet a full teaching resource. In the *Family* curriculum it is suggested that classes meet once a month for eight months. Sessions normally take a two-hour block of time. Each session includes 1) instruction, 2) experience, and 3) celebration. For the first hour of the session, persons meet in peer group classes—preschool, primary grade, junior high, and high school/adult. During the second hour each family comes back together as a unit to do something and discuss with each other what was learned separately and how, experientially, it relates to their own family. The two-hour block culminates in a specially planned sacramental service or paraliturgy. In the *Family* curriculum resources there are materials which may be reproduced and sent home with participants as a family packet. The sessions take place on a Saturday or Sunday and usually in a parish hall with five to eighty families involved. Normally the sessions are not tied into a formal observance of the Mass. Of the sessions in Cycle A, the formal educational content is related to faith topics, such as creation, covenant, and eucharist.

Other faith communities have done much the same kind of worship-learning unification, but instead of creating a program theme de novo, they have built a worship-education curriculum around the lectionary. Thus worship and education are integrated. These integrations are not necessarily done for intergenerational purpose, but, in effect, that is what happens when Christian community learners focus on the same Old Testament, Epistle, and Gospel lessons in the sanctuary and the classroom.[37]

In the Abernethy, All Saints, Gallagher, and Lectionary approaches to integrating worship and education, a sense of wholeness is created for the congregation and its members of all ages. In one sense, as Janet Fishburn describes it, "the congregation is (or becomes) the curriculum."[38] When people are worshiping together, interacting, and learning from each other they are providing themselves as the occasion for others to be "built up"—edified—in the faith. Whether it be through self-selected topical themes or liturgical year scripture lessons, the worship-education program approach brings educators, clergy, the laity, and young and old together.

As the centermost pieces of Judaeo-Christian religion, worship and education joined in a positively reinforcing way enable the faithful of all ages to pray, talk, work, and learn side-by-side. They create a most powerful faithing dynamic.

Assessment. When considered in terms of six variables—time, depth of involvement, holism, scheduling leadership, and commitment—there is much to be said in favor of this model of IGRE, even though it has some shortcomings by comparison to the other models.

First of all, consider *time*. Speaking exclusively about the All Saints form of the worship-education model, there is sufficient calendar time involved (eight to ten weeks) to make adoption of this model a valid experiment and experience. A congregation, for example, can try it out in the summer months, without forcing a major or prior restructuring of normal routines and organization. It becomes an experiment which fits into the life of a congregation, is significant and yet not unnecessarily disruptive. The weeks of the summer—or some other season—are not as long-termed as weekly classes nor as short-lived as a workshop or event. It is just enough time to be a good trial and, typically, a positive experience.

There is, of course, considerably more restructuring and reprograming involved for a church which opts for the Abernethy or lectionary forms of the model. They need not be taken on in toto, of course, as either might be tried for a quarter or a liturgical season and then evaluated.

In terms of clock-time, in all four of the forms discussed above there is anywhere from over an hour to just over two hours involved. That is fairly limited, placing some strictures on what can happen, but it is adequate for transactions to begin.

Second, in consideration of *depth of involvement*, this model should be described as "broadly strong but . . ." It calls for good interaction of persons, for example, but does not attempt to be interpersonally intensive as are family groups or IG camps. Still, when people share in small groups, this model moves well beyond superficial relations. Characteristically the model provides more social exchange than worship services alone permit but not as much as would be available at an all-families potluck dinner or on a retreat. In terms of educational intensity, the model does much or most of what the weekly class can do in any one session, though not when considered over calendar time. There also is worship exposure in this model but, again, it is not in the depth as would be experienced if the entire IG program stayed in the sanctuary.

In general, then, the model does not do in depth any single thing the other models can do—save one. In overgeneralized stereotype one might say that the family group model is stronger with regard to interpersonal learning; the forte of the weekly class is in cognitive religious understanding; the workshop promotes fellowship growth especially well; worship affects spiritual development; and an all-church camp enables more psychomotor (physical) learning. To describe the strength of the worship-education program model I use the expression "holistic learning." *Holism* becomes a third variable by which to compare the models. The worship-education model attempts to touch the whole person in multiple dimensions of his or her life. It is interested in the birth and rebirth of faith lifestyle in ways that are cognitive, affective, psychomotor, social, and spiritual. This model customarily works on all five of these fronts in the same block of time. At times, of course, the all-church camp, some family groups and workshops incorporate these multiple dimensions of holistic learning, too. They cannot do so, however, for as many people as the worship-education model does.

Beside time, depth of involvement and holism, *scheduling* is a fourth variable for consideration. The worship-education program, as noted, happens during church/synagogue "prime time," i.e., the weekly worship hour. So placed, it can attract and involve larger numbers of people. Intergenerational events which are out-of-town, day-off-demanding, weeknight-filling, and so on, simply cannot involve the numbers which one hopes to reach. So the usually scheduled moment for this program is one of its positive features.

Fifth, consider *leadership*. The model does not require the level of skilled personnel to make it happen as do most family learning groups or worship services. Yet, planner-doers are needed to make the program happen. These people can be ordinary congregational members who simply are interested in improving the level of their community's life and learning together. This is not to say that some expertise is not needed. Happily, the resident "religious professional" is regularly involved. The clergyperson's contributions can be very significant 1) in integrating the worship experience with that of the church/synagogue's formal educational thrust and 2) in promoting and facilitating the idea of generations learning together. Likewise, the religious educational staff, if there is such, will also help with planning, as this obviously is an educational program. These "experts," though, are often-as-not consultants. The leadership is of the laity. The laity seem willing to make a commitment to a program which has clear beginning and ending boundaries which this model has. Moreover, people commit to helping especially when they see that the whole has shared leadership. If the worship-education program is in a summer program, one can miss a planning meeting or go on vacation for a couple of weeks and still be a part of the total process. The involvement is of significant enough duration to effectively train persons to be sensitive and increasingly skilled in intergenerational work.

All in all, the worship-education program model is do-able. It represents more than just a cursory investment in intergenerational programing but is not so deeply investive as to turn people away in the initial stages. The model focuses on 1) general 2) interage 3) religious 4) education and 5) worship. In sum, it is *learning in and about faith in multiple ways with and from other-age people.* I will return to consideration of this model, more than any other, in chapter 8 of this book when developing a "Total Parish Paradigm" for IGRE.

6. THE ALL-CONGREGATION CAMP

Considering all things, the most experientially rounded intergenerational learning model is the week-long all-congregation (or IG) camp. In an all-ages six-day camp there is enough time, facility, space, movement, and people to let happen the very best of multiple possibilities in IGRE. Much of that positive opportunity is also found in weekend retreats.

Whether for a week or forty-eight hours, the all-congregation camp/retreat experience constitutes a sixth distinguishable model for IGRE.

A United Methodist study found that the week-long camp occurs primarily among larger membership churches. Churches of 200-700 members will more often schedule weekend retreats.[39] Small membership churches do their retreats more informally, having periodic church family "get away" occasions. All such activities create tremendous IGRE opportunities.

Many denominational judicatories own and operate camp, conference, and retreat house facilities. On the schedule one summer for Camp LaForet in Colorado was 1) an "intergenerational camp for young children and persons over fifty," 2) a more traditional "family camp" for all ages, and 3) an "extended family camp" open to persons of the Unitarian-Universalist denomination from all over the country. In addition, individual congregations booked the facility for week camps and weekend retreats.[40]

The extensive use of a camp such as LaForet for IG programs is widely repeated throughout the nation in other religious conference grounds. In Ohio, for example, from June to September, the United Church of Christ Conference scheduled eleven intergenerational camps of one description or another for its facilities.

Intergenerational religious learning occurs in IG camps and retreats through vigorous outdoor activity as well as quiet inside games. Growth occurs through interpersonal sharing, educational programs of mutual value, campfire worship services, a variety of musical/artistic/craft activities, through eating three-plus meals a day together. Full description of the all-congregation camp experience may be found in write-ups on camp experiences and in various publications related to camping, camp management, outdoor education, retreat planning, recreation, nature, learning, and specialized worship.[41]

An all-congregation camp of a week or a weekend's duration has many inherent advantages for intergenerational education. First of all, natural meetings of significance between different-age and same-age people happen in this less-structured framework. People simply have time to get acquainted. A week at the lake or over a Saturday night at a mountain retreat center can break individuals out of their backhome time traps. Intergenerational sharing happens easily at the horseshoe pit, beneath a shade tree, over a Coke, on the piano bench, by the pool, in two brown chairs, roasting marshmallows, hiking, and on and on. These meetings and sharings happen here more easily because new interactive patterns are created. The phone, TV, pets, organizations, business involvements, sports team practices, music lessons, and so forth, are left behind. There is space and time for good rapport between people—even if no intentional IGRE activities are planned. Interage acquaintances turn into friendship, as told in the case of young and old fishermen who found themselves tying trout flies together one evening and arranged a trip to the lake for the next morning.

With good planning, camp leaders will set up and facilitate both intentional family and beyond-family interchanges. One congregation's camp schedule, for instance, designated a daily "Family Tree Time." On the first day, nuclear families were encouraged to "find a tree in the woods that somehow looks or feels like your family. Once found, stay there to talk about your 'ancestral tree.' End by discussing possible future family branches." Later in the multifamily cabins, nuclear families shared discoveries from their tree discussions. On some retreats simulated extended families are created by including single grandparent types and unattached teenagers with other families. Then too, two or more families may for a week covenant to function as a larger-than-nuclear-family unit, caring for one another and one another's children. These several "family" formations can be encouraged by good camp leadership.

In the above, religious *community* seems to be the primary concern of the intergenerational camp. Expanded and improved human relations are certainly worth building. Running alongside community are other religious education goals. Learning about the Bible, improving interpersonal skills or developing family spiritual life are three educational objectives often pursued. For such learning, camp leaders invariably establish a theme. The theme provides a focus for learning, guides the selection of resource leaders and materials, and suggests learning concerns, visual displays, movies, music, and activities to fulfill the educational intent.[42]

Intergenerational camps and retreats are planned around still other foci. *Recreation* is one of these. All ages of people may just want to "get away" from routines and do something enjoyable ("rest" not excluded). Congregations in the northern tier of states book facilities for cross-country skiing weekends: young and old "schuss" together. *Spiritual enrichment* per se is yet another primary purpose where young and old learn to pray and meditate together. The list is not exhausted.[43]

Whatever may be the primary purpose for calling people of multiple ages together, lots of the other or secondary IGRE activities may transpire. To name and rename just a few, there can be IG crafts, choirs, table games, skits, all-age baseball, age-mixed doubles in tennis, nature walks, Bible study, painting classes, square dancing, disco dancing, star gazing, new games, serendipity exercises, singing, guitar strumming, morning watches, worship, and quiet conversation. For just these reasons the all-congregation camp is the most comprehensive-intensive IGRE program model we have considered.

To round out this section on the camp/retreat model for IGRE, the wider variations on it should be noted. The *work-service project* is one. Faith communities here take on a project such as building a play yard with members from an inner-city church, painting a house of an elderly farm widow, setting up a Vacation Bible School in a migrant camp or preparing cabins and grounds of a retreat center. These kinds of projects are generally of several overnights. The work related to them is something that multiple generations can do together. Doing together enables people to come together. In the coming together there is a great deal of learning-about-life-and-faith. Much of that intergenerational learning can happen even when the project is only of an afternoon's duration, aimed at cleaning up the meeting house yard.

All too frequently the work-service project is one involving only youth and a few adult sponsors. There is no reason why young people could not be joined by more adults, children, and whole families. It would be for the enrichment of all.

Similarly, there would be mutual upbuilding if, on religiously sponsored *travel tours,* the primarily retired folk travelers were joined by younger people. On these domestic and international trips, the older eyes-of-experience *and* the younger eyes-of-wonder might focus separately and then share perception.

Yet another variation on the IGRE overnight-plus model is that of the *RV (recreational vehicle) Caravan.* Camper and trailer trips can and often do involve persons of many ages. Some caravan excursions are several weeks in duration. Clearly they can be of educational significance on several fronts for the IG sojourners.

Generically, we may be talking about *playgroups* in the faith community as similar to week and weekend IG experiences. Play groups enable people of all ages to laugh, concentrate, romp, match wits, learn new games, enjoy doing, and so on, together. This is part of the faith lifestyle, too, and it is especially engendered in break-away occasions for a week or weekend at camp. Related to the playgroup category are actual intergenerational *play productions* such as the Unitarian-Universalists are commending to their congregations. Such plays can be done in a camp setting or back home in eight to twelve weeks of rehearsal ending with the presentation of a dramatic or musical show.[44]

Assessment. The puzzle piece which the camp and retreat model most clearly picks up, which the other models cannot incorporate so easily, is the one of intergenerational physical or psychomotor activity and learning. We learn from and with each other by hiking, canoeing, and horseback riding together. My mental picture in this regard is of a beautiful eighty-year-old who led camp nature walks. She invariably had a train of followers which included a perceptive forty-year-old mother and an unrelated four-year-old boy. Wonder-filled peda-gogical (walking together) discovery and sharing among those three was strongly present. Physical IGRE activity that promotes faithful growth occurs for others on the baseball diamond, round dancing, doing a trust walk, or playing capture the flag.

My suspicion is that some of the most intense and life-shaping personal encounters with God happen for individuals in outdoor settings. Those powerful personal moments (often quiet moments and in solitude) are shaped in great part by caring others, younger and older, who surround and encourage the occasion of those mystical peak experiences.

There are, of course, some problems and drawbacks with regard to use of the all-congregation camp model for IGRE. One thing is the difficulty of getting enough people to give enough time to make such an experience happen. Schedules have to be cleared and people convinced that something worth their while is going to transpire. In the past, camps and retreats have been too age- and/or sex-specific, as for youth or women only. Such retreats are not to be denigrated, but they do not have the positive learning possibilities which the IG camp provides.

Retreats can also be somewhat expensive—as compared with never leaving town. Even so, the cost to a family for the congregation engaging a conference facility is considerably less than almost any other vacation or weekend trip. When the campers do their own cooking, the cost is further reduced—and meal preparation becomes a significant IG lifestyle happening.

A third problem which IGRE camps occasionally encounter is that of togetherness becoming too intense. To share a cabin or bathroom with people of different habits and hygiene can be difficult at times. An emotional spilling over, though, just as often serves good learning ends for all involved. "We became just like a real family," someone quipped.

Another shortcoming of the camp model is the absence of the long-term. The good gained on retreat is hard to sustain back in the "real world." The high level of support and sharing does not continue easily. Still, people know that they return infinitely better acquainted with others than they would ever be in a hundred coffee hours of saying "Hello, ah . . . [reading the name tag] . . . Bobbie!"

One should note, too, that programing for an all-congregation camp is no mean undertaking. It takes considerable forework, resourcing, and organizing to do age-inclusive meals, worship, games, movies, dancing, crafts, classes, and so on. As this is the case, some family-camp directors do not try very hard to be multigenerational in programing. Instead they stay with traditional age-specific activities, thus restricting the great learning advantage which the full days and mix of people portend. That is a danger. If, on the other hand, planners build in generational interaction opportunities throughout the experience, more religious lifestyle growth will take place in the hours of a single weekend than most persons will receive in a year of hourly classes and/or worship services.

Conclusion

In the notes of this chapter, I have identified bibliographic and other resources for the six models of IGRE. By no means is the list exhaustive. More resources are emerging. Many denominational and independent publishers are starting to list books and materials under the heading of "Intergenerational." Those who do not so list will have help for the reader under the category of "Family Resources."

The programs of IGRE that are being resourced will fit and be understood by the sixfold classification of this chapter. There are thousands— yea, tens of thousands—of programs and activities which churches and synagogues have conducted and are conducting along IGRE lines. Though many, they still are basically one. Insofar as this book is able to forward the theory and practice of the many forms, it is at the same time forwarding a basic genre of religious education called intergenerational.

Notes

1. George E. Koehler, *Learning Together: A Guide for Intergenerational Education in the Church* (Nashville: United Methodist Church, 1977), p. 56.
2. George E. Koehler, "Foundations for Intergenerational Education: A Study Guide" (Nashville: Discipleship Resources, 1979), p. 4.
3. Marguerite R. Beissert, *Intergenerational Manual for Christian Education: Shared Approaches* (New York: United Church Press, 1977), p. 13.
4. Margaret M. Sawin, *Family Enrichment with Family Clusters* (Valley Forge, Pa.: Judson, 1979), pp. 61-71.
5. Jeanette Benson and Jack L. Hilyard, *Becoming Family* (Winona, Minn.: Saint Mary's College Press, 1978), pp. 120-121. Also see National Family-Centered Catechesis Committee, *Family-Centered Catechesis: Guidelines and Resources* (Washington, D.C.: Board of Education, U.S. Catholic Conference, 1979), pp. 24-27, for a ten-category list of "Some Models of Family Catechesis."
6. Sawin, *Family Enrichment,* p. 27. For case histories on family clusters, see Margaret M. Sawin, *Hope for Families* (New York: Sadlier, 1982). Also see her article "Family Enrichment—The Challenge Which Unites Us," *Religious Education* 75:3 (May-June, 1980), pp. 342-353.
7. See R. Ted Nutting, *Family Cluster Programs: Resources for Intergenerational Bible Study* (Valley Forge, Pa.: Judson, 1977).
8. See especially Joe H. Leonard, ed., *Church Family Gatherings: Programs and Plans* (Valley Forge, Pa.: Judson, 1978), pp. 21-29, where John and Virginia Pipe discuss "Communication." Along these same lines is the book by Robert Arthur Dow, *Learning Through Encounter in Experiential Education in the Church* (Valley Forge, Pa.: Judson, 1971).

For illustration of a Jewish congregation using Family Clustering for similar purposes, see Dov Peretz Elkins, *The Humanizing Jewish Life* (Rochester, N.Y.: Growth Associates, 1976).

9. In addition to the resources already cited in these notes, Sawin's *Family Enrichment*, pp. 137-156, has a full bibliographic listing. Much of her own writing is listed in the mimeographed bibliography: Margaret M. Sawin, "A Bibliography for Family Clusters" (Rochester, N.Y.: Family Clustering, 1977), pp. 8-9. The whole bibliography is an excellent resource.

10. See Herbert A. Otto, *The Family Cluster: A Multi-Base Alternative* (Beverly Hills, Calif.: Holistic Press, 1971); Benson and Hilyard, *Becoming Family*, pp. 9-44; and Janice P. Alper, ed., *Learning Together: A Sourcebook on Jewish Family Education* (Denver: Alternatives in Religious Education, 1987), p. 49. Also see Sawin, *Family Enrichment*, pp. 62-64, for a description of additional programs.

11. Augustus Y. Napier and Carl A. Whitaker, *The Family Crucible* (Toronto: Bantam Books, 1980), p. 274.

12. Consult, for example, the following bibliographic source listings: Sheldon Louthan and Grant Martin, *Family Ministries in Your Church: A Comprehensive Guide for Church Leaders* (Glendale, Calif.: Regal Books Family Life Library, 1977), pp. 25-61; Mary Ellen Haines, "Resources," in the issue "Is the Family Dead?" *Journal of Current Social Issues* 14:1 (Winter, 1977), pp. 94-96; Barbara W. McCall, ed., "A.D. Report: The Family Today," *A.D.* 4:5 (May, 1975), p. 34; and Lois Seifert, *Our Family Night In: Workbook of Family Covenant Living* (Nashville: The Upper Room, 1981), pp. 155-156. One sample resource available for individual family use is *Families . . . Walking Together* (Findlay, Ohio: Vision House, 1981), a kit with cassette and family activities guides.

See also, Edwin H. Friedman, *Generation to Generation: Family Process in Church and Synagogue* (New York: Guilford, 1986).

Supplemental to the literature on "The Church and Family" is a broad range of books, journals, magazines, and publications which may be found in even the most modest pubic library. The card catalogue or microfilm reader will have hundreds of listings.

13. See also Susan B. Lidums, *Church Family Ministry: Changing Loneliness to Fellowship* (St. Louis: Concordia, 1985), pp. 58-69, in which she discusses several "forms" for family ministry, some of which are intergenerational in character. An additional resource on building IG communities within a congregation is Harold J. Hinrich's *Caring Community Project* (Minneapolis: Division for Life and Mission, American Lutheran Church, 1987).

14. Definition of "house church" will vary from situation to situation. In some places house church is a periodic gathering of folk for casual fellowship, food, and conversation. In other situations it is an intense support community. See Philip and Phoebe Anderson, *The House Church* (Nashville: Abingdon, 1975), especially pp. 146-159, for a discussion of "A House Church Cluster of Families."

15. Joseph and Mercedes Iannone, "Family Learning Team Approach to Total Parish Education," *Pace II* (September, 1980), p. 1. See also Mercedes and Joseph Iannone, "Family Learning Teams and Renewed Understanding of the Parish" in *Family Ministry*, ed. Gloria Durka and Joanmarie Smith (Minneapolis: Winston, 1980), pp. 228-248.

16. In my investigations of publishing houses producing religious education materials, I found that most have resources that are family-cognizant if not explicitly intergenerational. To date the most helpful materials are those generated by the Joint Educational Development (JED) Project in which fifteen mainline Protestant denominations are participating. More is said about these materials in this section. One sample resource is the 1987 publication *Living the Word with All Ages: For Use with LTW Children's Resources* which is the title of six quarterly IG guides for fall/winter/spring in a two-year cycle.

The United Methodist Church publishing office, Graded Press, has materials which provide guidance for IGRE classes. See, for example, Ruth McDowell, ed., *Intergenerational Learning Experiences* (Nashville: Graded Press, 1980). Other publishing houses often identified with production of IGRE materials are Augsburg, Fortress, and Judson, some titles for which we have already mentioned. Fortress does, *Together: A Guide for Leaders of Intergenerational Events*. Judson does, Mel Williams and Mary Ann Brittain's *Christian Education in Family Clusters: 38 Sessions for the Church Year* (Valley Forge, Pa.: Judson, 1982) which is a curriculum guide for ninety-minute Sunday morning classes. Barbara Kortney's *To All Generations: Sunday Church School Intergenerational Events and Classes* (Philadelphia: Parish Life Press, 1983) is a brief representative resource for IGRE church school classes.

Pioneer work in the IG class done by Sharee and Jack Rogers is reported in a book (now out of print) called *The Family Together: Intergenerational Education in the Church School* (Los Angeles: Acton House, but no longer publishing, 1976). If found, it can be most instructive.

Two articles of interest to persons starting an IGRE classes are Carolyn Engelhardt's, "Church School for All Ages Together," *Spectrum* 46:4 (July/August, 1976), pp. 4-6, and Jo Ann Gilmour's "An Intergenerational Sunday Church School," *Baptist Leader* 37:2 (January, 1976), pp. 54-56. Journals such as the two just cited and *The Church School Today* (United Methodist) and *Church Teachers* (Donald Cooper, ed.—a National Teacher Education Program publication), regularly carry articles on IGRE classes and other interage expressions.

17. Grace Maberry, "One in the Spirit: Prospectus for Intergenerational Education," A Report on the Project Exploring and Developing Intergenerational Education (EDIE), Board of Discipleship, the United Methodist Church, March, 1979, p. 5.

18. After a number of years of doing IGRE church classes for all grades, one Presbyterian Church found that first and second graders were better served by an age-specific class because of reading gap differences. See Faye Burdick, "An Update on an Intergenerational Education Experience," *Alert* (February, 1984), pp. 15-17.

19. The United Methodist Church, *Planbook for Leaders of Children, 1981-82* (Nashville: Graded Press, 1981), p. 42.

20. "The Decade" plans are outlined in the National Conference of Catholic Bishops, *A Vision and a Strategy: The Plan of Pastoral Action for Family Ministries* (Washington, D.C.: Publications Office, U.S. Catholic Conference, 1978). Tabor Publishing (formerly Argus Communications) has Catholic resources under the title of "Family Ministry," such as Delores Curran's video program called *The American Family: It's Not Dying, It's*

Changing. Paulist Press has Catherine Martin's *Building Christian Community* (Paramus, N.J.: Paulist, 1986).

21. See *Union of American Hebrew Congregations Catalogue, 1987,* pp. 2, 10, 11 and 20; also, *Catalogue '87/88 Alternatives in Religious Education,* pp. 3, 4, 22, 23 and 30.

22. In April, 1987, I wrote some sixty-four denominational offices and curriculum publishers to resurvey the field for IGRE materials. Among the resources discovered, beyond those already mentioned or to be mentioned, are the Friends (Quaker) Church publication of *Walking Cheerfully,* by Barbara Henderson, Lorraine Wilson, and Karen Read (Philadelphia: Yearly Meeting, 1983), a six-session class on nurturing the light within; the Presbyterian Church, USA, quarterly publication *Alert* which has resources listed under "Intergenerational," many of which concern weekly classes; and the booklet from the Mennonite Church by Bertha Harder and Marlene Kropf called *Intergenerational Learning in the Church* (Newton, Kans.: Faith and Life Press, 1982), 81 pp., which provides guidelines for use in shorter-term classes.

23. A good starting place regarding workshops for IGRE is Beissert, *Intergenerational Manual,* pp. 13-15. Leonard, *Church Family Gatherings,* offers some excellent workshop-like program ideas for "when the whole church family gathers together." A six-hour workshop on intergenerational education itself is described in Donald and Patricia Griggs, *Generations Learning Together: Learning Activities for Intergenerational Groups in the Church,* (Livermore, Calif.: Griggs Educational Service, 1976), pp. 31-35. More action-oriented is an IG "Hunger Workshop" described in Donald E. Miller's *Story and Context: An Introduction to Christian Education* (Nashville: Abingdon, 1987), pp. 92-94. A five-session intergenerational workshop "to guide your family in discovering together what the Bible says about values" is presented in *Family Values Workshop: Family Guide* and *Leader's Guide* (Glendale, Calif.: Gospel Light Publications, 1979).

24. JED curricular resources are found under the general title of "Congregational Life/Intergenerational Experience" resources. Two representative publications are Trudy Vander Haar's *Advent* (New York: United Church Press, 1977) and Patricia and Roger Robbennolt's *Planning Guide for Pentecost* (New York: United Church Press, 1978). Other resource guides from JED are entitled *The Lenten Season, Holy Week, Harvest/Thanksgiving* and *The Festivals of Christmas.* In addition, one may order JED curriculum guides on the themes of The Lord's Supper, Mission, Peace, Stewardship, Creation, and other topics. These work in well for a workshop event.

A number of other publishers have special issue guidebooks which can be used in a similar matter. See, for example, the Ecumenical Task Force on Christian Education for World Peace, *Try This: Family Adventures Toward Shalom* (A United Methodist Church Publication, 1987) and *Peace Experiments* (A Unitarian-Universalist piece from 1985).

The *Planbook* of the United Methodist Church lists similar seasonal and topic-focused IG resource materials.

Lutheran publishers are generating material in the field too. See *Sunday Gathering: Six Intergenerational Events for the Sunday Church School* (Philadelphia: Parish Life Press, 1984) which sounds like it is a weekly class curriculum piece but mostly focuses on occasional holiday celebrations.

Other authors and publishing houses have prepared guidebooks and booklets which may be consulted for purposes of conducting IGRE seasonal workshops. From the Eastern Orthodox perspective, see Gaynell and Jim Cronin, *The Great Events Series: All Saints Day to Pentecost* (Louisville, Ky.: Ikonographics, 1980). It has resource filmstrips, cassettes and study guides. Also helpful is Patricia and Donald Griggs, *Teaching and Celebrating Advent* (Nashville: Abingdon 1975). Richard E. Murdoch in an article, "A Family Festival Cluster," *Religious Education 72:5* (September-October, 1977), pp. 528-533, talks about a Christmas-time event which helps families focus on the season.

Rabbi Nathan Rose tells of four "Preschool Holiday Workshops" on the Jewish holidays in *Learning Together,* pp. 61-73.

25. As an example, see a description of an evening IG Bible study on the parable of the Good Samaritan, which evening included both supper and worship: DeVere Ramsey, "From Two to Ninety-Two: A Design for Small Churches," *JED Share* 14:1 (Spring, 1987), pp. 12-13.

26. The several illustrative events described in this paragraph were gleaned from *New Forms Exchange, Learning Together: Resources For Intergenerational Study* and others.

27. John H. Westerhoff III and William H. Willimon, *Liturgy and Learning Through the Life Cycle* (New York: Seabury, 1980), pp. 40-41. This book is an excellent opening into the arena of age-inclusive worship and education. Also see the John H. Westerhoff III and Gwen Kennedy Neville coauthored book, *Learning Through Liturgy* (New York: Seabury, 1978).

Westerhoff is a pastoral theologian interested in religious education. His amplified thoughts on age-inclusive worship and the thoughts of others, such as Randolph Crump Miller, C. Ellis Nelson, and David Ng are reviewed more thoroughly in chapter 8 of this volume, the last section therein. For this chapter and section, I will underscore for closer reference only David Ng's "What Children Bring to Worship," *Austin Seminary Bulletin* (October, 1978), pp. 5-30, and David Ng and Virginia Thomas' *Children in the Worshipping Community* (Nashville: Discipleship Resources, 1980). The Ng and Thomas book has a complete bibliography on the subject of age-inclusive worship and education on pp. 146-154.

28. Arlo Duba, "Seminarians Who Have Never Been to Church," *Monday Morning* (December 3, 1979), pp. 10-11.

29. Virginia Sloyan and Gabe Huck, eds., *Children's Liturgies* (Washington, D.C.: The Liturgical Conference of the Catholic Church, 1970) is a Catholic worship resource which is adaptable for ecumenical and intergenerational groups. A Lutheran source is James H. and Rowena D. Robinson's *How to Involve Children in Worship* (St. Louis: Concordia, 1980). Among Episcopal Church resources, see Thomas B. Woodward, *To Celebrate* (New York: Seabury, 1973). A. Roger Gobbel and Gertrude G. Gobbel in an article, "Children and Worship," *Religious Education* 74:6 (November-December, 1979), pp. 517-82, talk of learning in services for both children and adults. They ask, "What shall we *do along with* children?" The Anglican Church of Canada proposes something of an answer to the question in their publications, *Life in the Eucharist: A Communion Preparation for Children* with its *Child Parent Book* and *Leader's Guide* Toronto, Ontario: Anglican Book Centre, 1986), 56, 63 and 70 pages, respectively.

30. See James Haas, *Make a Joyful Noise!* (New York: Morehouse-Barlow, 1973) and Thomas and Sharon Neufer Enswiler, *Wholeness in Worship:*

Creative Models for Sunday, Family and Special Services (San Francisco: Harper & Row, 1979).

31. James F. White, *New Forms of Worship* (Nashville: Abingdon, 1971), p. 34.
32. Westerhoff and Willimon, *Liturgy and Learning*, p. 8.
33. Three books by Jerry M. Jordan, *The Brown Bag: A Bag Full of Sermons for Children, Another Brown Bag (Filled with Sermons for Children)*, and *One More Bag* (New York: Pilgrim Press, 1978, 1980, and 1983, respectively) are exceedingly helpful in doing children's sermons. See also W. Alan Smith, *Children Belong in Worship: A Guide to Children's Sermons* (St. Louis: Christian Board of Publication, 1984).

Abingdon Press lists among its resources the following books: *50 Children's Sermons* by Graham R. Hodges, *Silly Putty and Other Children's Sermons* by William E. Parsons Jr., *The Squirrel's Bank Account and Other Children's Sermons* by S. Lawrence Johnson, *Little Threads and Other Object Lessons for Children* by Harvey Daniel Moore III.

Children's sermons for various lectionary readings are available, such as Michael L. Sherer's *Good News for Children: Object Lessons on Epistle Texts Series* (Minneapolis: Augsburg, 1986), Series A, B and C, 128 pp. each; Philip E. Johnson's series, variously titled, *Celebrating the Seasons with Children* (New York: Pilgrim Press, 1984, 1985, 1986, respectively); or Jim and Doris Morentz's *Children's Object Lesson Sermons* for various lectionary years (Nashville: Abingdon, 1983, 1984, 1985, respectively).

Not all the writers on liturgical life are convinced of the value of the children's sermon. Ng and Thomas in their book opt in favor of omitting it and creating instead a revitalized regular sermon; see pp. 43-49 and 134-135 in *Children*. Philip W. McLarty, however, is an advocate of the children's message; cf. his *The Children, Yes! Involving Children in our Congregation's Worship* (Nashville: Discipleship Resources, 1981), pp. 48-58.

34. William Beaven Abernethy, *A New Look for Sunday Morning* (Nashville: Abingdon, 1975), p. 35.
35. A description of a decade's experience with this model and its holistic impact on All Saints Church is given in the appendix of this book. Also in the closing chapter is a "Pretend" piece imagining what happens to a younger and an older person who participate in an All Saint's Church program. Also, see James W. White, "Interage/Intergenerational Education: A Six Summers' Case Study," an unpublished paper delivered at the Annual Meeting of the Association of Professors and Researchers in Religious Education (St. Louis: November 20, 1977), 26 pp. (mimeographed).

Many other worship-education integration programs are described in the literature, especially in the loose-leaf publications *New Forms Exchange* and *Learning Together.*

Also relevant to this model are McDowell, ed., *Intergenerational Learning Experiences;* Gustav K. Wieneke, ed., *Summer Sunday School: Resource I;* and Alan Jahsman, ed., *Summer Sunday School: Resource II* (Philadelphia: Fortress, 1972 and 1978, respectively). Many of the resources listed in the notes given heretofore are germane to the working of this model too.

36. Maureen Gallagher, *Family: Parish Religious Education* (Paramus, N.Y.: Paulist, 1974). See also the Paulist program *Paths of Life* and the Twenty-Third Publications' *Total Parish Family Program.*
37. See the curriculum, *Living the Good News,* developed by the Episcopal

Diocese of Denver, Colorado, 1978ff. It is built around the Episcopal Eucharistic Lectionary readings. In 1987 this curriculum was in use by about a third of the Episcopal parishes in the United States. From an Eastern Orthodox perspective much the same approach is suggested by Vasiliki Eckley in "The Church Year and Lectionary as Curriculum for the Local Church," *Religious Education* 77:5 (September-October, 1982), pp. 554-567. United Churches of Christ across the country report similar lectionary-based curriculum developments, as in the Wisconsin Conference where the *Covenant Curriculum* was initiated. See the article "Using the Lectionary," *United Christ News* (November, 1986), p. 5.

Another outstanding resource for the integration of worship and education is the JED publication, *Planning Guide for Worship: A Congregational Life/Intergenerational Experience* by John and Catherine Ambrose (New York: United Church Press, 1979). It is particularly helpful as it includes a planning guide, music leaflet, and suggestions for worship-education activities.

38. Janet Fishburn, "Worship and Education: Text and Context," *Worship Alive* (Nashville: Discipleship Resources, 1979), p. 3.
39. Findings of a survey on IGRE church practices, reported in Maberry, "One in the Spirit," p. 5.
40. Information from personal conversation with Pat Becker, Director, LaForet Camp, Black Forest, Colorado, May, 1984.
41. Elizabeth and William H. Genne, *Church Family Camps and Conferences* (Valley Forge, Pa.: Judson, 1979) is the best single resource on this topic. Also worth considering are John D. Rozeboom, *Family Camping: Five Designs for Your Church* (Nashville: Board of Discipleship of the United Methodist Church, 1973); Robert Picken Davis, *Church Camping: Administrative Manual for Sponsoring Units, Planning Committees and Director* (Richmond, Va.: Knox, 1969), especially pp. 55-64 and the annotated resources guide on pp. 132-141; Mary Calhoun, *Vacation Time, Leisure Time, Any Time You Choose* (Nashville: Abingdon, 1975); and *Intergenerational Camping* (Philadelphia: Lutheran Church of America, 1987).

Geared more toward the weekend type retreat is Jack and Marcia Byington, *The Family Weekend Experience Kit* (New York: Sadlier, 1976). Adaptable to a week or weekend camp is Ralph R. Hellerich's *We Look At the Church: A Resource for Families* (Philadelphia: Fortress, 1979); "Track III" in this book is excellent for five sessions in a camp setting, pp. 23-50. Especially recommended for a several-day experience is Meredith Sommer Dregni's *Experiencing More with Less* (Scottsdale, Pa.: Herald Press, 1983), based on the book, *Living More with Less,* and concentrating on lifestyle change. Also see "The Family Car (Family Weekend Camp)," *Church Educator* (April, May, June, July, 1986 issues), 2 pp. each, and Shirley Barish's "Six Kallot: Retreats for Jewish Settings," which is ostensibly for youth but easily adaptable for an IG setting; this resource is listed in *Catalogue '87/88 Alternatives in Religious Education.*

Resources for IG camps recommended by Joseph Bragg of the Christian Church (Disciples of Christ) are three publications of the Outdoor Ministry Committee of the National Council of Churches: *Lifestyles of Faithfulness, Stewardship of Creation,* and *Community.* Bragg's commendation was in a personal letter of June 22, 1987.

A few other special resources to assist in intergenerational camps and retreats are these: Clarence M. Bowman, *Worship Ways for Camp* (New York: Association Press, 1955); Andrew Fluegelman, ed., *New Games Book: Play Hard, Play Fair, Nobody Hurt* (Garden City, N.Y.: Dolphin Books, 1975); Donald E. Miller and Others, *Using Biblical Simulations,* Vol. I and II (Valley Forge, Pa.: Judson, 1973 and 1975); and Elizabeth McMahon Jeep and Gabe Huck, *Celebrate Summer! A Guidebook for Families* and *A Guidebook for Congregations* (New York: Paulist, 1972). Hundreds of other resources for programing within all-congregation camps could be listed.

42. This resource note might be inserted at several places. It fits here too and concerns AUDIO-VISUAL RESOURCES for IGRE programs generally. A partial listings of good IGRE resources films can include *Lilith Summer* and *Close Harmony* from AIMS Media, *Hello in There* from Franciscan Communications in Los Angeles, *Special Trade* from Barr Films in Pasadena and *Death of a Gandy Dancer* available from the Learning Corporation of America in New York. These twenty to thirty minute IG-useful films are available through the National Teacher Education Program (Scottsdale, Az.).

Bella Jacobs, Pat Lindsley, and Mimi Feil list IG-related films in their *A Guide to Intergenerational Programming* (Washington, D.C.: The National Council on Aging, February, 1976), pp. 25-28. Among those recommended are *The Shopping Bag Lady, Where Life Still Means Living,* and the Edward Feil production *When Generations Meet.*

The Generations Together program at the University of Pittsburgh has a 1986 videotape which presents their young-people-with-older-people programs. It is entitled *The Best of You . . . The Best of Me.*

John and Mary Harrell of Berkeley, California have some A-V resources that include filmstrips, cassettes, and guides which have IG applicability. Listings include *Living the Christian Year, Lord Come* (for Advent), *Christ is Risen* and *Ways of the Spirit* (on the Book of Acts). A number of IGRE reports indicate use of a filmstrip with cassette called *Whobody There* (Winona, Minn.: St. Mary's College Press, 1971) which is useful in various IG settings.

An excellent resource related to doing family group dynamic work are two films produced by Virginia Satir and others, called *Insight* and *A Better Place to Stand* (Minneapolis: Manitou Productions).

43. See Bob Stowe, "All-Age Church Programming," *New Forms Exchange* (New York: United Church of Christ, 1978).

44. Alorie Boyle Parkhill and Mary Ann Moore, *Doing Plays with Kids* (Sudbury, Mass.: by the authors, 1980).

PART II
Theory

Chapter 4

Foundations in
Faith Resources

As the story goes in the twentieth chapter of Acts, a lad named Eutychus was seated in the third story window of a house listening to St. Paul preach. Paul went on and on into the midnight hour, and Eutychus fell asleep. He then fell out of his window perch, dropping three stories. Everyone presumed Eutychus to be dead—everyone except St. Paul who, bless his quick-to-learn heart, proceeded to hold the lad. Marvelously, life was restored.

In this story, minimally, is a message about relying less on words and more on other sense modes, including touch, in teaching. More importantly, for intergenerational religious education, the story of Eutychus is a biblical precedent of young and old engaged together in mutual edification. For surely Eutychus taught St. Paul even as he was instructed.

What people are doing today in IGRE has Judaeo-Christian faith heritage. In this chapter basic foundation stones for IGRE are unearthed by means of three disciplines related to the faith. The resources dealt with are biblical, historical, and theological. Section one is on the Hebrew Bible and includes subsequent Jewish educational practice. Section two gathers insights from the New Testament record and from life in the early Christian church. The next two sections treat church history per se, looking for intergenerational examples in the 1900 years since the close of the canon. In the final section contemporary theological resources are considered. I argue that constructive underpinning for IGRE may be found in the categories of "process" thought.

The foundational/theoretical material of this chapter is given as though it were the architectural design by which IGRE models are built. It is quite the other way around. Most IGRE pilgrimages are "practice in search of theory." Programs, procedures, and models are sometimes

69

erected without knowing whether the ground for the same is solid stone or sinking sand. On the basis of reading about the models of IGRE in the previous chapter, it may seem that there is not much in the way of foundation theory for these many programs. Such a view may be in error, as no one operates in a vacuum. So while it may "feel as though" theory follows practice, in actuality IGRE models are based on a latent, almost subconscious precedent.

Someone once described the human animal as a creature existing in a clear plastic bubble or "blip." We never see this encasing blip because we are always seeing *through* it. And we build through it, too. The blip is our invisible but ever-operative philosophy. In religious education our modus operandi is informed and formed by faith heritage and thought. In the process of gaining insights from fields supportive of religious education, we will be able to shape IGRE to kindle faith anew.

Insights from the Hebrew Bible and Judaism

For IGRE the keystone verse in all the scriptures is Psalms 145, verse 4: *"One generation shall laud thy works to another."*[1] Many IG services of worship begin with those words. The verse contains the important biblical idea that the generations are related to each other and need each other for life together in God.

In the Hebrew scriptures, connectedness among generations is understood especially in terms of *berith*—"covenant." The word of Yahweh is that "I will establish my covenant between me and you and your descendants after you throughout generations" (Genesis 17:7). In discussing covenant in conjunction with family, Old Testament scholar Walter Breuggemann writes: "Biblical faith is essentially *covenantal* in its perception of all reality. . . . The family is first of all a community of covenant-making, covenant-keeping, covenant-breaking, and covenant-renewing. That is its principal mark. . . . The family in the Bible is always *intergenerational.*"[2] The sense of generational relatedness in covenant has been diminished in modern society by the stress on individualism. By contrast, in ancient Israel the notion of an "individual" (autonomous free agent) is virtually nonexistent. Identity was lodged in the covenant of the nation of Israel. To be cut off from the *berith* was to be, in Hebrew, an individual or "idiot," a nonhuman.

Speaking of "The Faith Community in History," religious educationist Donald Miller notes that in ancient times Torah was the heart of the community and that "Torah" had the double meaning of both covenant and instruction. "Keeping the covenant," Miller says, "was based upon remembering. The whole people were to remember the covenant, including young children, adults, and the elderly."[3]

For the early Israelite the business of knowing one's genealogy was strongly present. It was essential for understanding the world, as identity was wrapped up in generational connectedness. A good Jew would say, "I am Joseph, son of Jacob, son of Isaac, son of Abraham . . . and so on." Familial lineage was more important than place of origin or profession or position in society. One was to "honor father and mother" (who came before) and "beget heirs" (especially male-type), so the family could go on. The generations were linked together by blood.

Stated another way but negatively, the notion of generations-related is carried in the idea of God "visiting the iniquity of the fathers upon the children to the third and fourth generations" (Deuteronomy 5:9) or in the saying that "The fathers have eaten sour grapes, and the children's teeth are set on edge" (Jeremiah 31:29).

For each generation there had to be nurturing in the faith. In Israel it was done intergenerationally. The formula for faithing is classically stated in the great *"Shema! [Hear!] O Israel!"*: "Hear, O Israel: The LORD our God is one LORD, and you shall love the LORD your God with all your heart, and with all your soul, and with all your might. And these words which I command you this day shall be upon your heart; and *you shall teach them diligently to your children."* (Deuteronomy 6:4-7a, emphasis added). In these words the Deuteronomist lays a heavy charge on his readers.

By and large, Judaism took that charge seriously, establishing an impressive teaching tradition. In biblical and postbiblical times the teaching mandated has taken place in two primary locations—the home and the synagogue. Usually that teaching is conducted in intergenerational transactions.

In a Jewish *home* around the dinner table, especially at Passover, the faith is recreated intergenerationally. In Deuteronomy the basic instructions for the Seder are given: "When your son asks you in time to come, 'What is the meaning of . . . [the things being done and said in the meal]' . . . then you shall say . . . [what they mean, and the reader is instructed in what to say]" (Deuteronomy 6:20-25). There is a hint of an underlying dialogical learning model in this stylized ritual prescription. We learn by asking questions and responding—if not with answers then with questions. One Jewish child is reported to have asked, "Father, why do you ask so many questions?" To which the father replied, "And why should I not?"

In the Seder meal there is a high moment in which the youngest reader-child asks "The Four Questions." They are questions of: "Why is this night different from all other nights? Why do we recline? Why do we eat unleavened bread? Why do we dip the herbs twice?" Then, an explanation is given. During the meal there is a great deal of physical movement, as when the children search for a hidden matzoh. In some households the eldest unmarried daughter goes to open the door for Elijah; cases are reported where she opens the door to usher in her intended!

The meal stays concrete operational in its teaching devices. So one learns by eating such foods as bitter herbs, which is quite symbolic. The Seder meal in the home seems to have served for centuries as the great equalizer of the generations and as teacher for all. In the same vein Rabbi Ahad Ha'am is reported to have said, "More than Israel has kept the Sabbath, the Sabbath has kept Israel."[4]

The second primary faithing source in the Jewish tradition is the *synagogue*. At one time the Temple in Jerusalem was the central shrine for the religion. After the destruction of Jerusalem (586 B.C.) and of the Temple (70 A.D.) with resulting diaspora of Judaism, the local synagogue came to prominence. The synagogue was for learning Torah. Rabbi Raymond Zwerin notes that even today, "The synagogue is first of all for education, second for fellowship, and third, for worship."[5] That is a different prioritization on building-use from what Protestants and Catholics practice.

Traditionally synagogue learning was strictly for men and boys. Today most synagogue schools are for both boys and girls. Persons who saw the "Judaism" program on the television series "The Long Search" may recall an intergenerational Torah School in Jerusalem. In this school for advanced studies emphasis was decidedly on discussing—really, arguing—the meaning of texts. Young and old alike were encouraged to join the conversation.[6]

A paradigm example for intergenerational learning in the Hebrew Bible and subsequent Judaeo-Christian religion, is the story of the boy Samuel and the old priest Eli (1 Samuel 1-3). In that story there is a full cast of interage and male-female characters. There is barren middle-aged Hannah who straightens out old Eli and receives a blessing in return. There are the sons of Eli who will learn from no one. There is young Samuel who hears Yahweh's voice three times and each time goes to old Eli for instructions. Eli gives instructions so that through the boy he himself might hear the Word of Yahweh. Priest teaches pupil that pupil may teach priest, that they all might be called "Rabbi."

Insights from the New Testament and Early Church

Children and youth in the early church—much as today—must have asked of their elders, "Tell me about Jesus as a child." Eventually, one story made it into the canon: Luke 2:41-48. It is the account of the boy Jesus in the Temple. An amazing aspect of that story is that Jesus' parents did a full day's travel away from Jerusalem before they missed him! Luke indicates that Mary and Joseph simply assumed their son was in the safe company of others in the traveling party. A trustful extended family must have been in operation. The assumption that Jesus was present proved to be in error. So Mary and Joseph went back to Jerusalem. They then spent three additional days searching for their son. The last place they thought to look for him was in the Temple! When they finally found him he was "sitting among the teachers, listening to them and asking them questions." We also read that "all who heard him were amazed at his understanding and answers." Apparently there was considerable give and take with these older teachers in the Temple.

One other thing to note in the Lukan passage is Jesus' place-putting of his parents. His first words to them were, "How is it that you sought me? Did you not know I must be in my Father's house?" This statement suggests a new understanding of family. By saying he needs to be in God's house, Jesus affirms that human solidarity includes more than immediate family or clan. Luke especially is one to emphasize that Jesus identifies with poor, the dispossessed, women, foreigners, and *children.*

The Synoptic Gospels all have accounts of Jesus-as-an-adult with children. In Matthew 19:13-15/Mark 10:13-15/Luke 18:15-17 Jesus invites children to stand beside him, to sit on his lap or to come near that he may lay his hands on them and pray. If the disciples had had their way, these youngsters would have been prevented from approaching. Jesus, however, says, "let them come"—as if to indicate that his message is for children too.

Jesus does, in fact, teach the children a lesson, though not with words. He invites them to the inner circle of the adult followers and gives them concrete instruction in the Kingdom of God. He does so by letting them experience him as a physically warm and loving person. At the same time, Jesus uses the children as a foil to teach the adults an abstract conceptual lesson about the nature of the "Kingdom of God." He engages in an IGRE parallel learning arrangement!

Closely related to the story of the blessing of the children is another Synoptic Gospel passage. In Matthew 18:1-6/Mark 9:33-37/Luke 10:46-48 Jesus is given to say, "Truly, I say to you, unless you turn and become like little children, you will never enter the kingdom of heaven. Whoever humbles himself like this child (one invited to stand beside him), he is the greatest in the kingdom of heaven." The point of his statement is that older people need childlikeness to be receptive to God's reign. The discovery of that essential childlikeness for the disciples, Jesus suggests, is facilitated by being appreciative of a child's perspective. For the child in this story there is also a great learning going on. He/she is affirmed as "Okay" now.

In most of the stories of the Bible involving younger people there is reciprocal interaction with adults going on. We have already seen that with Samuel and Eli and with Jesus and the elders. In the Hebrew Bible the same might be found in the accounts of Joseph and his brothers, Ruth and Naomi, David and Saul, Shadrach/Meshach/Abednego and the king and others. In the New Testament it is seen in the story of adolescent Mary and Elizabeth, young John and Jesus, Timothy and Paul, and, of course, Eutychus and Paul. The two-way relations become faith paradigms.

The primary advocate of relatedness in the apostolic church is St. Paul. In several of the letters he speaks of the "whole people of God," as well as of the connectedness of the Body of Christ. In 1 Corinthians 12:12-13 he writes: "For just as the body is one and has many members, and all the members of the body, though many, are one body, so it is with Christ. For by one Spirit we were all baptized into one body—Jews and Greeks, slaves or free—and all were made to drink of one Spirit." In Galatians 3:28 he says that in Christ there is "neither male nor female." We would add for him, "neither young nor old."

Paul holds high the ideal of familial spiritual connections. In his letter to the church in Rome, he makes his strongest case for who Christians are in relation to one another and God: "For all who are led by the Spirit of God are sons of God. For we did not receive the spirit of slavery to fall back into fear, but you received the spirit of sonship. When we cry 'Abba! Father!' it is the Spirit himself bearing witness with our spirit that we are children of God, and if children then heirs, heirs of God and fellow heirs with Christ . . ." (Romans 8:14-17a). As sons and daughters of every age—and all heirs of God with Christ equally—the faithful are encouraged by St. Paul to be the whole people of God together.

It appears that intergenerational cohesiveness might have been the case in the early church too. Several passages in the Book of Acts suggest that children were regularly included in the life of Christian communities. Age-inclusiveness is hinted at two times in the sixteenth chapter, for example. In Acts 16:15 we learn that Lydia, a woman and first convert to Christianity on the soil of Europe, was baptized "with her household," which household was likely to have included children. Again, in Acts 16:33 there is a suggestion of the same as Paul's jailer in Philippi was baptized "with his whole family." We are probably not wrong in thinking, either, that the Agape meal of the early church was every bit as multigenerational in exchange as was its antecedent Seder meal.

People of all ages in the early church may have learned together too. In the catacombs of Rome, for example, there are drawings on the walls dating back to the first century. A sketch of Jonah emerging from the whale very likely was a teaching aid to the faithful of every age to see, discuss, and reflect upon.

From such elementary efforts a systematic education program evolved. Something of its nature is seen in the *Didachē* or *Teaching of the Twelve Apostles,* one of the chief extrabiblical documents of the early church. It describes how Christians learned together at the beginning of the second century. In it the catechumen, young or old, is addressed as "my child" by the anonymous Syrian teacher. In traditional Jewish style, this teacher described "two ways" of life to the learner. Though the "right" way is clearly indicated, a dialogic model is suggested for learning. Part of the concern for the relationship of generations is seen in the *Didachē,* chapter 4: "Thou shalt not take thy hand from thy son and from thy daughter, but from youth on thou shalt teach them the fear of God."[7] In instructions regarding the eucharist, the author records that the whole church should be gathered together from the ends of the earth, even as the scattered grain is gathered into one loaf. The feeling one gets from reading the *Didachē* is that all people, young and old, may learn from "the Lord," the apostles, and each other.

Insights from a Millenium-Plus of Church History

In chapter 1 we noted that in traditional societies intergenerational exchange occurred on a daily—if not almost hourly—basis among people. It occurred because families were larger, extended, and usually lived together. The faithing of individuals was done intergenerationally in such families. St. Basil of the fourth century provides a case in point. In his earliest years Basil was educated by his grandmother who took him to the country for instruction. Later he was instructed by his rhetorician father. All the members of his family were Christians, and he was reared accordingly.[8]

The church, then, through most of its history has educated in cultures that were structurally intergenerational. Nothing extraordinary had to be devised in the way of any special programs of IGRE intent as most everything was intergenerational anyway. In this section I want to identify five things happening in the history of church up to the Protestant era which had intergenerational dimensions to them. IGRE was carried on through 1) religious instruction, 2) art, 3) worship, 4) season observances, and 5) life rites.

1. *Religious Instruction.* From the New Testament accounts we hear that most new members came into the primitive church simply on profession of faith. Later the church established religious instruction courses, notably the catechumenate for persons of varying ages. Candidates went through a rigorous two to three year period of instruction,

prayer, fasting, and good works before they were baptized and/or con-firmed into the church. Each catechumen (meaning "one under instruc-tion") had a sponsor, usually of a different age, with whom to work. The sponsor vouched for the candidate's eventual worthiness to receive the sacraments. Instruction in classes was likely of the order suggested in the *Didachē.*[9]

If the candidates for church membership were literate they might have read something like Augustine's *Enchiridion,* which means "hand-book" or "manual." Written for his spiritual "dearest son Laurence,"[10] Augustine explains the meaning of faith, hope, and love. Catechetical leaders might also have read Augustine's *Concerning the Teacher,* a semi-Socratic dialogue on communication between himself and his real fifteen-year-old son, Adeodatus. The conclusion of the dialogue is that learning is by truth, which is Christ, who is within.[11]

With the passage of historical time, the Mediterranean Sea became a Christian lake. The Greco-Roman world was Christianized. By the sixth century the custom of *infant* baptism became almost universal and confirmation emerged as a rite distinct from baptism. It lost some of the intergenerational character which had been present in the earlier bap-tisms of multi-age candidates.

Where intergenerational dynamic waned in one area, it waxed in another. Beginning in the fourth century and continuing through the next thousand years plus of the church's history were the monasteries and nunneries where interage learning continued and thrived. Though the monastic orders were sexually segregated, there was a wide range of ages involved in the life of the typical commune. White haired abbot, young tonsured novitiate, *and* children of all ages would be together regularly. Millar reports that a pattern was established early on whereby parents sent their children to monastic schools for general education as well as religious training.[12] One can well imagine, especially within self-sustaining communes, that a great deal of interage learning went on in the garden, the milk shed, the tannery, the scroll shop, as well as in the chapel. The learning and support was mutual, as suggested by this word picture of an older St. Basil:

> The great Cappadocian patriarch was an educationalist of no mean order. It is pleasant to picture him, worn with ill health, fatigued with the cares of his high office and unremitting labors for the preservation of orthodoxy and Christian unity, turning for solace to the boys of his schools. . . . It is not unlikely that he found the greater part of the inspiration for his best work in the classrooms and playgrounds of the schools he had founded.[13]

2. *The Arts.* In addition to person-to-person IG religious instruction in the history of the church, a second major contributor to all-age

learning was the arts, even as suggested above in use of catacomb pictures. Byzantium frescoes operated in much the same visual-education way. All through the period of the early church and during the "Dark" Ages, there were moments of graphic and architectural achievement. Then came the flowering of the Middle Ages. The great cathedrals of Europe sprang up in the twelfth through the thirteenth centuries. They spoke powerfully to all people, inviting the faithful to worship and to elevate thought to God. Within these cathedrals stained-glass art was developed and refined to make the windows of the cathedrals great teaching tools across the generations. In the lead and glass, stories of the Bible and church history were communicated effectively.

The greatest artistic piece, however, was done by St. Francis of Assisi. It was he, according to tradition, who set up the first manger scene. It became a classic art form, an expression of the collective unconscious. What Francis' grotto creche scene said to observers was that heaven and earth, animal and human, rich and poor, wise and foolish, man and wife, parent and child, *young and old* are intended to be together in God's Peaceable Kingdom.[14]

Integral to the period of the Middle Ages were the morality plays which came into vogue. These street and cathedral presentations worked with biblical themes, life problems, and "how to be saved" issues. People of all ages witnessed and/or participated in them. As a "G-rated" production, eight-year-old and octogenarian were instructed and could share reflections.

As for music, it really was *not* that much a part of the church for the first fifteen hundred years. The chants or plainsongs which were done stemmed from Hebrew and Greek traditions. Codified by Pope Gregory in the late sixth century the use of such chants was restricted primarily to monks and other persons who could read. In the Renaissance, with the invention of the printing press and the rise of literacy, new musical shape in the church occurred with part singing, chorales, and hymns for all.

3. *Worship.* More than through catechetics or the arts, religious education was carried through Christian worship itself. For most of church history, the synonym for worship is "Mass." Central to the Mass is the *action* of it. The action is what made worship an intergenerational learning experience. There is abstract symbolic mystery in the Mass for adults to ponder, and there is visible and concrete doings to hold the attention of the young. In a Catholic or Orthodox Mass there is movement, color, sounds, smells, and more. With enough action young people can go right along learning with the eldest persons present, each asking questions and offering interpretation.

At this point one might ask, "How did all this action in worship

develop historically?" My hypothesis is that the more dramatic moments in the Mass—such as bell ringing, lifting the host, kneeling to
receive the wafer, and so on—may well have evolved precisely as an
accommodation to younger worshipers, to hold their attention. The
action of the Mass conveys the sense, "Stay awake, children. Look up.
There is something here you need to know!" Without rituals which have
drama and movement, people—including adults—become disinterest-
ed, restless, bored, and sleepy.

For most of the centuries that Christian people have assembled, they
have done so intergenerationally and in a ritual life which evolved to
involve everyone present. People learned together. They heard the scripture lessons. They recited creeds. They responded to the chants. They
received the Host. And they did these things standing, sitting, kneeling,
and occasionally with face on floor! More than anything else, what was
happening interactively in the pews was that people were modeling the
role of "worshiper" one for another. As always, the lifestyle of faith was
being caught more than taught.

4. *Liturgical Calendar.* In addition to catechetics, art, and worship, a
fourth education feature evolved over the first two-thirds of the history
of the church: the Christian calendar year. It too worked to bring generations together.

At one time in the Middle Ages, it is reported, so many holidays were
on the calendar that the soldiers complained that they did not have
enough days to fight. Then as now, holidays generally served to unite
disparate generations. On holidays people worship, go to fairs, compete
at sports, eat, talk, dance together. In time the regional holy and saint
days were integrated into a Christian calendar year. The calendar indicated to the faithful that life has a pattern to it. The basic format of the
liturgical calendar includes the birth, ministry, and death/resurrection of
Christ's life. Everything else is placed around these. Interestingly
enough, the longest season turns out to be that of the "Sundays after
Trinity" up to twenty-eight in all. The liturgical color for this season is
green—green for growing/becoming/learning under the intergenerational dynamic of Father, Son, and Holy Spirit.

5. *Life Rites.* Related to the seasons of the Christian calendar year
were rituals marking life passages for people. With all religions Christianity is involved with the whole human life saga. Beliefs and practices
were devised to ritualize womb-to-tomb events. Seven sacraments—
baptism, communion, confirmation, marriage, ordination, confession,
and extreme unction—were identified as key rites to be observed in the
life cycle.

These rituals became for surrounding witnesses meaningful and educative events. In those days babies were born in homes. Everyone in the

family knew what was happening. They fully participated in the birth-
ing rituals and the closely attendant baptismal rites. And likewise younger siblings and older friends and family gathered to be attentive to the
child receiving first communion. Puberty was marked by confirmation
ceremonies. Adulthood usually was signified by marriage or, for some,
the taking of ecclesiastical vows. People fought. They lied, were unfaith-
ful, gossiped, sinned, and were forgiven. They got sick, died, and were
buried. All of these things happened to people of various ages, and it all
took place in the presence of persons of different ages—in the intergenerational extended family. The sacred social rituals of the church helped
educate each and all into the meaning and mystery of life.

The historic rituals of the church affirm that no one should mourn or
rejoice in isolation. The rituals which emerged for seasonal and life-
event moments affirm that people are made for one another. The rituals
helped—and help—with learning about life together.[15]

Insights from the Protestant Era On

The above elements which enabled generations to learn together over
historical time have not gone out of existence. Religious art, the liturgical calendar, and so on, are still with us. Even so, events of the last five
hundred years have changed some things in the culture and in the
church, effecting new interage teaching-learning responses. Let me indicate two major historical changes and two creative responses to those
changes.

With the Protestant Reformation change occurred in worship. A de-
emphasis on the Mass in Latin transpired. Martin Luther said that
people should hear "The Word" in the vernacular. In emphasizing the
Word, Luther elevated preaching to near-sacramental status. Meanwhile
five of the seven earlier sacraments were dropped as nonbiblical. In
time other Protestant Reformers expunged worship services of much of
the former visual and physical action. Puritan sabbath services in America, for example, were remarkably plain. People may have heard the
liturgy/Bible/sermon in their native language, but the use of the dea-
con's head knocker and feather tickler suggests that for many people the
services were awfully long and not particularly engrossing. In pictures of
Pilgrims going to church we see that children went too. One may ask if
they understood what was said. If the answer is in the negative, then
pulpit overtalk may help account for why, in part, by the beginning of
the nineteenth century, less than 10 percent of the population in the new
United States was church-affiliated.

A second major cultural event of the last several centuries is related to
understanding childhood. With the Renaissance new conceptualizations
of "man" came into being. In time "childhood" was seen differently too.

Prior to the late eighteenth century, children were considered "imperfect adults," *tabla rasa* (blank slates) to be written upon. They needed molding until finally worked into acceptable adult shape. In the medieval mind, childhood did not have distinguishable characteristics for which any particularly special educational attention needed to be directed. Hence, children grew up within the adult world. In a sense, they did not really exist.

The person who helped turn thinking around on this subject was Jean Jacques Rosseau. His book, *Emile,* is the story of raising a child natureally. It helped people perceive childhood as qualitatively and quantitatively different. Said he, "Nature wants children to be children before they are men. . . . Childhood has ways of seeing, thinking, and feeling peculiar to itself."[16] Children began to be understood as a truly *different generation* in the human family.

In the twentieth century we have seen elaboration of the categories of childhood with the classification "teenager." Adolescence is something new in people's perception, for up until very recently teenage persons too were just adults in process. More recently Kenneth Keniston has spoken of the category of "youth" or postadolescent adult. This eighteen to twenty-six-year-old age group is now seen as having characteristics uniquely its own.[17] Through the writings of Gail Sheehy (author of *Passages*) and Daniel Levinson *(Seasons of a Man's Life)* other important qualitative differences in people who enter their middle years are being identified. All in all moderns have discovered that "different-age folks are different." One of the consequences of this new appreciation has been to segregate ages into peer groups which, as noted, begins to have other problems.

A socio-religious response to emerge from the changing conditions of recent history has been to place greater emphasis on the home as the locus for religious education. Though the sacraments were deemphasized in Protestant circles, the concept of the "priesthood of all believers" with the "centrality of the scriptures" were together underscored. These two emphases began to play out at the family dinner table. Luther's *Table Talk* discourses suggested a pattern of educational interaction for subsequent generations. In European cottages and frontier American cabins the split log table became an altar upon which a family Bible was placed and interpreted. All ages together were instructed and could share generation-to-generation.

Susanna Wesley, mother of John and Charles, is said to have taken each of her nineteen children aside for one hour per week of individual Bible study. Her home-life example is not an isolated instance. Learning was generation-to-generation.

A second development in religious education was the response to the changed historical situation in late eighteenth-century England. This was the Sunday school movement which so flowered in America at the turn of the last century. Though the Sunday school was a very grade and sex-conscious enterprise, it was a historically successful and enjoyable creation. There was action in it for those who participated. With the development of uniform lessons all learners in the Sunday school studied the same topic the same week. Enabling graded classes to be more interactive, church architects developed the "Akron Plan" for church interiors. The Plan had a center stage where the Sunday school superintendent sat. Around and above him were three or more balcony tiers for classes of adults and children. Arranged by age and sex these classes participated jointly in the opening exercises. Separate doors were then drawn around each cluster of students, so they could study at their own level of interest and ability for another thirty to forty minutes. At the end of the hour, the doors were reopened and all persons together took part in the closing ceremonies.

Cultural/societal/ecclesial situations differ over time. Not all intergenerational educational mechanisms of the past work well now. The multigenerational home has mostly passed. Except in some fundamentalist Christian circles, Sunday school for adults and, to a lesser degree, for children is not thriving. Still we see how these worked in the past. Christians are challenged to revitalize such or find effective alternative forms in continuing to "go . . . baptize . . . and *teach*" (Matthew 28:19-20).

Insights from the Categories of Process Theology

In addition to the supports which the Bible and history give to the idea of intergenerational education, further under-girding may be found in contemporary theological thought. I find work done in process theology particularly helpful.

During the 1950s and '60s American religious education was strongly influenced by neo-orthodox theology. Neo-orthodoxy placed emphasis on the existential situation of the human, a correct formulation of historic dogma, the importance of decision making, the giving of glory to God alone, appreciation of the pervasiveness of sin, and the need for people to respond to God by service in the world. Educational curricula of this time was heavily influenced by such theological input, to wit: The United Presbyterian "Faith and Life Curriculum." One logical consequence in childrens' curriculum, for example, was to throw out the song, "Jesus Loves Me." That kind of song, the neo-orthodox curriculum writers argued, is too egotistically sinful. "Emphasis should be put on *our* loving God and the neighbor," curriculum enactors concluded. The point is that what we believe makes an impact on what we do educationally.

There is no shortage of theological formulae today. Liberation theology, the theology of hope, evangelical-fundamentalism, neo-liberalism, and continuing neo-orthodoxy all may be found. In religious education circles there is widespread interest in process theology. The philosophy of Alfred North Whitehead and the theological company of Hartshorne, Weiman, Williams, Loomer, Ogden, Teilhard de Chardin, and others has been well-received. Religious educators affiliated with the professional publication *Religious Education,* for example, often write from a process perspective.[18] I share the enthusiasm.[19] The reason process thought is so well-received is because it does such a good job of describing how 1) God, 2) the world, and 3) humankind really are and how they are going. These three categories, God/world/humankind, are seen in process thought as more alike than dissimilar. They share common characteristics. So that the way we describe people (as "changing," for example), may also be descriptive of the world and of God.

In this final section, five words are presented which are frequently found in the writings of process theologians. I think they also will instruct IGRE. The words are 1) becoming, 2) relating, 3) loving, 4) creating, and 5) enjoying. All these words are "ing" words or linguistic verbals. In English, verbals may be participles or gerunds, but first and foremost, they are verbs of action used as predicate adjectives *and* nominatives. The difference between an adjective and a noun sometimes cannot be clearly drawn. So to say, "God is becoming" may be to use "becoming" as an adjective *and* as a noun—but active as a verb nevertheless. So these process theological words are verbals, suggesting that God/world/people are active rather than passive. The "ing" words also describe what is going on in time present, not time past.

1. *Becoming.* Becoming is the primary word in process theology. It is a veritable synonym for "process"—and probably for "growing" too. To say that the world or God or people are in the process of becoming is to acknowledge that "what is" is not what "will be." There is room for expansion, change and, hopefully, improvement.

Let us first consider God as becoming.

The Greek categories of "being" which influenced Christian theology for so many centuries are giving way to an emphasis on becoming. God as the Unmoved Mover and First Cause is not the way to think of God. God is not "the same yesterday, today, and tomorrow," unless the sameness is in the constancy of change. God is best understood as that one who is in process too.

Especially we note that people are becoming, changing, moving, and maybe even progressing. Humans do not have an unchanging nature but are, in fact, malleable and dynamic. Instead of being static creatures we are clearly a species on a pilgrimage involving growth and change. This becoming is not, of course, unidirectionally forward or inevitably progressive, but there is hope for fuller realization of potential. Furthermore, becoming is not restricted simply to the young. People of every age can wear the lapel button: "BE PATIENT, GOD HASN'T FINISHED WITH ME YET!" Life is not an aborigine's one-possibility thing. It goes on beyond puberty, beyond Catch-30's, beyond forced retirements. In the process of becoming every person needs others to aid him or her. We are not born alone. We seldom die alone. And we do not grow alone. Interaction with other people helps us with our becoming. Process theologian Norman Pittenger states the case this way: "We belong with our fellow humans. We should not be able to develop our capacity to understand ourselves unless we had others around us and with us." Pittenger illustrates the point, saying that a baby becomes whole by interaction with others. That which is true for babies is true for adults too. "Healthy growth depends always upon acceptance of those others, with whom we live and in sensitive relationship with whom we begin to live well."[20]

The world, too, is in process of becoming. I will say more about this idea under the category of "creating," but the point for the moment is that everything is alive and has potential. The world is ongoing, and there is evolving taking place not just with humans or in the animal kingdom but with all entities. The world is lively.

So, God, people, and world are becoming. The development of each is related to all, and all are interacting. As each becomes more nearly what he/she/it was intended to be, such becoming adds to the becoming of the others. God, for example, becomes more because Jacob can say to Esau, "In your face I see the face of God" (Genesis 33:10b).[21] This is part of what process theologians mean by "the consequent nature of God" (see below) developing from human becoming.

2. *Relating.* Especially relevant for purposes of intergenerational education is the category relating. Whitehead says the world is "organismic," meaning that everything is connected. Another synonym which might be used is "societal." More than people in years past, we know from recent ecological investigations that to tug at any single thing in nature is to find it attached to the rest of the world. When the world appeared divided, isolated and every thing a "thing-in-itself," we could go about the business of industrial "development" or whatever without much concern for relating. No more.

Events in the world of nature relate strongly to societal happenings. Nature historian, William Cronon, says: "It is almost as though the trees and the soil and the animals, wild and domestic, were active protagonists, for the impact they had on the (American) colonists was at least as profound as the impact of the colonists on the land."[22] The relationship is two-way.

Process theology asserts that God too is relating to the world and to humankind. Whitehead describes God as having a "primordial" and a "consequent" nature. Primordial is suggestive of a creating God who gives "aim" to all things. God's consequent nature is that which God becomes as a consequence of receiving what the ongoing world and humanity offer back—what we become. In this sense what God will be is not determined until people respond and act. In the primordial and consequent natures of God we see how people and world and God are relating.

In the relating of God and humankind and world one should note that the relating is dynamic. God's consequent nature—or what God shall become—is in part determined by humankind's offering to the world. Process theology does not work with a hierarchial understanding of divine-human connectedness. Neither has it a top-down understanding of human-human connections. We give and receive in more equal measure. This applies across generations as well. Our consequent nature changes as we relate.

The point to be underlined for IGRE purposes is that people's humanity is insured only through relating which is meaningful. Contrary to mythic hyperbole, there is no "self-made" man or woman. One cannot be human alone. Only humans make us human. A newborn baby literally has to be stroked or the spine shrivels up and the infant dies. Remus and Romulus notwithstanding, wolf-reared children do not reenter society as humans. And the physically sickest people in society are *not* those most exposed to others' germs. More than age, it is isolation which puts people in an early grave. And so on and so on. Relating is what keeps life human.

3. *Loving.* To speak of God/world/humanity as loving is to indicate the character of the relating just discussed. Loving is the active principle in the world by which things are moved. By loving, God lures humanity into new becomings. By loving, we move one another and the world. Below is one of the best known quotations from process thought on the nature of God. It is Whitehead's statement about the "Galilean origin (or vision) of Christianity":

> This vision does not emphasize the ruling Caesar, or the ruthless moralist, or the unmoved mover. It dwells upon the tender elements in the world, which slowly and in quietness operate by love; and it finds purpose in the present immediacy of a kingdom not of this world. Love neither rules, nor is it unmoved; also it is a little oblivious as to morals. It does not look to the future; for it finds its own reward in the immediate present.[23]

This loving is also described by Whitehead and others as luring, persuading, and inviting. According to process theologian Norman Pittenger, God is "pure unbounded Love," the "cosmic Lover."[24]

The "chief exemplification" or "classic instance" of the loving God *and* the loving human is Jesus Christ. If Jesus was anything he was loving. He was the lover nonpareil. He loved/lured/persuaded people into dynamic relationship with God so they might become all that is possible for them to become. The Galilean did not force or command except by his outgoing love. He loved and lived, died and was raised for *all* people. And now, according to the process thinkers, the Risen Christ, who is ahead of us, now beckons/calls/lures/loves humankind into the future for the enhancement of the consequent nature of God and the world.

The implications of loving for the educational task are many. First and foremost, loving is the style by which the best religious education, including intergenerational expression, is guided. These sundry persons in and around churches and synagogues are not just anybodies who come together for worship, fellowship, and learning. They are some-bodies. Their becoming is most effectively enhanced by loving. "Of people" we should "be a little more careful than of any other thing." Not that there is no room to "afflict the comfortable." There is. The big reminder, though, is that people are best motivated by relationships which honor and respect them as persons. Though we highly value the love received from same-age peers, we also are moved by the kind of attention given by persons younger and older. Few things are nicer than a child on one's lap or a shoulder rub by grandma!

Another thing to note about loving and IGRE is that faith communities in the United States have no other option, other than loving, in religious education. Required attendance in religious instruction, for example, cannot be had in this country, as in some. The church/synagogue is a voluntary organization, which is an advantage. Less-coerced learners participating in religious education programs are people more open to being loved and loving. Those responsible for IG learning opportunities get to "lure" (love) their mixed educational pilgrims into growth and the process of new becomings. Insofar as they do, it enables all to participate in and experience the nature of God, world, and people as loving.

4. *Creating.* When the term "creating"—or especially, "creation"—is used, the first mental association is likely to be with the Genesis 1 story. We think of God as creator "in the beginning." Process theology, however, emphasizes that God is ongoing creator, which is more than being sustainer of a once-and-for-all-time created universe. The creation is not completed. So the creating goes on. It goes on for God and also for the world and for people.

The best synonym for creating is probably "innovating" or "novelty." "Behold!" Yahweh says (according to Isaiah 43:19), "I am doing a new thing!" This assertion about God's activity is likewise affirmed for the world and people in process thought. The creation of the new, of the novel, is how process (becoming) takes place. It may be that people in North and South America are especially open to this idea. From the first years of American history we have been a nation emphasizing the new—New World, New England, New Haven, New York, New Jerusalem. We are a people prizing novelty and creativity. If an advertiser says something is "NEW," Americans buy it. This openness to the novel may also account in strong measure for why process thought has been so readily accepted in America.[25]

Creating and innovating are intriguing to consider. They often happen when new mixes of ideas, elements, or ages occur. Insofar as faith communities facilitate such mixing for creativity, we join God in the work of making things new. Insofar as we create imaginative programs which significantly involve and benefit people, we are co-creating. Based on the plethora of reports on IGRE programs spoken of in the previous chapter, it would appear that there is a great deal of creativity ad novelty happening yet in the faith communities.

5. *Enjoying.* The idea of "enjoying" by God/world/people is a category in process thought that John Cobb and David Griffin, in particular, have lifted up.[26] The notion here is that all things—rocks, trees, bees, and people—have an initial aim in life. That aim or purpose is to become the most that it is possible for them to become: If a flower, then a bright and pleasant-smelling one; if a mouse, then an active and squeaky one. When this happens all things reach some state of existence that is optimally satisfying. The entities find fulfillment or great enjoyment in time. Enjoying is not shallow "Ha-Ha" laughing (though it might know laughter) but is more accurately seen as deeper, having to do with significant realized meaning. To enjoy the mountains, a child, good music, even a sermon may be to find life fulfilling, enjoyable. It might be that we should think of enjoying as close to what Abraham Maslow means in speaking of "peak experiences." In older language, it might be considered the answer to the Westminster catechetical question, "What is the chief end of man?" The answer: "The chief end of man is to know God and *enjoy* him forever." On God's part we might say that the Holy One is *delighting* in the world and enjoying the praise which divine love inspires. In *Chariots of Fire,* track star Eric Liddell says of God, "He made me fast, and when I run I feel his pleasure."[27]

It just may be too that the world advances on enjoying and enthusiasm. Teilhard de Chardin puts it this way: "Although we too often forget this, what we call evolution (of the world) develops only in virtue of a certain internal preference for survival (or, if you prefer to put it so, self-survival) which in man takes on a markedly psychic appearance, in the form of a *zest for life.*"[28] Life with vitality is "very good" for God, humanity and the world.

The obvious point in consideration of enjoying for intergenerational education is that IGRE should be enjoyable too. In the movie, "Oh, God!" God (George Burns) says that he is a comedian playing for people who are afraid to laugh. Insofar as that is true for Christians and Jews it may account for why much of Sabbath school and CCD education is so deadly. We are not really attuned to delighting and enjoying with God. The relevant word then, reads something like this: Provide IGRE offerings for people to enjoy; let classes, retreats, workshops, sermons, sing-a-longs, and programs meet and fulfill genuine needs; let people spark each other and there will be light; enable *joy* (hope/realized potential/meaning/faith) to come *in*to each learner—or, to well up from with*in* each learner—and, thus, all may together *en*-joy God/world/humanity.

* * * *

Insights from the faith for intergenerational religious education can be found in the Hebrew scriptures and Jewish tradition. Resources are available in the New Testament witness and in Christian history both pre- and post-Reformation and in contemporary theology. In devising specific IGRE programs people may not have realized from what a wealth of resources they were already drawing. Hopefully this chapter discloses some of the underlying faith resources (latent or new) which will be work-enhancing. Such base supports are present and can be helpful when consciously built upon. In general the witness of the scriptures, the experience of our Jewish and Christian foreparents, and the categories of process thought together act as macrotheory from within the faith tradition for intergenerational life and learning.

Notes

1. Revised Standard Version. See also Psalms 148:1 and 12-13.
2. Walter Brueggemann, "The Covenanted Family: A Zone for Humanness," *Journal of Current Social Issues* 14:1 (Winter, 1977), pp. 18-19.
3. Donald E. Miller, *Story and Context: An Introduction to Christian Education* (Nashville: Abingdon, 1987), p. 43.
4. Quoted in *Learning Together: A Sourcebook on Jewish Family Education* (Denver: Alternatives in Religious Education, 1987), p. 78.
5. Raymond Zwerin, Rabbi, Temple Sinai, Denver, Colorado, personal conversation, 1979.
6. "Judaism," Public Broadcast System Television Series: *The Long Search* (Fall, 1979).
7. *Didachē* or *Teaching of the Twelve Apostles,* ed. Roswell D. Hitchcock and Francis Brown (New York: Charles Scribner's Sons, 1885), p. 11. For addi-

tional detail on this document, see Gerald S. Sloyan, "Religious Education: From Early Christianity to Modern Times," in *Source Book for Modern Catechetics,* ed. Michael Warren (Winona, Minn.: St. Mary's College Press, 1983), pp. 111-112.

8. L. Millar, *Christian Education in the First Four Centuries* (London: Faith Press, 1946), p. 50.

9. See Teleketics, *The Changing Sacraments—Godparent Gussie: Baptism/Confirmation* (Los Angeles: Franciscan Communications Center, 1974), a filmstrip.

10. Augustine, *Confessions* and *Enchiridion,* Vol. VII of *The Library of Christian Classics,* trans. and ed. Albert C. Outler (Philadelphia: Westminster, 1955), pp. 337-339 for introduction to the book.

11. Augustine, *Concerning the Teacher,* tran. George G. Leckie (New York: Appleton-Century-Crofts, 1938), p. 56.

12. Millar, *First Four Centuries,* p. 135.

13. Ibid., p. 75. (Were Millar writing in these times, I suspect his wording would be different here.)

14. See James W. White, "Creches and Communion," *The Christian Ministry* 8:6 (November, 1977), pp. 31-32.

15. In our day the marker events of human life are not so well ritualized or attended by people. Consider funerals. Very often when an older family member dies, geographical distance prohibits third generation persons— meaning children—from attending. That is a social ritual tragedy. There is no better occasion than a funeral for the young to learn about and deal with death. They need to be there to ask what is going on, see their father cry (yes) and give comfort. They have that to offer. They always have.

16. Jean-Jacques Rosseau, *Emile,* trans. and ed. William Boyd (New York: Teachers College Press, 1966), pp. 38-39.

17. See Kenneth Keniston, *Young Radicals: Notes on Committed Youth* (New York: Harcourt, Brace and World, 1968), p. 264ff.

18. See, for example, the Symposium Issue: "Process Thought and Religious Education," *Religious Education* 68:3 (May-June, 1973); also, Iris V. and Kendig Brubaker Cully, eds., *Process and Relationship: Issues in Theology, Philosophy, and Religious Education* (Birmingham, Ala.: Religious Education Press, 1978).

19. See my "In Process: A Theology for Adult Christian Education," *Lumen Vitae* 37:4 (1982), pp. 413-430.

20. Norman Pittenger, *Unbounded Love: God and Man in Process* (New York: Seabury, 1976), p. 36.

21. Pursuant to this idea, see Richard A. Rice, "Theological Affirmations for Intergenerational Education," paper delivered at the United Methodist National Consultation on Intergenerational Education (Nashville: February 19-21, 1979). Rice emphasized the church as community and that God is revealed through persons of all ages.

22. D. Kimball Smith, "Historian of the West," *Yale Alumni Magazine* 48:4 (February, 1985), p. 17.

23. Alfred North Whitehead, *Process and Reality: An Essay in Cosmology* (New York: Free Press, 1969), p. 404.

24. Pittenger, *Unbounded Love,* p. 52.

25. For elaboration on "novelty" as a special American value and goal, see James W. White, "Credos of the Academy: College Presidents' Inaugural

Addresses as an Indicator of Religious Positions in and of Higher Education," *The Iliff Review* 35:1 (Winter, 1978), p. 47.
26. John B. Cobb Jr. and David Ray Griffin, *Process Theology: An Introductory Exposition* (Philadelphia: Westminster, 1976), pp. 54-57.
27. W. M. Weatherby, *Chariots of Fire* (New York: Dell, 1981), p. 87.
28. Pierre Teilhard de Chardin, *Science and Christ,* trans. Rene Hague (New York: Harper & Row, 1968), p. 212.

Chapter 5

Social Scientific Theorists
[And Some]

When asked to identify fellow social scientists whose theory might be consulted in support of intergenerational education generally, Lawrence Senesh, professor emeritus at the University of Colorado, said, "No one can be pointed to as the father or mother of intergenerational education."[1] He noted further that there is no systematic body of knowledge or any clearly catalogued literature for the philosophical foundations of this field.

At the same time, there is some very helpful macrotheory to be found in academic disciplines close but not directly related to intergenerational life and learning. In this and the following chapter I want to lift up some of the basic and relevant social-scientific thought that has been formulated which has applicability for IGRE. We begin by considering key ideas apropos to intergenerational learning provided by a social philosopher (George Herbert Mead), a social psychologist (Erik Erikson), a family psychotherapist (Virginia Satir), and an anthropologist (Margaret Mead). None of these four contributors ever use the phrase "intergenerational education"—much less "IGRE"—yet each is talking exactly about such in his or her own seminal way.

The above-mentioned social scientists have had their work complemented by others who have addressed issues somewhat similarly in the field, or they have extended work begun by the primary person. So, in these pages we shall also consider such thinkers as Martin Buber, Sigmund Freud, Margaret Sawin, and Mary Mead Bateson. (These latter names and others constitute the "[and some]" of this chapter.)

The next chapter also presents social-scientific theory, it being a review of reflection being done on "stages of human development" in regard to cognition, moral reasoning, faith construction, and adult life structure. At that chapter's conclusion I do a summary lifting up of recurring themes from the various social scientific thinkers identified in *both* chapters. Together, these two chapters provide a first draft for the missing systematic theoretical base for intergenerational religious education.

The Social Philosopher: George Herbert Mead (and Martin Buber)

George Mead, the early-twentieth-century behaviorist, sociologist, and philosopher at the University of Chicago, is without question the person with whom to begin a search for foundations in IGRE. His insights into how and why people learn from one another are truly foundational. Mead speaks often of "the social self." What he does from a modern social-scientific point of view is reassert what Aristotle said twenty-four hundred years ago, namely, that the human is a "social animal."[2] Mead describes our situation thusly: "All living organisms are bound up in a general social environment or situation, in a complex of social interrelations and interactions upon which their continued existence depends."[3] A baby at birth, he contends, does not have a "soul" somehow implanted. Rather, the infant becomes a human being in the process of interaction with others. A feral (wolf) child can never be human. Our humanness is shaped only with and through others. Mead says:

> Human nature is endowed with and organized by social instincts and impulses; that consciousness of meaning has arisen through social intercommunication; and finally that the *ego*, the self, that is implied in every act, in every volition, with reference to which our primary judgments of valuation are made, must exist in a social consciousness within which the *socii*, the other selves, are as immediately given as is the subject self.[4]

In this summary statement there are kernels of Mead's basic theoretical contributions. Especially evident is his notion that both mind (thinking) and self (identity) are the result of social interchange.

Taking clues from the late-nineteenth-century philosopher Wilhelm Wundt, Mead came to see "the gesture" as the primary mechanism for formation of mind and self. By gesture he means spoken communication primarily. Language is the basic gesture employed by humans in social exchange. Its effect is to shape mind and self. In particular the "significant gesture" is most determinative. By significant gesture Mead is talking about communication which evokes an *expected* response in the other person. When the expected response is given back, this triggers the speaker's already-anticipated next gesture. It is in the rightful anticipation of an expected response from the other that the communicator "takes the role of the other" or "enters into the perspective of the other." This role-taking ability, Mead contends is uniquely human. It is essential to the process of a person's full development. It is what makes human cooperation possible. Mead was fond of using baseball imagery in speaking of role-taking: If a ground ball is hit with two runners on base, for example, each player on the field can rightfully anticipate the action of fellow players. Our learning to think as others think—and rightfully anticipate their thinking and actions—is what shapes our own mind, thinking, and responses.

The above may also be explained and understood in terms of a social "act." A simple yet complete human act has at least three parts: 1) the originating communicator's extended gesture with 2) the generated response of the recipient which is basically the 3) same response evoked in the originating communicator. Mead's favorite illustration of this phenomenon is someone shouting "Fire!" in a theater. That word (gesture, significant symbol) evokes the same response in the one who shouts as it does in those who hear it. The shouter knows beforehand what its effect will be. The gesture "Fire!" stands for, initiates, and expects the whole oncoming act. Human life is made up by an ongoing series of social acts among people.

Especially with regard to the understanding of "self" does Mead's thought bear fruit for intergenerational religious education. Each self, Mead says, is an "I" and a "me." The I and the me comprising each self are inseparable but can be distinguished for heuristic purposes. The "I" may be understood as the initiating, novel side of the self which offers the gestures. The "me" is the self who hears and responds to what is said or done. The "me" is the self made an object to the self. One's self-concept (the "me") is shaped by responses to the "I." *Those responses always come from other people.* When a child distinguishes between "I" and "me," we may at that point suggest that his or her concept of self is emerging. Over time and through thousands and thousands of inter-*actions*, a clearer and sharper picture of the "me" begins to emerge. Each shared collective act shapes "me."

Gradually there emerges a kind of "generalized other" to whom each person perceives him or herself to be related—even when alone. The generalized other is all the attitudes of others to the self which have become incorporate in the self. The generalized other is the attitude-shaping community with whom the "I" interacts. Freudians might suggest that the generalized other is the superego or conscience. Paul Pfuetze suggests that "God" might be another name for the generalized other.[5] I would describe it as one's ideal of what it means to be fully human. In any case, the self is a construction of "I" and inseparable "me"—one person living in relation to others.

As mind and self of an individual develop through *socii,* so at the same ongoing time there evolves in that society itself some shared understandings. A "community of meaning" exists when people agree upon significant symbols and respond similarly to these and other gestures which are offered. As people are able to take roles or perspectives of others in shared communities of meaning, there emerges greater universal meanings. Mead was a social reformer. He had visions of expanding communities of meaning which would bode well for the whole human family: "Any self is a social self, but it is restricted to the group whose roles it assumes, and it will never abandon this self until it finds itself entering into a larger society and maintaining itself there."[6] The sharing of significant symbols needs to be expanded beyond family or clan. In that way universal meanings may come into being for individuals and their societies.

I have spent considerable time on Mead in this chapter because his thought has important IGRE implications. *Religious* mind and self may emerge in persons if significant gestures and the exchange of symbols occur in the community of faith. Participation and communication, then, are crucial in religious socialization. In this light, consider one of the Judaeo-Christian ideas/ideals about humanity and the world, the notion of "God's Kingdom on Earth." The religious education concern, of course, is to facilitate actualization of this great hope in people and in the world. Such facilitation may begin simply by repeating the above actual phrase (as word gesture) together with others in worship—a form of participation. To give meaning to the phrase, there needs to be communication around and about it so that the words become truly significant for all. In trying to say what "God's kingdom" means, the oldest persons might speak of commitment to world literacy, middle-age persons to nuclear disarmament, youth to inclusive friendships, and children to a clean earth. All these notions and more, of course, are involved. Mead makes the ethical assumption that "sharing experience is the greatest good."[7] Such sharing begins to shape the Generalized Other (capitalization intended) for all. Extending communication may enable perspective-taking, the establishment of universal meanings and an emerging conception of self as one committed to and working for the coming larger kingdom. The kingdom's coming is predicated on the development of mind and self in *socii.*

In his book on George Mead, Paul Pfuetze discusses the thought of Martin Buber as well. He notes that while Mead was an American, a pragmatist, and a social scientist, Buber was a European, a humanistic scholar, and a Jewish existentialist. Ostensibly these two were quite different. Nevertheless, Pfuetze finds a great deal in common between them. Like Mead, Buber believes that we become human only with other selves. We may in our life have "I-it" relations with things and "I-you" relations with acquaintances, but "I-Thou" relations with special people are of essential importance. The concept of "I-Thou" for Buber is not two pronouns and a conjunction but one word. It is very similar to what Mead is talking about in describing the "self" as constituted by "I" and "me." Buber says, "I become through my relations to the Thou; as I become *I,* I say, *Thou.*"⁸ Pfuetze describes the situation for both Mead and Buber with these words:

> One grows by giving and receiving within a community. The human organ-ism is born into, is nourished by, participates in, and communicates with a world of persons. Thus the individual comes to full stature as a human person in the reality of relationships with other persons and things and events—and, Buber would add, with God. In the mutual recognition of other selves . . . the human self develops and has its being.⁹

For Buber the ideal relationship between people is dialogic. The dia-logue involves inclusion. There needs to be a crossing over or "experi-encing the other side."¹⁰ This crossing over is especially incumbent upon the older or teacher-member of the dialogue. The teacher needs to begin "from above" on a loving plateau so that the learner experiences inclusion and can respond with trust. In this way the younger or other-member of the dialogue learns to relate with still others.

As people in friendship enter into deeper I-Thou relations, they often find themselves in relation to a "Third." Buber does not hesitate to call this Third "God." God is discovered in the between-actions. George Herbert Mead is not inclined to make such a theological statement, but he would agree that in the between-actions one's humanity is found.

The Social Psychologist: Erik Erikson (and Sigmund Freud)

The second major theoretician to consider in foundation for intergen-erational education is Erik Erikson. Erikson's greatest influence is in the field of social psychology, whereas Mead most heavily impacted sociolo-gy. Both thinkers describe the individual as a being fundamentally in relation to other people.

Before discussing Erikson we need to consider both his mentor, Sig-mund Freud, and his contemporary, Erich Fromm. Freud seemed to describe psychological neuroses as individual and internal in origin. Erikson takes the view that human psychological problems and their resolution are more often social. Fromm is equally adamant on this point: "We believe that man is primarily a social being, and not, as Freud assumes, primarily self-sufficient and only secondarily in need of others. . . . In this sense, we believe that individual psychology is fundamentally social psychology."¹¹ Fromm's statement may be a little unfair to Freud when considered alongside the following by the Viennese physician: "Each individual is a component part of numerous groups, he is bound by ties of identification in many directions, and he has built up his ego ideal upon the most various models."[12] Some of the "various models" upon whom the individual builds are parents, siblings, and so on. This may be seen in a layout of the states of sexual development which Freud delineated. His descriptive states are: Oral Period of Infancy (sucking, biting); Anal Period of Infancy (holding, releasing); Phallic State with Oedipal (castration complex) feelings for boys and Electra (penis-envy) feelings for girls; Latency, when the sex drive for the opposite-sex is displaced by orientation to same-sex peers; and Genital Stage sexuality in puberty.[13] These stages involve others with the individual, but Freud almost suggests that the stages are gotten through *in spite of* others.

Erikson, Freud's pupil, has greater appreciation of the interrelations. He is a *social* psychoanalyst. Partly this means that Erikson emphasizes the ego (reason) more than the id with its subconscious impulses. Erikson is generally more sanguine about the developmental opportunities in healthy personality.

In his writings Erikson identifies eight "Ages of Man"—sometimes called "stages" or "phases" of development. These ages encompass life from birth to death. (Freud's stages ended with puberty.) Each of Erikson's ages has a social-psychological developmental task associated with it. The task involves a handling of polarities. To deal successfully with the task is also to attain something of the "virtue" associated with it. An example of one task (and problem polarity)—with its attendant virtue—is "Acquiring a Sense of Industry . . . [while] Fending Off a Sense of Inferiority. . . [leading to]—A Realization of Competence." This is the description for Stage 4. All of the psycho-social stages with their favorable lasting outcomes or basic virtues can be described as follows:[14]

TASK		PROBLEM		OUTCOME	AGES
Basic Trust	vs.	Basic Mistrust	:	Drive and *Hope*	1
Autonomy	vs.	Shame and Doubt	:	Self-Control and *Willpower*	2-3
Initiative	vs.	Guilt	:	Direction and *Purpose*	4-6
Industry	vs.	Inferiority	:	Method and *Competence*	7-11
Identity	vs.	Role Confusion	:	Devotion and *Fidelity*	12-20
Intimacy	vs.	Isolation	:	Affiliation and *Love*	21-32
Generativity	vs.	Stagnation	:	Production and *Care*	33-55
Ego Integrity	vs.	Despair	:	Renunciation and *Wisdom*	55 on

In the column on the right in the above schema, I indicate the approximate chronological ages at which people confront these developmental tasks. Erikson believes that everyone everywhere must work on these tasks. Most people succeed in the struggle. If they do not find a satisfactory resolution at the usual time of crisis, in later years they may work on the task. Ideally such remedial work is not necessary if adequate nurturing and learning during the critical periods are provided. Any task once done, however, is never completely finished. The "Sense of Basic Trust," for example, must be maintained by infant and octogenarian.

The Eriksonian idea most important to intergenerational religious education is this: *A satisfactory working through of any development task is dependent on social interchange.* Taking clues from Erikson, religious educationist Donald Miller writes, "The faith journey is not to be seen as isolated and independent, but as social and interactional."[15] Both adults and children have developmental work to do. In doing that work well, the generations are catalysts one for the other. Erikson notes:

> Parents who are faced with the development of a number of children must constantly live up to a challenge. They must develop with them. . . . This weak and changing little being (their child) moves the whole family along. Babies control and bring up their families as much as they are controlled by them; in fact, we may say that the family brings up a baby by being brought up by him.[16]

Further consideration of Erikson's stages reveals the social interaction which is going on. In the first stage of psycho-social development the infant is acquiring a sense of basic trust. That trust is predicated on the parents'—especially the mother's—conveying a sense of well-being and order to the baby, including a trust of the unknown and unpredictable. Their exchange is a "cradle of faith." The mother-parent, in turn, usually finds her own assurance with regard to uncertainties and fears through more formal religious beliefs and practices. Her faith, cognitively, is more nearly a societal/cultural inheritance. At the second stage of development the father of the baby figures more prominently in the development picture. Here again, even as the child's sense of autonomy increases, the father himself is learning "caring," related to his adult developmental task of generativity.

The ingredients in mature, healthy personality for Erikson can be summarized as *"individual happiness combined with responsible citizenship."*[17] In discussing the larger society, Erikson joins hands with Mead, anticipating a better construction of the world. His own life reflected that concern. During the "loyalty oath" controversy of the McCarthy era of the 1950s, Erikson at the University of California refused to sign. He followed that course because of two concerns: 1) what the signing would say to his students who were in identity formation and 2) what it meant in his own agenda of integrity. Erikson writes:

> In our country, probably more than in any other large country, the child is the adult's partner. We treasure as a promise of things to come the simple daily observation that wherever the spirit of partnership pervades a home and wherever childhood provides a status of its own, a sense of identity, fraternal conscience, and tolerance result.[18]

As will be seen in the next chapter, considerable expansion of Erikson's work on developmental stages has been done by others. Something which no one has done—and which informed and careful observers need to do for our understanding—is to observe and describe the interactions of people at various stages and the dynamic outcomes on developmental tasks. One attempt in this direction was suggested by J. Richard Fowler.[19] Fowler observed that children and parents are experiencing critical personal transitions at the same time. Parents, age thirty-eight to forty-four, for example, may be going through a "mid-life transition" at the very time their teenage children are engaged in "identity formation." It is not clear, Fowler observed, exactly how the family dynamics would operate in this case, but they would be working! Would the two generations, for example, here have empathy one for the other? If some of the mutual concerns were aired in the presence of a third person—say, someone at Stage 8 who had attained the virtue of wisdom—would that be beneficial to the other two? We suspect it might, even as Erikson has affirmed that *all* ages have growing to do and *all* have need for one another in the becoming process.

The Family Psychotherapist: Virginia Satir (and Margaret Sawin)

The names of Kurt Levin and Harry Stack Sullivan are often mentioned in a discussion of interpersonal dynamics. The individual most associated with this topic in recent years is Virginia Satir. As a family psychotherapist, Satir consistently refuses to see an "identified patient" for one-to-one counseling. Rather, she will see such a patient only with others in his or her immediate family. Satir's contention is that change or growth in one member of a family necessarily affects all others. So all need to be together in the therapeutic process—just as they have been together in the process of "creating" the identified patient.

In discussing the contemporary family, Satir quotes Nathan Ackerman to this effect:

> The family is called upon to make up to its individual members in affection and closeness for the anxiety and distress which is the result of failure to find

a safe place in the wider world. Individuals pitch themselves back on their families for reassurance as to their lovableness and worth . . . (which) imposes upon the family an extra psychic load. Is the contemporary family equipped to carry this extra load? No—not very well! The family tries, but achieves at best a precarious success; often it fails.[20]

Agreeing with this analysis, Satir tries to equip the family to do its work better. She contends that the family is engaged fundamentally in the business of enabling its members to develop self-esteem, that is, a sense of self-worth. Self-esteem, she says, is a drive more basic than sex.[21] The sense of self-worth is especially related to other people—notably family people—who help develop and maintain it or decrease and destroy it. Satir writes that we are "dependent on others. We need them to help us get many of the things we want (or not prevent us from getting them). We are also dependent on others to validate our existence and worth."[22] In her book, *Peoplemaking,* Satir ties four ideas together, those of: 1) self-worth, 2) communications, 3) family rules, and 4) links to the larger society.[23] She is convinced that these four factors in family life can change in a positive direction. Like Erikson she is optimistic about the possibilities of people improving their situation. Satir writes, "I mean this to be the most important message in this book: *there is always hope that your life can change because you can always learn new things."*[24]

Sounding this positive note, let us consider what Satir identifies over and over again as the key factor for enhancing self-worth: effective interpersonal communications. Communications even affect a person's physical health. Satir believes that if one wants to be literally sick, all he or she need do is become disconnected from other people.[25] Conversely, health comes with good connecting. Healthy connecting involves words *and* "metacommunications," that is, body stance, tone of voice, facial expressions, and so on. Often as not our communications with others are unhelpful statements and poses involving: Placating: "Whatever you say, dear."; Blaming: "It's your fault!"; Computing: "If one were to consult informed authorities . . ."; and Distracting: "And hasn't the weather been strange lately?" What is needed more than anything else is "leveling" or talking straight: "I WANT X AND Y." Leveling, Satir believes, is needed everywhere from family life to international relations.

In *Conjoint Family Therapy,* the author-counselor has more instruction for the professional therapist. In *Peoplemaking* there is more help for laypeople in the way of ideas for improving communication. In both books the theme is helping people become whole by improved interpersonal relations and communication. Satir's focus stays on the family, especially the family in counseling, but her insights have applicability in group structures other than the nuclear family. She urges other societal institutions to do their utmost to contribute to strengthening family communications.[26] The church/synagogue, for example, could be a major contributor in constructive peoplemaking, doing something so simple, one might imagine, as setting aside time in worship for people to talk to one another. Instead of just saying, "Hello" to neighbors in the pews, members of the congregation might converse a little more significantly. The worship leader might suggest a sharing topic for all: "What is your favorite story in the Bible?" or "How are you feeling this Mother's Day?" Satir says that just *asking questions* of people helps to reestablish a sense of self-worth.[27]

Convinced that young and old can share across the age barriers, Satir writes,

> Once you as an adult grasp the notion that a human being at any age is a *person,* whether at birth, two weeks, fifteen years, thirty-five years, or eighty years, your job as a peoplemaker will be easier. You have more in common with your children than you thought. For example, the disappointment that a grown man experiences at losing a desired job is no more painful than that of a four-year-old who loses his favorite toy. The experience of disappointment is the same at any age. The feeling in a child who is the brunt of a tirade from an angry mother is no different from the woman's feeling when she has been the brunt of a tirade from her angry husband, or vice versa.
>
> There are very few things a child feels that the adult does not know something about from his own experience.[28]

It is for these reasons that Satir holds that the purpose of the family is both to "grow new people" and "further the growth of those already here."[29] The end result of the communicating and intentional peoplemaking is that children eventually become peers to their parents. As peers, they become friends. As friends, each is valued and develops a sense of self-esteem.

Someone who has done much to incorporate Virginia Satir's ideas into a feasible program related to religious institutions is Margaret Sawin. Earlier in this book (chapter 3), we examined her work in "Family Clustering." With Satir she sees "families as systems."[30] Pulling on any one member of a family moves all others; helping one member helps all. To enable functioning families to do their peoplemaking work better, Sawin believes that the church and synagogue can be of inestimable value. They are, she contends, "the only agencies in Western society which include the entire family in their clientele."[31] They can help nuclear families of whatever size and description to become stronger. They can create beyond-kin extended families which edify (that is, "build up") each member. The building up, Satir would say, is with self-esteem.

The Anthropologist: Margaret Mead (and Mary Mead Bateson)

Since the 1920s when she observed "growing up in Samoa" and wrote her famous book by the same title, Margaret Mead has been a foremost analyst of generational relations. By the 1970s she was saying that we are witnessing a new worldwide pattern of generational learnings. There are, she says, three cultural styles operating in the world. These she describes by the words *"postfigurative,* when the future repeats the past; *cofigurative,* in which the present is the guide to future expectations; and *prefigurative* for the kind of culture in which the elders have to learn from the children."[32] In the past most people lived in a postfigurative culture. In such a culture, where three generations were present, the generation of the grandparents is primarily determinative of the way life will be for the other two. Almost everything is determined beforehand. A sense of timelessness and unchangeableness pervades the society. "The essential characteristic of a postfigurative culture is the assumption, expressed by members of the older generation in their every act, that their way of life . . . is unchanging, eternally the same."[33]

There have been times in history—and certainly in the recent present—when the all-determinative importance of the oldest generation has not weighed as heavily. This is so in a cofigurative culture, a culture in which "the prevailing model for members of the society is the behavior of their contemporaries."[34] The examples Mead gives of such cultures are those in which distinct breaks from the past have occurred. The breaks may be brought on by new technologies, changing modes of work, or a predominately younger generation moving to a new country. In such wise the generation of the grandparents either literally or figuratively gets left behind. Their experiences and knowledge are not particularly helpful in the changed situation. Frequently generational gaps occur because parents—but especially grandparents—relinquish control of the educational system. Education is given over to nontraditional others. The past then becomes shadowy. Grandparents are no longer role models, and parents can no longer designate marriage partners or career paths. In such a world peers become all important in determining behavior. Most observers would agree that the cofigurative model has predominated in the United States with our age stratification, teenage culture, and the rest. Few elderly even pretend to have part of this culture, Mead says.[35]

In recent years with those persons born after World War II, a third culture began to emerge. Mead calls it the prefigurative culture: "As I see it, children today face a future that is so deeply unknown that it cannot be handled, as we are currently attempting to do, as a generation change with cofiguration within a stable, elder-controlled and parentally modeled culture in which many postfigurative elements are incorporated."[36] The splitting of the atom, the invention of computers, overpopulation, ecological unbalance, the breakdown of cities, space exploration and much more, she says, "have brought about a drastic, irreversible division between the generations. . . . Even very recently, the elders could say: 'You know, I have been young and *you* never have been old.' But today's young people can reply, 'You never have been young in the world I am young in, and you never can be.' "[37] The break among generations is wholly new and universal. Mead says,

> Today nowhere in the world are there elders who know what the children know, no matter how remote and simple the societies are in which the children live. In the past there are always some elders who knew more than any children in terms of their experience of having grown up within a cultural system. Today there are none.[38]

The problem is doubly complicated because the middle generation grew up in a rapidly changing world too. Today's parents are like the first pioneers on a strange continent, but their children are most like explorers on a new planet. Mead says, "We (adults) have to realize that no other generation will ever experience what we have experienced. In this sense we must recognize that we have no descendants, as our children have no forebears."[39] For all the parties present there is no common current vocabulary by which to dialogue.

While all of this sounds very unhopeful—as distinct from Erikson's or Satir's words—Margaret Mead still believes that our most human characteristic is the ability to learn and to teach. Adults, especially, are going to have to learn new modes of thinking and behaving which will help keep the future open.

> So the freeing of men's imagination from the past depends, I believe, on the development of a new kind of communication with those who are most deeply involved with the future—the young who were born in the new world. . . . The development of prefigurational cultures depend on the existence of a continuing dialogue in which the young, free to act on their own initiative, can lead their elders in the direction of the unknown. Then the older generation will have access to the new experiential knowledge, without which no meaningful plan can be made. It is only with the direct participation of the young, who have that knowledge, that we can build a viable future.[40]

It may be that Margaret Mead's analysis is overly responsive to the situation presented by the world's youth culture of the late sixties. Still, much of her reflection continues to hold true. The young are born into a very different world than that of their parents. Likewise, the parental world is different from the grandparental experience. These differences highlight the reality of the generation gaps. Those gaps, though, can be bridged and sometimes are, by the young, more than their elders. Sociologist Gunhild Hagestad, taking cues from Mead, says that in the family and society "young members often serve as 'cohort bridges' to older generations by mediating, interpreting, and making human sense of technological and cultural change."[41] One might imagine, in this context a young person teaching his/her elder to operate successfully various hi-tech instruments.

More broadly, the intergenerational sharing called for could guarantee the continuation of *Homo sapiens* on earth. In an article on creating a viable future, Margaret Mead's daughter, Mary Catherine Mead Bateson, says that we need a new paradigm or "relationship mediation" to inform our thinking. Older paradigmatic images were usually patriarchal or matriarchal. They no longer serve, Bateson says.

> Let me therefore suggest another mediation, the mediation of "The Adoption of the Child," through which we can discover both compassion and responsibility through a sense of a share in parenting. I believe each person trying to decide how to live, what action to take [etc.] . . . In making such decisions (we) want to be responsible to the future need to be sure we have a relationship with at least one real, flesh and blood child.[42]

Given what appears to be increasing deprivation of the children of the earth, such an adoption might bless the young with physical necessities. The adoption would be good for adults too, providing greater meaning. It would be excellent for the whole human community. Bateson remembers her mother saying, "In this nuclear age, as nice as the Russians are to their children, their children live because we don't blow them up. We are the only people who can look after the children in Russia. And vice versa."[43] The needs and hopes of children and adults worldwide, Bateson believes, are reciprocal. Her mother agrees.

* * * *

At this point we are halfway through the presentation of basic social-scientific theory which can contribute to the work of intergenerational religious education. We have examined foundational work by people in the distinct but related fields of social-philosophy, social psychology, family counseling, and anthropology. All have been saying how and why we are related one to another across the ages. More than that, they assert that for the continuation of human life—both individual and collective—we need to improve upon learning from and with each other.

Notes

1. Lawrence Senesh, a personal conversation, Boulder, Colorado, May 28, 1980.
2. J.A.K. Thomson, *The Ethics of Aristotle: The Nicomachean Ethics Translated* (Baltimore: Penguin Books, 1965), p. 277, and books 8 and 9, generally.
3. George Herbert Mead, *Mind, Self and Society: From the Standpoint of a Social Behaviorist* (Chicago: University of Chicago Press, 1934), p. 288.
4. George Herbert Mead, *Selected Writings,* ed. Andrew J. Reck (Indianapolis, Ind.: Bobbs-Merrill, 1964), p. 97.
5. See Paul E. Pfuetze, *The Social Self* (New York: Booman Associates, 1954), p. 84.
6. Mead, *Selected Writings,* p. 192.
7. Mead, quoted in Pfuetze, *Social Self,* p. 49.
8. Martin Buber, *I and Thou,* (New York: Charles Scribner's Sons, 1958), p. 11.
9. Pfuetze, *Social Self,* p. 233.
10. Martin Buber, *Between Man and Man* (New York: Macmillan, 1966), p. 96.
11. Erich Fromm, *Escape from Freedom* (New York: Rinehart, 1941), p. 290.
12. Sigmund Freud, *Group Psychology and the Analysis of the Ego* (New York: Bantam Books, 1960), p. 78.
13. Sigmund Freud, *A General Introduction to Psychoanalysis* (New York: Perma Books, 1955), pp. 312-347. See also, Calvin S. Hall, *A Primer of Freudian Psychology* (New York: Mentor Books, 1954), pp. 102-113.
14. Erik H. Erikson, *Childhood and Society* (New York: Norton, 1963), p. 274. This format for the tasks was developed by Henry Maier to describe Erikson's ages. See Henry W. Maier, *Three Theories of Child Development: The Contributions of Erikson, Piaget and Sears* (New York: Harper & Row, 1969), p. 53, for the detailed example above.
15. Donald E. Miller, *Story and Context: An Introduction to Christian Education* (Nashville: Abingdon, 1987), p. 235.
16. Erikson, *Childhood,* p. 69.
17. See Maier, *Three Theories,* p. 27.
18. Erikson, *Childhood,* p. 418.
19. J. Richard Fowler, "Child and Adult: Growing Together." Paper read at the International Convention of the Religious Education Association, Toronto, Canada, November 26, 1979.
20. Virginia Satir, *Conjoint Family Therapy: A Guide to Theory and Technique* (Palo Alto, Calif.: Science and Behavior Books, 1964), p. 26.
21. Ibid., p. 55.
22. Ibid., p. 89.
23. Virginia Satir, *Peoplemaking* (Palo Alto, Calif.: Science and Behavior Books, 1972), pp. xi and 3.
24. Ibid., p. 27.
25. Ibid., p. 79.
26. Ibid., p. 293.
27. Ibid., p. 230, and *Conjoint,* p. 141.
28. Ibid., pp. 229-30.
29. Ibid., p. 113.
30. Margaret M. Sawin, *Family Enrichment with Family Clusters* (Valley Forge, Pa.: Judson, 1979), p. 7. Also, Margaret M. Sawin, "The Theoretical

Foundations of the Family Cluster Model," an unpublished paper, Rochester, New York, p. 3.
31. Sawin, "Theoretical Foundations," p. 6.
32. Margaret Mead, *Culture and Commitment: The New Relationship Between the Generations in the 1970s* (Garden City, N.Y.: Anchor Books, 1978), p. 13.
33. Ibid., p. 14.
34. Ibid., p. 39.
35. Ibid., p. 60.
36. Ibid., p. 62.
37. Ibid., p. 63.
38. Ibid., p. 75.
39. Ibid., p. 76.
40. Ibid., p. 88.
41. Gunhild O. Hagestad, "Multi-generational Families, Socialization, Support and Strain" in *Intergenerational Relationships,* ed., Vjenka Garm-Homolova et al. (Lewiston, N.Y.: Hogrefe, 1984), pp. 107-8.
42. Mary Catherine Bateson, "Caring for Children, Caring for the Earth," *Christianity and Crisis* 40:5 (March 31, 1980), p. 68.
43. Ibid., p. 69.

Chapter 6

Developmental Theory
For The Generations

People perceive things differently. They perceive differently not just because of years lived but also because of other human variables. In this chapter we consider some of the important differences in people which time—but especially experience—shape. Our goal is to come to greater appreciation of the fullness and complexity of the human animal who is involved in intergenerational life. Our guides here are the social scientists who have looked most closely at what they term human development.

The developmentalists describe "stages" into which people may move in the course of their lives. An explication of these stages reveals how very different and complex we really are. Understanding these differences might even suggest that IGRE is nigh to impossible. Perhaps. Yet, it is with these differences that educators must work. Happily, the developmentalists reviewed in these pages give helpful clues on how best to proceed. These clues will be identified as an additional theoretical base for IGRE.

In the previous chapter we noted that Erik Erikson, following Freud, is a developmentalist. His "Ages of Man" description is in regard to stages in social-psychological life. People also may be staged according to intellectual or *cognitive development.* So says Jean Piaget. We shall look at his analyses. Second, we consider *moral reasoning* stages as described by Lawrence Kohlberg, William Perry, and Mary Wilcox. Third, James Fowler's efforts to classify *faith development* stages are presented. And fourth, there is a review of the theory and findings on *adult passages* which Gail Sheehy, Daniel Levinson, and others have offered. In the conclusion of this chapter I pull together the findings of this and the previous chapter to see what is being said overall about the theory and practice of intergenerational life and learning by these many important contributors.

Cognitive Development: Jean Piaget

In an interview Jean Piaget once said, "I always preferred the workings of the intellect to the tricks of the unconscious."[1] Piaget joins with Erikson in attempting to describe normal and healthy personality. Piaget's focus is different from Erikson's, however, in that he is less concerned about social and emotional aspects of the ego. He is more focused on the intellect per se. He is a *cognitive* developmentalist, describing his work as that of "genetic epistemology."[2] By that he means he is engaged in experimental (observational) philosophy which seeks to answer questions about how and when people know. Especially he has made studies of children's intellectual development.

In approaching Piaget the word with which to begin is "equilibrium" or "equilibration." He writes: "The psychological development that starts at birth and terminates in adulthood is comparable to organic growth. Like the latter, it consists of activity directed toward equilibrium."[3] Piaget believes that mental development proceeds by moving through to new stages or plateaus of cognition. At each stage the developing person has a distinctive way of thinking about the world. Each stage has its own equilibrium involving relative stability and increasing complexity. Having attained equilibrium at one stage, a child may eventually be challenged—by inner and outer pressure—to "think again," that is, significantly change and expand his or her way of perceiving. The reformulation of the thinking process will likely lead to a new and more complex way of reasoning—and a new equilibrium. For Piaget, the more advanced the better.

Depending on whether one reads the early or the late Piaget, there are six or four "phases" of cognitive development. It is simpler here just to describe the four phases and use that description as a reminder that people think differently. They have different mind-sets or conceptual/perceptual abilities.

The first phase of intellectual development is called the *sensorimotor stage*. It begins at birth and continues to about age two. There are many substages within it.[4] As the name suggests, the sensorimotor stage is characterized by organized motor responses by the infant. One responds to persons and things which enter into his or her sense world.

The next stage is described as *preoperational*, meaning that the two- to seven-year-old child operates more by intuitive thought than by logic. Whatever appears is what is real. A child may say, "The moon follows me around." So it seems. Though still mostly egocentric, this age child is slowly learning to take the perspective of others. He or she is now able to think about things as separate entities, with language an increasingly important tool.

Starting around age five to eight the child can enter the *concrete operational* phase. For the first time the young thinker has reversibility: He or she can logically rethink a series of previous events, e.g., "where I might have left my gloves." The child is also capable of conservation, that is, knowing, for example, that the size of a ball of clay is not changed when the shape changes. The child is adept at handling concrete problems that can be seen or felt.

The fourth and final phase of cognitive development is that of *formal operations.* Such may occur from age eleven on, though for many people formal operational thinking is never attained. The main intellectual characteristic of phase four is that abstract conceptualization, symbolic representation, and historical perspective-taking are now possible. One can "think about thinking." Piaget once described this stage as that where "hypothetico-deduction" is possible, meaning that various problems can be entertained in the head before deciding on the matter or deducing a plan of action. The successful formal operational thinker achieves a level of equilibrium which is more complex and richer in ideational possibility than any which came before.[5]

Piaget's theory on the stages of cognitive development has a number of implications for IGRE. The first truth of consequence from Piaget, obviously, is that important differences in thinking exist among people—especially children. The young, for example, necessarily offer different interpretations on the meaning of the Bible, the effectiveness of prayer, and so on. To talk about God's "Spirit" to a concrete operational child may only be to have described "Casper the Ghost—with a hole in him!" Taking clues from Piaget, Ronald Goldman made close observations of the religious thinking of children in England. He noted age differences in belief and talk about the existence of God, for example: "After 13 years most children find it unnecessary and inappropriate to support their convictions with physical evidence. . . . Again, it is interesting that 13 years appears to be the time when anthropomorphic elements tend to be left behind and higher theological concept occurs."[6] Much before this critical age any abstract articulation of the faith will fall on deaf ears.

A second insight to be gleaned from Piaget is with regard to the mechanisms which trigger change. In elaborating on Piaget's work, David Elkind writes: "Mental growth is clearly determined by three major sets of factors: maturation, physical experience, and social experience. . . . [A] fourth factor, equilibration, [is the] overriding factor that determines the mode of interaction of the other three."[7] Bearing these things in mind we know that cognitive development or stage change does not occur simply because an internal time-clock switches to "ON." Though physical maturation is partly involved, equally critical are interactive experiences with things and people.

For the individual involved in a cognitive stage change, Piaget says what is going on is a process of *adaptation:* The individual is adapting to his or her environment. It is a twofold process: "All needs tend first of all to incorporate things and people into the subject's own activity, i.e., to 'assimilate' the external world into the structures that have already been constructed, and secondly to readjust these structures as a function of subtle transformations, i.e., to 'accommodate' them to external objects."[8] An explication of the two words—"assimilation" and "accommodation"—in the above quotation adds helpful ideas three and four from Piaget. *Assimilation* involves "horizontal decalage," that is, adding on to the layers of the self. An assimilating person broadens his or her cognitive horizons. That person fills out the cognitive stage by adding educational experiences and additional information to the structures of his or her knowing mind. *Accommodation* requires internal changes, modification. It often precipitates a stage change as people have to move, shift, accommodate for impinging outside reality.

One of the things which promotes growth is when a note of "cognitive dissonance" is sounded in the person's experience. This dissonance or conceptual/perceptual conflict may cause a reworking of one's mode of thinking. Most often, cognitive conflict is set up by interchange with other people—often by people at different stages of intellectual development.

People facilitate cognitive development for others in additional ways. Piaget has observed that the child is "egocentric." Nothing pejorative is involved in using the term egocentric. It is simply to say that the child necessarily builds the world around him or herself. Taking the role of others or "thinking like mother thinks" is simply not possible for young children. Through the years/because of the years and because of what seems like endless discussions with others, a child's egocentrism begins to give way. He or she is able to think in terms of a broader social circle.

In his writings Piaget describes the child's progress in thinking as moving from primary interaction with the *physical world* to that of *social relations* and finally on to that of the *ideational.* He suggests that by about age fifteen a person's mental furniture is in place. What Piaget looks for in the stage-fulfilled individual is the attainment of formal operational thinking, that is, thinking which is in equilibrium: "In reality, the most profound tendency of all human activity is progression toward equilibrium. Reason, which expresses the highest forms of equilibrium reunites intelligence and affectivity."[9] Piaget's statement is certainly as much a statement of hope and faith as it is one of realized observation. The point is that the attainment of full cognitive potential is a desirable human/interhuman outcome.

Stages of Moral Reasoning: Kohlberg, Perry, Wilcox

Of special interest to religious educators is work built on Piaget's cognitive developmental base. Lawrence Kohlberg, William Perry, and Mary Wilcox are today describing structural-developmental "stages of moral development"—or, better, "moral reasoning." In this section their contributions are considered.

Harvard educator, Lawrence Kohlberg, has been a most creative contributor to contemporary thinking about moral development. Of himself he writes: "Inspired by Jean Piaget's pioneering effort to apply a structural approach to moral development, I have gradually elaborated over the years of my study a typology scheme describing general structures and forms of moral thought which can be defined independently of the specific content of particular moral decisions and actions."[10] He describes his approach to the understanding of the stages of moral reasoning by such terms as "cognitive-developmental," "progressive," and "interactionist." We shall use all three expressions.

What Kohlberg is doing is different than, say, what maturationists do. A maturationist, such as Rosseau especially, or, in some ways, Erikson, holds that the emerging individual is innately good and, if allowed to unfold naturally, unhindered in negative ways, that inherent goodness will come forth. The human, then, may be most likened to a *budding plant*. Kohlberg considers such an understanding as "romanticism." It is not his approach. Neither does he advocate moral education through "cultural transmission" with direct teaching of values. Classically John Locke and, contemporaneously, a behaviorist, such as B. F. Skinner, would be cultural transmitters. They stress setting up the environment in such a way as to get the moral truths 1) out of the realm of ideas and 2) into the mind and behavior of the learner. Like a *machine,* the cultural transmitters suggest, a moral person can be built. Kohlberg's approach is a third way. He discusses it as follows:

> The cognitive-developmental metaphor is not material [i.e., the person is not like a plant or machine]; it is dialectical; it is a progression of ideas in discourse and conversation. The dialectical metaphor was first elaborated by Plato, given new meaning by Hegel, and finally stripped of its metaphysical claims by John Dewey and Jean Piaget, to form a psychological method. In the dialectical metaphor, a core of universal ideas are redefined and reorganized as their implications are played out in experience and as they are confronted by their opposites in argument and discourse.[11]

As a dialectical model, what Kohlberg is saying about the development of moral reasoning is that changes and processes going on *inside* a person are meeting with objects, challenges, and people *outside*. By these meetings the person progressively moves into advanced stages of moral reasoning.

As noted, Piaget himself did some work on understanding moral development. Kohlberg expanded it immensely. By the end of his life, Kohlberg began calling his schematic understanding the "Levels and Stages of Moral Development." It has been presented in several places and always in somewhat different ways.[12]

TABLE NO. 1. SUMMARY OF LAWRENCE KOHLBERG'S
"LEVELS AND
STAGES OF MORAL DEVELOPMENT"

LEVEL I — Preconventional or Premoral Reasoning
(Dominant in middle-class children, ages 4-10)
Moral value resides in external, quasi-physical happenings, bad acts, or in quasi-physical needs rather than in persons or standards

Stage 1 — Orientation toward punishment
"You'll get in trouble!"
Obedience to rules to avoid punishment
Deference to perceived powerful authorities

Stage 2 — Orientation toward satisfying one's own needs (sometimes others)
"You scratch my back/I'll scratch yours."
Obedience to rules to obtain rewards, get favors

LEVEL II — Conventional Role Conformity
May appear in preadolescence; is the major level of adults
Moral value resides in performing good or right roles, in maintaining the conventional order, and in fulfilling the expectations of others

Stage 3 — Orientation to "Good Boy/Nice Girl" understanding of self
"A scout is trustworthy, loyal . . ."
Conformity to stereotypical images and avoidance of disapproval of others

Stage 4   Orientation to the maintenance of the social order
"Do your duty" and "Show respect" for authorities,
rules, and the social order of family, peers, class
Conformity to avoid censure and resultant guilt
There is self-acceptance of the subculture morals and
mores

LEVEL III Postconventional or Self-Accepted Moral Principles
(Seen in adulthood, if at all)
Moral value resides in conformity by the self to shared
and shareable standards, rights, and obligations

Stage 5   Orientation to the social contract
"What if everybody. . .? So I will or won't . . ."
Conformity to standards *agreed upon* by the *whole* society
Aware of relativism in values in different societies but
makes tentative judgments on well-thought-out criteria

Stage 6   Orientation to conscience and highest universal principles
"What is the truly just and loving thing to do?"
Conformity to right as defined by conscience in accord
with self-chosen ethical principles (e.g., Kant's Cate-
gorical Imperative)
Perceiving persons as ends and not means

It is Kohlberg's contention that the levels and stages of moral development described in Table No. 1 are sequential and invariable—that is,
one may not skip a stage, and once a stage is attained there is no
regression. These stages are also believed to be universal both as to place
and as to various religious faiths.

(Kohlberg's methodology wittingly or unwittingly suggests that no
difference will be found between men and women. That assumption has
been challenged by Carol Gilligan who wondered why men tended to be
scored into stages higher than women. To Gilligan the answer seemed to
be that *women perceive and value in different ways.* Women especially
emphasize "relationships-with-people-in-time," more so than "justice"
or "individual rights" considerations in making moral choices, which
latter stance often characterizes male approaches. Such a critique of
Kohlberg underscores the importance of human interaction (relation-

ships) for moral development of women and—looking forward to the future—for men.[13] Joining Gilligan in this understanding of relationship is Maria Harris. Though she operates out of personal hunches rather than out of an empirical research base, Harris suggests that the experience and "power of sisterhood" be brought in to help relationships, reconciliation, and completion, not just of human relations but "in relation with earth, too, and with sun and moon and stars and ground."[14] Were these factors entered into Kohlberg's computation it is likely that women would be scored higher in stage classes.)

Kohlberg thinks that no more than 5-10 percent of any given population reaches a postconventional stage of moral reasoning. Such persons, however, are not necessarily more "moral"—as that word is popularly understood. A person reasoning at Stage 5 may not be any more sexually straight or philanthropically generous than someone operating at Stage 2. Stage difference means only that *people offer different reasons for their moral actions.* Nevertheless, the assumption in this stage structuring often is that "higher is better." Certainly it is more complex and inclusive.

One of Kohlberg's strategies for scoring or classifying persons is to present "moral dilemmas" for their response. Consider, for example the question: "Is it right for a poor man to steal a costly drug to save the life of his sick wife?" Regardless of the answer(s) given to the question, the key concern is to find out from the person, "Why do you say that?" By asking "why" questions in a structured interview, it is possible for a trained interviewer to discern the stage of moral reasoning at which a respondent operates. Let us note, in addition, that by using moral dilemmas and discussion, there is healthy stretching on the part of the respondent. Such can be constructive horizontal decalage for stage completion and advance. In this sense, more is also better.

Kohlberg describes his position as "interactionist epistemology." One knows via interaction with others. Note then: *The most decisive factor in moral development is other people.* Kohlberg believes that an individual can comprehend one stage above the stage at which he or she currently reasons. The comprehending of and moving toward a stage above is facilitated if a stage-above person models this higher plateau of reasoning. The modeling is needed for growth.

One of Kohlberg's colleagues at Harvard is William Perry. He too is a follower of Piaget and someone concerned about understanding moral development—especially that of college students. In a ten-year period between 1954 and 1963, Perry and his colleagues conducted extensive open-ended interviews with undergraduate students. Without imposing prior categories on students' self-descriptions of their college experience, the researchers tried to see if, in fact, there was a pattern in or "form" to intellectual and moral thinking during four years of college. In the book reporting findings from the study, Perry describes the classification spectrum in thinking by students on intellectual issues: "In its full range the scheme begins with those simplistic forms in which a person construes his world in unqualified polar terms of absolute right-wrong, good-bad; it ends with those complex forms through which he undertakes to affirm his own commitments in a world of contingent knowledge and creative values."[15] Described in broad, ideal-type terms a student might begin his or her college career with a Simple Dualism. With such the individual sees the world as we/good/right vs. others/ bad/wrong. There would be lots of deference and conformity to Authority. Authorities are persons seen as having *"the* right answer—the Truth, the Absolute."* In time, the student's Simple Dualism begins to fall apart and a Complex Dualism comes to be. At this stage, Multiplicity is seen. Multiplicity involves an awareness of differing views on truth and values. Even though these differing interpretations are acknowledged as present, the student still believes that only one Answer will be true and right. Then there can come the thinking form of Relativism in which it is thought that everybody's ideas are just as good as anybody else's. Part of what is going on is that the person chooses not to choose: There are just too many intellectual and ethical options. Finally, Perry contends, the student—usually in his or her senior year—breaks out of Relativism and gives the self to Commitment in Relativism. In effect the individual says, "In spite of all the problems of conflicting creditable claims, I am making a commitment. I assume responsibility. Here I stand!" Perry describes the highest level as constituting "a maturity in which a person has developed an experience of 'who he is' in his Commitments both in their content and in his style of living them."[16]

The above is a sketchy presentation of Perry's description of intellectual and ethical forms. Nevertheless, the sketch serves as an introduction to two important points related to our IGRE study. The first is that the *learning experience itself*—in this case, college education—seems to induce positive changes in the direction of better thinking and decision making. That should be heard as a positive word for educators broadly. Second, note that part of the motivation for intellectual and ethical advance may have been generated by *the interviewing itself*. The interviewers were persons genuinely interested in what their subjects had to say. One interviewee is reported as saying to his interviewer, "I don't know what *you've* learned from all this research but *I've* learned that the most important thing that could happen around here is that every student should have an interview like this at the end of every year."[17] Knowing that "someone is interested in what *I* think and do, in how *I* think and act!" makes an individual more reflective and improvement-conscious. Perry believes (and I concur from my reading of his study) that the interviewers did not have an inordinate biasing or "Hawthorne Effect" on the students—that is, actually causing the changes. Still, for *our* IG interests, it would be all right if they had. Perry reported in passing on a study in which an interviewer at another college held weekly individual and group sessions with a sample of students for several years. The result of this intensive and extensive tracking of students was that thirteen out of the test group of thirty students ended up on the honor roll. The control group of thirty-one noninterviewed students had only five so recognized. The interpersonal factor makes a difference!

In addition to the work of Kohlberg and Perry on moral development, let us consider that of Mary Wilcox also.[18] Wilcox's observations on "social perspective-taking"—the ability to see the self and the self in relation to others—are especially relevant in intergenerational learning. She notes that in the earliest years of life the self alone is the center. The young child is necessarily involved in pure egocentrism. Only slowly does the egocentrism give way. Authority for children is vested in "big" people, seen to be in the right. They must be obeyed to avoid punishment (cf. Stage 1 of Kohlberg). At the next stage, though still very much egocentric, the child can enter into "dyadic instrumental" relationships. Here mutual backscratching arrangements with others are effected. Even so, the child cannot yet really understand the thinking of another person. At Stage 3, however, some of the necessary empathetic appreciation begins to emerge. The face-to-face relationships with persons of one's most important reference group figure prominently in decision making. These others help form a self-image of what "Good Boy" or "Nice Girl" is. At the next stage of development, triadic relations between the self, others and the society begin to emerge. The individual incorporates rules/laws/standards of this wider society into the self. Conduct and thinking are governed by these. Within a Stage 5 mode of social perspective-taking, there can even come a time in which the individual, as it were, steps outside his or her society and begins to take the perspective of persons in other societies. With such a social perspective often comes criticism of one's own societal structures, values, customs, and so on. If an individual attains a Stage 6 level of moral reasoning, that person is operating in terms of a universal humanity which is guided by the highest principles of justice and love for all persons everywhere.

Wilcox says that "the developmental journey is a fluid and fluctuating PROCESS of interaction," and she agrees with Piaget and Kohlberg that "the social environment is the primary stimulus to growth and development."[19] Rejecting notions that moral or values education should be 1) done only in the home or church or 2) limited to teaching "traditional" and agreed-upon values or 3) conducted through values clarification exercises, Wilcox proposes a fourth way of teaching. This fourth way considers the whole person in the learning process. In this model of moral education the teacher inputs significant content, stresses communication, considers emotional feelings, works on right and left brain aspects of the mind, uses the physical abilities of each person, and does it all in a supporting community.

In Wilcox's theory the moral development of the whole person involves factoring in a number of considerations. One of these is what Jerome Bruner describes as the "enactive" model or representation.[20] Physical involvement with verbal reflection—especially self-conscious "labeling"—occurs in the enactive mode. Development is also enhanced, Wilcox says, by "exposing the learners to conflicts in reasoning, letting them hear persons who reason at higher stages, providing role-taking experimental opportunities, using moral dilemmas in the classroom, and more."[21] Key to development in moral reasoning always is development of *improved social perspective-taking.* Wilcox believes that progress in role-taking abilities forms the context for stage advance in moral reasoning.

Faith Development Stages: James Fowler

In the previous chapter we looked at psycho-social theory of development as articulated by Erik Erikson. In this chapter we have reviewed Piaget's cognitive and Kohlberg's moral structural-developmentalist theories. These three theoretical strands have been woven together in a development theory having to do with faith structures. The person who has done this is James Fowler at the Candler School of Theology in Atlanta, Georgia. Fowler's beginning in this area was the listening to "religious pilgrimage stories" at Interpreters' House in North Carolina. At the same time he was reading Erikson. Then he joined Lawrence Kohlberg for collaborative work at Harvard where he continued research interviews with people to ascertain faith stages.

In lectures, articles, and books Fowler introduces his work by reflection on the meaning of the concept of "faith." Faith, he says, is more than a noun. It is closer to being an active verb. Faith or *faithing* essentially involves *knowing* and especially *construing* (constructing) an ultimate environment: "Faith, then, is an active mode of knowing, of composing a felt sense or image of the condition of our lives taken as a whole. It unifies our lives' force fields."[22] Faith is both rational and passional. It has a "logic of rational certainty" and a "logic of conviction" in it. Though faith's content—that is, *what* is believed and trusted—may vary among people, cultures, and religions, the human progression in ways to construe an ultimate environment is similar.

For the purpose of this book—namely, to identify theoretical bases for

IGRE—a most important thing to share from Fowler is what he says is going on vis-á-vis the self, other people, and the ultimate environment. Basically Fowler draws a triadic figure for understanding the dynamics of faith building. See Figure No. 1.

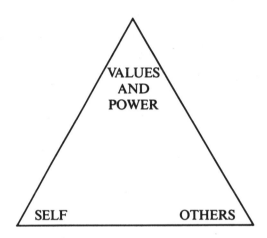

Figure No. 1. FOWLER'S TRIADIC CONSTRUCT
OF FAITH BUILDING

Fowler contends that each self is always in relation to other people *and* to some center of values and power which is shared with these others.[23] The self, others, and the values/power may all change—or, better, be expanded—as faith-stage advances occur, but always one is thinking and acting with regard to a center of shared meanings and authority. To illustrate what he means, Fowler observes that when we meet new people what usually happens in conversation is that we cast about for mutual interests. Behind our probing is the search to discover common causes, commitments and loyalties with the other. Finding such, we both become persons in relation to transcendent meaning. He writes:

> "World Maintenance" involves a tri-polar or covenantal relationship between persons, and between them and shared visions of excellence of being. . . .
> "Reality" is a shared construct which is covenantly maintained. . . . The maintenance of "reality" requires constant renewal and transformation. The trust and loyalty to each other . . . must constantly be developing and revivifying. A principal contribution of institutional religions in cultures is their generation of renewing power and passion in the mainly tacit covenant which sustains a people's interpersonal trust and their shared visions of excellence of being.[24]

Fowler here sounds like someone quoted earlier, namely, Martin Buber. His words also echo the reflections of Josiah Royce and H. Richard Niebuhr. In fact, they are all persons to whom Fowler acknowledges indebtedness for his tri-polar conception of faith relationship.[25]

That to which humans give themselves in triadic relationship also redounds to persons of faith. Fowler says, "We invest or devote ourselves because the other to whom we commit has, for us, an intrinsic excellence. . . . The centers of value and power that have god value for us, therefore, are those that confer meaning and worth on us and promise to sustain us in a dangerous world of power."[26]

In the faith development structure there are, Fowler believes, six distinguishable stages, universal, invariant, and sequential. (Please consult Table No. 2 for a description.)[27]

The first three stages of Fowler's schema are somewhat linked to biological development. The latter three are attained (if at all) only by processes having to do with life experiences, hard thinking, and significant interactions. In making a stage advancement the individual may be involved in such things as conflict with authorities, reconciling identities, competing allegiance claims, inconsistencies discovered in the self, contradictions in thought, and encounters with transcendent mystery. Few people ever reach Stage 5—the Conjunctive—without first suffering major life tragedies or defeats. "The oppressed," Fowler says, "get to Stage 5 before the comfortable."[28]

Fowler lists seven horizontal classification variables, "aspects," or "competences" which fill in the meaning of the six stages.[29] They are as follows:

A. Form of Logic (modified Piaget on cognitive development)
B. Role-Taking (social-perspective as understood by Robert Selman)
C. Form of Moral Judgment (modified Kohlberg)
D. Bounds of Social Awareness (extent of primary indentifications)
E. Locus of Authority (to whom/what one is attentive)
F. Form of World Coherence (model for an ultimate development)
G. Role of Symbols (ways of using symbols, myths, and rituals)

These variables elaborate each faith stage. Persons working in IGRE would want to look at these aspects in order to appreciate more fully the differences which exist in people's faith stance—that is, in their knowing, construing, and "mode-of-being-in-relation" to others.

Happily, for purposes of this book, Fowler has related his stage development constructs to the question of "religious socialization." He says,

> The development of faith competences and the movement from one stage to another cannot be the *direct* result of education or schooling. Rather, in precisely the fashion described by the religious socialization theorists faith

TABLE NO. 2. STAGES OF FAITH DEVELOPMENT AS DESCRIBED BY JAMES W. FOWLER

Stage No.	Faith Stage Name and Characterization	Earliest Age Seen	Descriptive Characteristics
0	Undifferentiated Preimaging Construer	0	Trust overcoming fears of abandonment Cf. Erikson's first two stages Seeds of courage, hope, love infused in primal faith grounding
1	Intuitive-Projective Naive Theologian	2	Intuitive or imitative of adults' images, mixed with one's own novel and fantasy-filled constructions Awakening to consciousness, others, and reality beyond the everyday Greatly influenced by visible faith of primal adults
2	Mythic-Literal Young Empiricist	7	Literal interpretation of faith stories, relying on episodic & narrative Learning the lore/language/customs of one's religious community Concrete and one-dimensional symbols and concepts Ultimate environment seen as a consistent/caring/just ruler or parent
3	Synthetic-Conventional Logician Conformist	12	Synthesizing of beliefs/values of important others to self Structuring the ultimate environment in interpersonal terms "Those who count" inform faith most in one's unexamined "ideology"
4	Individuative-Reflective Ideological Theologian Demythologizer	18	Self (identity) and outlook (worldview) differentiated from others' Reordering of conflicting dichotomies into more explicit meaning system Rationally and analytically deciding on issues for oneself Greater self-awareness of one's own choices and exclusions
5	Conjunctive Remythologizer Theologian of Balance	Mid-Life	Recognizing equal validity of conflicting claims, cherishing paradoxes Accepting relativity of one's worldview, yet making commitments "Second Naivete" entered as symbols and concepts are reunited Espoused values are congruent with action taken Boundaries and inner structures become porous and multiplex Multiple names and metaphors used for the holy
6	Universalizing Theologian Saint	40 or more	Direct participation in the Ultimate Commitment to inclusive community beyond class, nation, and religion Moral and ascetic actualization of universalizing apprehensions Self-denial or kenosis—"pouring out" for others' sake Leaning into the future of God for all being Possible martyrdom to visions incarnated

development occurs as a person wrestles with the givenness and crises of his/her life, and draws adaptively upon the models of meaning provided by a nurturing community (or communities) in construing a world which is given coherence by his/her centering trusts and loyalties.[30]

Even as others have done, Fowler emphasizes the crucial role which community plays in faith development. Community facilitates faith development by offering intellectual stimulation, affection, advanced stage modeling, challenge, interaction, sponsorship, and one thing more.[31] Fowler uniquely emphasizes symbol/myth/ritual/metaphor as important to faithing. Religious communities need to provide just these kinds of socialization experiences.

One of the best illustrations of a faith community working on several levels of faith development at the same time has been provided by Clarence Snelling. In leading worship, he did intentional presentations appealing to the multiple faith stages of people in the congregation. First in the children's sermon and then in the adult sermon—both being based on the parables of Jesus—Snelling used verbal, visual, tactile, interpersonal, conceptual, and symbolic material which were appropriate to at least five stages of development. Stage 5, the Paradoxical-Consolidative, was usually given conceptualization at the end of the sermon. "It served," Snelling said, "as a kind of lure for people—not excluding myself." Snelling reported, further, that people generally responded positively to what he said *and* "always to very different things done in the service!"[32]

The developmental understanding for faith which Fowler presents is not just descriptive. It is also normative. Stage advancement is something for which persons of faith should strive—both in and for themselves and in and for others. The goal would be Universalizing Faith.[33]

Fowler endorses the idea of advance stage movement without necessarily prescribing any particular religious tradition as a better facilitator. At the same time, he insists that people *have* to have an actual religious tradition or framework with history. They need particular symbols, myths, and rituals for fuller stage developments to take place. "There is likely no way toward Stages 5 and 6 except through the powerful and particular *contents* of specific religious traditions. As Santayana is supposed to have said, we cannot be religious in general."[34] The contents of faith have 1) centers of value, 2) images of power, and 3) master stories to which people may relate. Institutional religions with their particular symbols play an important role in enabling a person to advance, at first vicariously and then, actually, in faith stages. In the Christian tradition, of course, such symbols as the Trinity, the Bible, the cross, even the word "God," are important. The most significant symbol for Christians is a person: Jesus of Nazareth. He is the across-generation Other with whom one symbolically (at least) interacts and who is—by many observers' reckoning—a Stage 6 person in thought, life, and death. The Christ lures young and old forward across the years and generations.

Adult Life Developmental Phases: Gail Sheehy and Daniel Levinson

The discussion on development in this chapter opened with acknowledgement of Sigmund Freud's contributions to understanding *children's* bio-psychological stages. These pages come to a conclusion with a presentation of *adult* developmental stages. What links Freud's and Erikson's child-watching with recent adult-watching is the notion that, just as the child experiences bodily changes and finds him or herself in psychological and social growth situations, so the adult undergoes changes—including physical changes—involving psycho-social reorientation. Neither adolescent identity formation, for example, or adult midlife crises, for another example, are going to be missed.

People working in life-span development psychology remind us that "development is a lifelong process. No single period in the life-span can claim general primacy for origin and occurrence of important and interesting developmental changes."[35] Change and development are influenced by people's age (year of birth), historical conditioning, and by unique, nonnormative events. Nonnormative influences (accidents, deaths, whatever) especially influence the second half of life, making for increased individual expression and special personality profiles for interage interaction.

Two prominent writers on adult growth stages are Gail Sheehy and Daniel Levinson. Sheehy describes what goes on as "predictable crises of adult life."[36] Levinson says that life has regular "seasons" to it: "To speak of seasons is to say that the life course has a certain shape, that it evolves through a series of definable forms."[37] The forms/passages/seasons/cycles/crises of which the authors speak are unavoidable periods in adulthood. One may not avoid being in Middle Adulthood (Levinson's category), for example. Having attained that age, though, would not mean necessarily that one reasoned at a Stage 5 (Kohlberg's category) level. To speak of developmental periods of adult life, then is to talk more of a "maturationalist" than of a "progressivist" or "constructivist" conceptualization of development.[38]

Gail Sheehy's descriptive work on adults is based in large measure on journalistic interviews she did with 115, mostly upper-middle-class, Americans. She relies also on Levinson, Roger Gould, and others who have done more controlled studies. Sheehy's colorful descriptions of adult passages and her excellent writing style made a major impact on recent thinking about adults. Table No. 3 is a presentation of her categories.[39]

TABLE NO. 3.
ADULT PHASES OF GROWTH
AS DESCRIBED BY GAIL SHEEHY

Name of Phase	Ages Involved	Characteristics
Pulling Up Roots	18 on	Leaving home Separating of self from parents Experimentation in lifestyle
The Trying Twenties	Mid-20s	Doing what "I should" do Sense of ability to do most anything Commitment to marriage, children, single life, or job
Catch-30	28-32	Expressing oneself on heretofore neglected aspects of that self Earlier commitments (marriage, job, something) are abandoned or reformed
Rooting & Extending	Mid-30s	Doing what "I want" to do More settling down but with success orientation: "Becoming your own person."
Deadline Decade	35-45	Mid-life crises occur Time push felt Awareness of one's own mortality
Renewal/ Resignation	Mid-40s	Doing what "I must" do Equilibration regained Modifying life plans

It is obvious from looking at the table that this classification of adult phases is not very precise as to ages involved. Still, the adult reader of Sheehy's book has the feeling that she is "on to something fundamentally true." Sheehy's description of women, for example, as Caregivers, Nurturers-Who-Defer-Achievement, Achievers-Who-Defer-Nurturing, Late-Baby Superachievers, and so on, all describe women we know. Her categories add to the richness and complexity of understanding adults. They help us appreciate that the "typical adult" in a learning situation is, in fact, a multifaceted person.

Sheehy is not, it will be observed, prescribing a path for molding a "philosopher-king" a la Plato. She is mostly *describing* adult life. Furthermore, she does not do much in the way of suggesting how people might receive help with their predictable crises, except to "be aware"

122   INTERGENERATIONAL RELIGIOUS EDUCATION

that such crises are coming. It is as though one has to undergo all the unavoidable passages alone. Even so, Sheehy believes that humans have the power within themselves "to animate all of life's seasons."[40] *Passages* itself is a testimony to the value of shared communication. The shared communication is especially helpful with information on parent-child relations, career changes, why people marry, the testimonial woman, the corporate wunderkind, effects of climacteric and menopause, a no-panic approach to physical aging, and so forth. These topics and categories all suggest concerns upon which educators could focus, especially educators concerned about how people of varying ages and stages can come together most beneficially.

Daniel Levinson and colleagues at Yale University are more prescriptive than Sheehy, especially with regard to intergenerational exchange. Levinson says,

> Relationships between generational levels are important in all societies. While acknowledging the differences between generations, we can also learn to increase the interaction between them. At every age, all of us carry within ourselves aspects of every generation. Coming to know and use these aspects is a relevant task in every era. . . . A special task of middle adulthood is to become more aware of both the child and the elder in oneself and in others. Work on this task allows us to transcend in some measure the generational barriers and to relate in a more fully human way to persons of all ages.[41]

Such a recommendation is based on in-depth, over-time studies of forty adult males, ages thirty-five to forty-five, from four occupational subgroups. Five to ten interviews lasting one-to-three hours each were conducted in the course of the study. Starting into the project Levinson and his research team did not know what they would find. Coming out of it, they had some pretty clear notions about the "life structure" of men in their middle years. Broadly conceived, Levinson describes the total life structure as having five overlapping eras: 1) Childhood and Adolescence (0-22), 2) Early Adulthood (17-45), 3) Middle Adulthood (40-65), 4) Late Adulthood (60-80), and 5) Late, Late Adulthood (80 to death). For more detail see Figure No. 2.[42] In his book, Levinson focuses mainly on early and middle adulthood.

Jose Ortega y Gasset said that around age forty there is a separation between generations: The pre-forty generation is involved in "initiation" and the post-forty generation in "dominance."[43] The psychoanalyst Carl Jung indicated, similarly, that the early forties is a watershed age, with "individuation" occurring then. Individuation means taking more responsibility, working through life's polarities, having a clearer identity, and being less dependent. Levinson's studies agreed strongly and empirically.

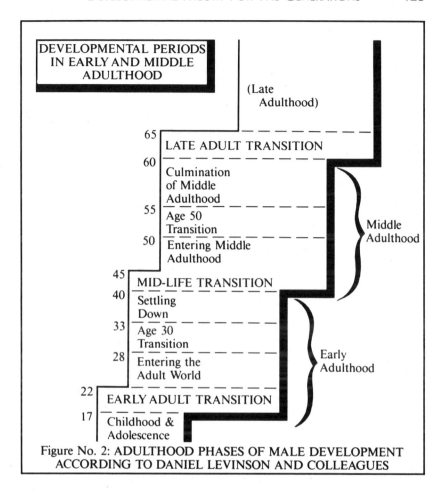

Figure No. 2: ADULTHOOD PHASES OF MALE DEVELOPMENT
ACCORDING TO DANIEL LEVINSON AND COLLEAGUES

More so than Sheehy, Levinson is cautious not to speak beyond what the data directly indicate. He does not generalize much on the adult stages as they affect women, for example, or regarding men who are younger or older. Still, what he unequivocally communicates is that men *are* going through processes of crisis and change. He calls these "transition" times and he sees them as part of the cycles of life. In the cycles and during the transitions, men can be helped, Levinson believes. The last chapter of *Seasons* is devoted to providing guidelines for healthy development during the early and middle adult years. He speaks of three "sets of tasks."

Developmental task number one is that of "Building and Modifying the Life Structure." This task is an ongoing process. Levinson urges people to be aware that in life they will be involved in terminating existing structures, exploring others, and making choices about direction. Interrelated choices are critical in the life structure. Certainly people know about the importance of choosing at age eighteen, because as teenagers we are told to expect to make choices at that age. Similarly, adults need to know that such choosings will be present at age fifty as well.

Second, Levinson talks about "Working on Single Components of the Life Structure." By that he means that life has various parts which periodically must be reassessed and acted upon. He identifies five components: 1) Forming and Modifying a Dream, 2) Forming and Modifying an Occupation, 3) Love-Marriage-Family, 4) Forming Mentoring Relationships, and 5) Forming Mutual Friendships. These single components are all involved in the total life structure. They will have different decisions or priorities made about them in the development process. Levinson discovered that with regard to component four above, most young men find older adults who serve as mentors for them as they launch their careers. Mentors help the early adults "realize the dream."[44] After age forty, mentors disappear, but mentoring *by* those mentored persons begins.

> Good mentoring is one of the special contributions that persons in middle adulthood can make to society. Given the value that mentoring has for the mentor, the recipient and society at large, it is tragic that so little of it actually occurs. We are held back by limitations in our individual development and in our institutional structures. These limitations serve to intensify intergenerational conflict and undermine relationships between youthful and middle-aged generations.[45]

Levinson urges professional and employment institutions to do more to facilitate mentoring.

It is possible that the institutional church could facilitate mentoring, but the life structure component for which religious organizations could be most helpful, is component five—"Forming Mutual Friendships." Here is the problem, though: "In our interviews, friendship was largely noticeable by its absence. As a tentative generalization we would say that close friendship with a man or woman is rarely experienced by American men."[46] As an institution concerned as much about "fellowship" as with "faith," surely the church/synagogue could be instrumental here. Andrew Greeley says that fulfilling the need for "belonging" (read: "friendship") is one of the primary reasons that religious institutions can hope to be around in the year 2000.[47]

The third task of Levinson's developmental prescription is called "Becoming More Individuated." In using Jung's concept, Levinson notes that the primary concerns here have to do with handling life's polarities. The polarities are those regarding Young/Old, Masculine/Feminine, Destruction/Creation, and Attachment/Separation conflicts. These all must be worked on continuously. Of the several, "The Young/Old polarity—the splitting of Young and Old, and the effort to reintegrate them—is *the* polarity of human development. It is the basic polarity to be worked on in every developmental transition."[48] This polarity is, it would seem, *not* best worked on by adults in isolation from either those younger or those older than they. The working out is best done together in multiple-age groups. If somehow middle-aged persons have been envying the young, then in knowing youth better, these adults might come to rejoice in their own unique steadying experiences. If such adults are fearful about death, then in knowing older people they might come to rejoice in prospects for their own ongoing fulfillment in later years. These mid-age adults would have much to give younger and older persons too.

Collective Summary Insights

The group of social scientists whose work we have reviewed in this and the previous chapter are of a similar mind: Young and old, we are made for each other. Aristotle was right. We are social animals. The *socii* is essential for *Homo sapiens*. By means of abbreviations for the names of theorists we have considered, I want to indicate in conclusion which writers have addressed most poignantly which recurring themes. These themes constitute some of the theoretical bases for intergenerational religious education. Here is a summary list of social scientists by name abbreviation.

MB for Martin Buber	MM for Margaret Mead
EE for Erik Erikson	WP for William Perry
SF for Sigmund Freud	JP for Jean Piaget
JF for James Fowler	VS for Virginia Satir
LK for Lawrence Kohlberg	MS for Margaret Sawin
DL for Daniel Levinson	GS for Gail Sheehy
GM for George Mead	MW for Mary Wilcox

Sometimes what these people have said has been specifically repeated by others. In other cases contributions stand more alone but are significant and usually consistent with what others have lifted up.

From George Mead's statement that "any self is a social self" to Daniel Levinson's remark in this chapter that "all of us carry within ourselves aspects of every generation," we have heard again and again the powerful refrain that *we make and keep life human by intergenera-*

tional action. The social matrices are generative of human mind (GM) and necessary for the expanded abilities of thinking (JP, WP). A man or woman's conception of self is also given by social act (GM). Significant social exchange provides people with a sense of self-esteem (VS), as well as the ability to affirm existence at every stage along life's way from acquiring Basic Trust to claiming Integrity (EE).

It is obvious to most observers that children need adults in order to survive and make it to adulthood (SF). We are also seeing that, just as much, adults need children to be fulfilled (EE) and perhaps even to survive into the future (MM). Within closer proximate chronological ages there is need for people to be in relation with one another. Toddlers need older children to imitate. Elementary grade-school-age children need to be in relation with youth (MW), youth to be interacting with modeling adults (WP and Robert Havighurst), and middle-life adults to be in mentoring relationships with younger adults (DL). Lawrence Senesh, whose remarks opened chapter 5, says the oldest generation has much to give and also much to receive. Each and every person at any age is or can be helped in his or her "being and becoming" by intergenerational experiences.

Our theorists share some common ideas on how the human community works. Many of the writers articulate a "stage-developmental" understanding of life's progression. The stages include physical-maturational components (SF, EE, JP), social-psychological factors (EE, MW, DL), and also cognitive (JP, WP), moral (LK, WP), social perspective-taking (GM, MW, JF), and faith (MB, JF) aspects. The developmental stages are seen as sequential, invariant and, for some (EE, JP, LK), universal. The various stages are spoken of in several of the developmental constructs (SF, EE, GS, DL) as "unavoidable" in life: Everybody, if he or she lives, will go through late adulthood, for example. With some of our thinkers, however, the stages are viewed as hierarchial (JP, LK, MW, JF): Not everybody, though he or she lives to be ninety, will attain Commitment in Relativism (WP). For this reason the developing person needs stretching experiences in order to "move up" to advanced developmental stages. Stage growth is possible, they say, because we first assimilate (JP) enriching experiences. Horizontal decalage fills us out. Assimilation prepares us for stage advance. The change may be brought on by accommodation of new data or understandings which did not fit our former operational stage (JP, LK, JF). By these processes the human-person-in-community becomes.

Key to making and keeping life human are significant gestures (GM), especially in the form of *language* and meta-language communication (VS, MS, JF). In addition to language we also can share *feelings* across the generations (VS) and relate to common *centers of meaning* (GM,

MB, JF). There is a great deal that keeps people identifiably together, among which are *life crises* (SF, EE, MM, GS, DL). These crises take different form with distinctive content for people at various life stages, but to survive and to thrive there is critical assistance which others can provide (EE, MM, LK, MW, DL). We have, in short, the necessary tools for realizing more of the potential in all people—if we but use them. These "tools," especially, are other people.

Our theorists offer some concrete ideas on how best to facilitate intergenerational exchange for the growth of persons. One thing they (VS, MS) say which is critically important is that families and groups be together and learn together. The reason for this is that if an individual learns something or changes in some way, it affects all others in the family or group. We need to be together to be able to grow singly and mutually (VS, MS). To promote stage advance, conflict is sometimes involved (EE, MM, GS) and even failure and defeat (JF). We can also help one another by several other means. Here are some that have been endorsed: leveling (talking straight) and asking questions (VS), interacting (JP), experiencing the other side (MB), using moral dilemmas in teaching (LK, MW), modeling advanced thinking and acting (LK, MW, DL), challenging (WP), teaching as much as learning (MM), and mutually defining communities of meaning (GM, JF). Development is further enhanced by action and interaction in other ways, including physical contact (MW), cognitive-affective relations (JP, LK), and symbolic investment (JF). The use of symbol, myth, and ritual in a specific faith tradition goes by the name of religious socialization (JF).

There is an openness—and, in some cases a strong endorsement (EE, MS, MM, MW, JF, DL)—for religious institutions to be involved intentionally in the human interactive development process. The church/synagogue, our theorists say, can do much to bring generations together and facilitate such things as family communication (VS, MS), cultural understanding (MM), ethical reflection (LK), definition of the Generalized Other (GM) or ultimate environment (JF), as well as helping with mentoring, the formation of mutual friendships, and the handling of the Young/Old polarity (DL). Though differences always remain among generations, the idea that religious organizations might help young and old to become friends and peers (VS) to one another is an attractive one.

These insights from the social scientists compel us to appreciate the complexity of human life across the generations. In the first few months of life a baby is remarkably different week-by-week (SF, JP). Any few years of adult age difference are also fraught with distinctive life structure differences (GS, DL). In general there is enough complexity among people to tempt the educator to give up on the idea that generations could ever possibly communicate their unique age-level concerns—much less be of help to one another on life structure tasks (EE, DL). Yet these very differences, if accounted for, can help the work of IGRE. For one thing, they suggest areas of educational attention for which generational interfacing might be helpful. And too, as we have seen, the theorists give us some good ideas on how to proceed effectively (EE, VS, JP, LK, MW, JF, DL).

Most of our analysts are strong believers that people can teach, learn, and grow together to help one another become complete persons. They also suggest that a better world may be the outcome of significant shared life together (GM, EE, MM, LK, JF). Together we may construe a vision of Ultimate Environment (JF) that will call us *all* forward together.

Notes

1. Elizabeth Hall, "A Conversation with Jean Piaget and Barbel Inhelder," *Psychology Today* (May, 1970), p. 27. See also Henry W. Maier, *Three Theories on Child Development: The Contributions of Erik Erikson, Jean Piaget, and Robert W. Sears* (New York: Harper & Row, 1969), p. 84.
2. Jean Piaget, *Six Psychological Studies,* ed. David Elkind (New York: Vintage, 1968), p. v.
3. Ibid., p. 3.
4. For a detailed outlining of this phase and its substages, see Piaget, *Six Studies,* pp. 8-17, and Maier, *Three Theories,* pp. 103-118.
5. There are a number of excellent and comprehensive treatments of Piaget's stage thinking. I especially recommend Mary M. Wilcox, *Developmental Journey: A Guide to the Development of Logical and Moral Reasoning and Social Perspective* (Nashville: Abingdon, 1979). Her fold-out chart attached to the book back cover is an excellent summary source. Piaget, *Six Studies,* pp. 8-70, and Maier, *Three Theories,* pp. 102-154, should also be consulted.
6. Ronald Goldman, *Religious Thinking from Childhood to Adolescence* (New York: Seabury, 1968), pp. 96-97.
7. David Elkind, "Editor's Introduction," Piaget, *Six Studies,* p. xiii.
8. Piaget, *Six Studies,* pp. 7-8. See also Maier, *Three Theories,* p. 95.
9. Piaget, *Six Studies,* p. 70.
10. Lawrence Kohlberg, "The Child as Moral Philosopher," *Psychology Today* (September, 1968), p. 25. Piaget's primary contribution is *The Moral Judgment of the Child,* written in 1932. For a recent statement on Piaget and Kohlberg, see Robert H. Platman, "Piaget's Contribution to Religious Education," *Reach* 10:3 (Winter, 1980-81), pp. 4-6.
11. Lawrence Kohlberg and Rochelle Mayer, "Development as the Aim of Education," *Harvard Educational Review* 42:4 (November, 1972), p. 456.
12. See the summary schema found in Lawrence Kohlberg, "Education for Justice: A Modern Statement of the Platonic View," *Moral Education,* pp. 72-73. This paper is found in Lawrence Kohlberg, *Collected Papers on Moral Development and Moral Education* (Cambridge, Mass.: Center for Moral Development and Education, Harvard Graduate School of Educa-

tion, Spring, 1973). See, also, Wilcox, *Developmental Journey* throughout
and on the fold-out chart inside the back cover.

13. See discussion on Gilligan's *In a Different Voice: Psychological Theory and
Women's Development* (Cambridge, Mass.: Harvard University Press, 1982)
in James W. Fowler, *Becoming Adult, Becoming Christian: Adult Development and Christian Faith* (San Francisco: Harper & Row, 1984), pp. 37-47.

14. Maria Harris, "Completion and Faith Development," in *Faith Development
and Fowler,* ed. Craig Dykstra and Sharon Parks (Birmingham, Ala.: Religious Education Press, 1986), p. 125.

15. William G. Perry, Jr., *Forms of Intellectual and Ethical Development in the
College Years: A Scheme* (New York: Holt, Rinehart and Winston, 1970), p.
3. (The capitalization of key words in the sentences of this paragraph is a
style used by Perry.)

16. Ibid., p. 154.

17. Ibid., p. 27.

18. For a report on moral development, a la Perry's above, see Mary Wilcox,
Clarence Snelling, and Edward H. Everding, "Interpretation and Truth in
Adult Development," a paper presented at the Annual Meeting of the
Association of Professors and Researchers in Religious Education, November, 1979. See also, Mary Wilcox, "Response . . . from the Moral Development Perspective," *Faith Development and the Adult Life Cycle,* ed. Kenneth Stokes (New York: Sadlier, 1982), pp. 134-140.

19. Wilcox, *Developmental Journey,* pp. 22-23.

20. See Jerome S. Bruner, *Toward a Theory of Instruction* (Cambridge, Mass.:
Belknap Press, 1978), p. 11.

21. Wilcox, *Developmental Journey,* see pp. 183-201.

22. James W. Fowler, *Stages of Faith: The Psychology of Human Development
and the Quest for Meaning* (San Francisco: Harper & Row, 1981), p. 25.
The concepts, words, phrases, and language in these paragraphs may be
found in Fowler's writings. They were first provided in personal conversations with Fowler and through lectures delivered in his course on "Faith and
the Life Cycle," Iliff School of Theology, August 2-12, 1976.

23. For a more detailed description of this triadic model, see Jim Fowler and
Sam Keen, *Life Maps: Conversations on the Journey of Faith,* ed. Jerome
Berryman (Waco, Tex.: Word Books, 1979), p. 20. See also Fowler *Stages of
Faith,* p. 17. Sometimes Fowler calls this third the CSV, "centers of supraor-
dinate value," as in *Faith Development and Fowler,* p. 17.

24. James W. Fowler, "Faith, Liberation and Human Development: Three Lectures," *The Foundation* (Atlanta, Ga.: Gammon Theological Seminary) 79
(1974), p. 7.

25. See Fowler, *Life Maps,* pp. 19-20, and *Stages of Faith,* pp. 5 and 204.

26. Fowler, *Stages of Faith,* p. 18.

27. Table No. 2 is constructed from material in several sources: class notes (see
note 22); personal analyses shared by James Fowler and Jerome Berryman;
a handout schema mimeographed by Fowler showing "An Outline" of the
Stages of Faith; a paper by James W. Fowler, "Stages in Faith—the Structur-
al-Developmental Approach," delivered at a Symposium on Moral Devel-
opment, Fordham University, Spring, 1975, pp. 12-13; Fowler and Keen's
Life Maps, pp. 42-95; *Stages of Faith,* p. 113 and then pp. 119-213; his
"Stages of Faith and Adults' Life Cycles," *Adult Life Cycle,* pp. 187-195;
Becoming Adult, pp. 52-71; and in his article, "Faith and the Structuring of
Meaning," *Faith Development and Fowler,* pp. 28-31.

28. Quote taken from lecture notes of August 12, 1976. See also Fowler and Keen, *Life Maps*, p. 80, where Fowler says that disadvantaged persons confront Stage 5 earlier than the more advantaged.
29. Fowler, *Life Maps*, pp. 39-41 ff. and 96-99. Also, Fowler, "Stages of Faith," pp. 14-30; *Stages*, pp. 242-257; Stokes, ed. *Adult Life Cycle*, pp. 188-194; and *Faith Development and Fowler*, pp. 31-37 and 286. The ordering of these seven aspects varies from publication to publication.
30. James W. Fowler, "Faith Development Theory and the Aims of Religious Socialization." Paper read at a special meeting of the Religious Education Association, Milwaukee, Wisconsin, October 24-26, 1975, p. 16.
31. See Fowler, *Stages*, pp. 286-287.
32. Clarence H. Snelling Jr., notes from a conversation, Cincinnati, Ohio, October 30, 1980.
33. See James Fowler, "Stage Six and the Kingdom of God," *Religious Education* 75:3 (May-June, 1980), pp. 231-248.
34. Fowler, "Religious Socialization" p. 20.
35. Paul B. Baltes and Hayne W. Reese, "The Life-Span Perspective in Developmental Psychology," in *Development Psychology: An Advanced Textbook*, Marc H. Bernstein and Michael E. Lamb, (Hillsdale, N.J.: Erlbaum 1984) p. 523, but also the whole article, pp. 493-531.
36. She so subtitles her book. Gail Sheehy, *Passages: Predictable Crises of Adult Life* (New York: Dutton, 1976).
37. Daniel J. Levinson with others, *The Seasons of a Man's Life* (New York: Knopf, 1978), p. 7. A helpful summarizing of Levinson and others' work in the field is done by Rita Preszler Weathersby and Jill Mattuck Tarule in their *Adult Development: Implications for Higher Education* (Washington, D.C.: American Association for Higher Education, 1980), pp. 6-9 and throughout.
38. See Fowler, "Stages," in *Adult Life Cycle*, pp. 185-186.
39. Sheehy, *Passages*, pp. 2-32 and throughout her book.
40. Ibid., p. 354.
41. Levinson, *Seasons*, pp. 27-38.
42. Ibid., p. 57.
43. Ibid., pp. 28-29.
44. Ibid., p. 98. (Parenthetically let it be noted that in generational relations these young adults who look for mentors often serve as "role models" for adolescents. Teenagers imitate or incorporate aspects of the young adult role models in their own "ideal self" image. On this point, see Robert J. Havighurst and Hilda Taba, *Adolescent Character and Personality* (New York: Wiley, 1949), p. 80.)
45. Levinson, *Seasons*, p. 254.
46. Ibid., p. 335.
47. Andrew Greeley, *Religion in the Year 2000* (New York: Sheed and Ward, 1969), pp. 167-175.
48. Levinson, *Seasons*, p. 210.

Chapter 7

Insights From Religious Educationists

Perhaps the most famous and frequently quoted statement on religious education is that of Horace Bushnell: "What is the true idea of Christian education?—I answer . . . That the child is to grow up a Christian, and never know himself as being otherwise."[1] Were I to nominate a "to be famous" statement in the field of *intergenerational* religious education, there are two I would offer. The first is by the writer-satirist Kurt Vonnegut.

> Whenever my children complain about the planet to me, I say: "Shut up! I just got here myself. Who do you think I am—Methuselah? You think I like the news of the day any better than you do? You're wrong."
> We are all experiencing more or less the same lifetime now.
> What is it the slightly older people want from the slightly younger people? They want credit for having survived so long, and often imaginatively under difficult conditions. . . .
> What is it the slightly younger people want from the slightly older people? More than anything, I think, they want acknowledgement and without further ado that they are, *without question,* women and men now.[2]

The other statement is by a religious educationist, Gabriel Moran: "We need learning within families, learning between children and other adults, learning between the very old and the very young, learning between families and all of society's 'outsiders' (the divorced, widowed, homosexual, 'retarded,' etc.)."[3]

Through the previous three chapters we have considered the thought of various religious, social scientific, and developmentalist writers, all with regard to theoretical foundations for intergenerational religious education. With only a few exceptions, I have not focused upon what

131

professionals in the field of religious education have said. In the pages of this chapter, they speak.

The contributions of religious educationists to understanding IGRE are grouped in terms of six key categories: 1) relationships in community, 2) socialization, 3) conscientization, 4) whole person learning, 5) the facilitational environment, and 6) worship. These six categories are decidedly interrelated but for examination purposes can be isolated. Similarly, the educationists who are discussed here in many cases have addressed all six categories but may be shown only as involved with one or two.

The presentation order for these six categories suggests, first, that for IGRE to occur, *relationships in community* which includes family and congregation are essential. What is going on in such communities is *socialization* of persons. Such learning can profitably be aided by recent reflections on "learning with" as spoken of in the literature on fostering *conscientization.* And that teaching/learning will be more effective if it involves the *whole person* —cognitively, affectively, and physically. In IGRE, planners need to be attentive to *the facilitational environment,* gathering insights from secular and religious educationists and researchers. Finally, intergenerational consideration must be given to the primary expression of the faith community's life, namely, *worship.*

Relationships in Community

In Christianity, relationship is of the essence. That is true in great measure because relationship is so significant in Judaism too. Additional reason for it being so in Christianity may be attributed to the fact that religion has functioned for two thousand years with the doctrine of the Trinity. Traditionally understood, in the Godhead are *three personae existing on dynamic relationship* with each other, yet the three are one. One might say, "Christians relate because God does so first" (see 1 John 4:19).

Whatever the origin of the emphasis, it is certain that contemporary Christian religious educationists stress relationships as a *sine qua non* of faith. Learning and growing in the religious life take place, they say, primarily in the company of significant others in the family and the community of believers.

Horace Bushnell, whose words began this chapter, says that the nurture of persons in faith takes place, first and most powerfully, in the family. In his 1861 classic, *Christian Nurture,* he wrote:

And this is the very idea of Christian education, that it begins with nurture or cultivation. And the intention is that the Christian life and spirit of the parents, which are in and by the Spirit of God, shall flow into the mind of the

> child, to blend with his incipient and half-formed exercises; that they shall thus beget their own good within him—their thoughts, opinions, faith, and love, which are to become a little more, and yet a little more, his separate exercise, but still the same in character.[4]

Fifteen centuries earlier, St. Augustine is reputed to have said, in effect, "Give me a child for the first six years of life, and I'll make him/her a Christian forever." Bushnell pushed the idea a little further, saying that more is accomplished in the first *three* years of a person's life then in all the other years combined.[5] He even believed that nurture began in the prenatal phase. Especially what happens in the first few years is not an oral transmission of propositional truths but an attitudinal and general affection transfer of religious dispositions. The sense of caring, loving, trusting, faithfulness, and so on, at deep psychic levels are learned during the formative years.

Recently Bushnell's speculations have received empirical support in the work of Ana-Marie Rizzuto. This social scientist claims that the effect of close interpersonal interactions (as between mother and infant in face-to-face feeding) is to program the child in his/her private representation of God for the rest of that person's life. God's face is given through the mother's countenance. "All children," she says, "arrive at the house of God with their own God under their arm."[6] Religious educators may then contribute to the shaping of the God-image, but the basic contours have already been provided before formal religious education begins.

So far as Bushnell is concerned, beyond immediate family, the community of the CHURCH is vitally important in the shaping of a person's faith. He says both the child and the parents exist in the context of the church. Thus baptism, for example, should be a rite observed with utmost seriousness by both the parents *and* the surrounding body of believers. In the ongoing life of a young person in the church, Bushnell was willing to have them be considered members of the body and come to the Lord's Table—even before they were confirmed! It was a radical notion in its day.

Some fifty years after Bushnell, George Albert Coe updated the interactive nurture position. Coe asked, "What, then, is Christian Education?" and answered, "It is the systematic, critical examination and reconstruction of *relations between people*, guided by Jesus' assumption that persons are of infinite worth, and by the hypotheses of the existence of God, the Great Valuer of Persons."[7] With such a high regard for the human and for human interactions, it is not surprising to find Coe insisting also that "personality can grow, or its growth be arrested, through friendship, affection, and loyalty."[8] Using the social gospel language of his day, Coe stressed the importance of social relationships for the communication of the faith.

In our own time, three articulate representatives of the Bushnell-Coe tradition are Randolph Crump Miller, C. Ellis Nelson, and Donald E. Miller.

Randolph Crump Miller talks about both the family and the total parish as agents of religious education, these being the two cells of society by which a learner comes to faith knowledge in a social process.[9] In his book *Clue to Christian Education,* Miller writes,

> The purpose of Christian education is to place God at the center and to bring the individual into the right *relationship* with God and his fellows within the perspective of the fundamental truths about life. The major task of Christian education today is to discover and impart the relevance of Christian truth. The key words here are relationship and relevance.
>
> Theology is a description of relationships. It may be defined as "truth-about-God-in-relation to man."[10]

In stressing relationships, Miller leans on both Martin Buber (whose "I-Thou" insights we considered in chapter 5) and Reuel Howe who spoke often about "the language of relationship."

With C. Ellis Nelson the key phrase is "community of believers." It is, he says, in the context of a community of believers "where faith begins"—the title of his best known book. "My thesis is that faith is communicated by a community of believers and that the meaning of faith is developed by its members out of their history, by their interaction with each other, and in relation to the events that take place in their lives."[11] Among the words in Ellis' statement, the one with a fresh ring to it is "events." By events Nelson suggests that the life of faith is built on accidental and planned happening/incidents/events which impact the individual with great meaning. Such events, occurring in the context of the community of believers, have a threefold effect for the person: They establish a *perceptive system* in relation to a worldview, form a *conscience* according to a value system, and create a *self-identification* out of personal relations within a social group.[12] Nelson holds that the church has not yet approached its potential for beginning and continuing the faith development process. This process needs much more deliberate planning of events, facilitating of the people interactions and more. Speaking rhetorically, Nelson asks, "Why this insistence on the communal nature of the church? Because it is by this process that faith can be incubated and nurtured. Faith is concomitant of human association. That is why the church must be a gathering of Christians which is permanent enough to allow individuals to know each other in various facets of their life and regular enough in its meetings to be able to develop a sense of solidarity in Christ and in their mission to the world."[13] Worship, fellowship, searching the scripture and confronting controversial issues are all to be part of the life of the community of believers which facilitates faith. He calls this "socialization"—which we shall consider in the next section.

Most recently Donald Miller has spoken of "the faith community as teacher," defining a community as a group of persons sharing common commitments, norms of behavior, symbolic culture, and living within a shared environment. What distinguishes this community is that it is "related to and affected by the widest horizon of meaning, the final center of value, its ultimate concern, and the sense of absolute dependence—by faith in God." The result of significant community life, Miller believes, will be "education for global participation" and, ultimately, impact which will "influence the fundamental values of a culture."[14]

In these soundings from the thought of Bushnell, Coe, Nelson, the Millers, and others, we hear time and again of the importance of relationships in community. It should be pointed out, though, that—except in very recent years—the explicit concept of "intergenerational life and learning" does not appear in the literature. Even so, there is basic compatibility between the idea of IGRE and that of relationships in community.

One place where I find some difference from IGRE understandings (as suggested earlier by Erik Erikson, Margaret Mead, and some others) is on the matter of how much learning is from-child-to-adult. With most of the religious educationists the emphasis seems to be from-older-to-younger. There is not much talk of learning *from* children.

In these discussions let me call attention to two other things. One is that the writers may be asking families to do too much. Single parent families and extended families separated from their relatives by geography are especially taxed. The hope is that the church-as-extended-family can be helpful. The other caveat is with regard to "community." Gabriel Moran is only too right-on when he observes we seldom have community in the modern age but, rather, "communal relations."[15] That is certainly true in the church/synagogue and is one of the limiting realties.

These notations made, still let us reaffirm with the religious educationists that *relationships in community* (of *family* and *congregation)* facilitate the all-important third relationship in community—that of persons with God. Randolph Crump Miller says (and Rizzuto implies) that "the child moves from faith in his parents to faith in his parents' faith to faith of his own shared in the larger community of the Holy Spirit."[16]

Socialization

The social-scientific term for what is spoken of above is "socialization." It suggests the processes by which a person is brought up in collectives to function successfully therein. In describing socialization, Berard Marthaler notes that social scientists in three disciplines use the term—but each with a somewhat different concern. *Anthropologists,* he observes, ask questions about how the culture is transmitted from one generation to another. *Sociologists* are interested in knowing how institutions are continued and changed. *Psychologists* want to know how people internalize the culture and societal values. When these three disciplinary concerns are directed to the matter of religious socialization, there are three distinct but related foci: 1) the maintenance and transmission of a religious tradition (the handing on of the symbols of faith, the communication of meaning); 2) the question of religious affiliation (belonging to a religious institution, incorporating persons into a society of believers); and 3) the search for self-identity and values derived from faith resources (religious growth, broadening one's valuation horizon).[17] One of the things which makes religious socialization different from what is usually thought of as religious education is that socialization is decidedly broader than schooling. It stresses informal as well as formal occasions for regenerating the faith.

In their book *Generation to Generation,* anthropologist Gwen Neville and religious educationist John Westerhoff say that religious socialization is "a process consisting of lifelong formal and informal mechanisms, through which persons sustain and transmit their faith (worldview, value system) and lifestyle, and this is accomplished through participation in the life of a tradition-bearing community with rites, rituals, myths, symbols, expressions of belief, attitudes and values, organizational patterns, and activities."[18] Sometimes Westerhoff will describe socialization by the term "enculturation," and when he does so, he especially picks up the interpersonal theme so vital in IGRE: "While much socialization literature has a tendency to emphasize how the environment, experiences, and actions of others influence us, enculturation emphasizes the *process of interaction between and among people of all ages.*"[19]

Westerhoff's emphasis on interaction should not be missed, in that socialization is sometimes erroneously characterized as a unidirectional process. He clearly wants there to be sustaining interaction in the faith community among the generations, as noted in his oft-quoted words:

> True community necessitates the presence and interaction of three genera-
> tions. Too often the church . . . sets the generations apart. Remember that
> the third generation is the generation of memory, and without its presence
> the other two generations are locked into the existential present. While the
> first generation is potentially the generation of vision, it is not possible to
> have visions without memory, and memory is supplied by the third genera-
> tion. The second generation is the generation of the present. When it is
> combined with the generations of memory and vision, it functions to con-
> front the community with reality, but left to itself and the present, life
> becomes intolerable and meaningless. Without interaction between and
> among the generations, each making its own contribution, Christian com-
> munity is difficult to maintain.[20]

Westerhoff's thinking is underscored by social scientists Vern Bengston
and Dean Black. They also insist that socialization is not unidirectional.
There always is bilateral negotiation going on. "The old learn from the
young," they say, "just as the young learn from the old."[21]

In light of these several statements, it seems clear that when it emphasizes these interactions, IGRE is a form of socialization. A question
remains, though. That is the question of whether IGRE is also to be
considered as "catechesis" and promoted as such. In the discussions of
religious socialization, "catechesis" pro and con positions invariably are
taken. In Greek the word for catechesis is *katechein,* which means "to
echo" or "to hand down." The handing down in the early church was
usually by oral transmission and was, therefore, interpersonal. It was
also a transmitting that had as much to do with lifestyle and affection as
with information. In later centuries, however, propositional truth became the near-sole concern in Catholic and Lutheran catechetical
classes.

In an attempt to breath new life into this venerable concept the 1971
General Catechical Directory, published in Rome, described catechesis
as "the term to be used for the form of ecclesial [or pastoral] action
which leads both communities and individual members of the faithful
to maturity of faith."[22] Such maturity is to be gained through a deepening involvement in 1) the *word* especially through explicit teaching,
2) the *community* where the faith is shared, 3) *worship* which is celebrative, and 4) *service* in the world because of social conscience.[23] "Ultimately, it is the church community," says Marthaler, "by its lifestyle,
purpose, and spirit which evangelizes, catechizes, and provides the context in which all grow to maturity in Christ."[24]

"Catechesis," then is a concept which is not intended by its advocates
to apply only to propositional transmission. Some persons have attempted to make the term somewhat more holistic in reference. One of
the Protestants who likes this Catholic-background term is John Wester-

hoff. He urges that the Religious Education Association support and encourage use of this concept.[25]

Personally I am not convinced that the idea of catechesis works too well, at least so far as IGRE is concerned. It has three discernible drawbacks. One is simply that the term is so Roman Catholic in association that it will not sell well in ecumenical and interfaith settings.[26] Indeed, the official Catholic documents clearly state that the only true catechesis is that which is under the direct political control of the Catholic hierarchy. Second, protests notwithstanding, catechesis still suggests too much of a one-way, older-to-younger, heavily cognitive, faith transmissive, and "imprinting" aura to it.[27] Third, catechesis—and to some extent also socialization and enculturation—implies that religious faith is timeless, changeless, and overly enamored of the status quo in religion and society. The truth is—or should be—otherwise. The religious education we need cannot be vested only in the elder generations. In summarizing various religious education models, Seymour and Miller note as one of the "problems" with the faith community (or the religious socialization/catechetical) approach is the "difficulty of intentionally using enculturation structures; apparent assumption that a church community is faithful."[28] As evidenced by statements quoted above by the proponents of socialization, status-quoism is considered to be neither necessary or desirable; but if in practice it were to be the case, then certainly that would not be descriptive of what IGRE is about.

Part of the corrective for the dangers pointed to in my third reservation above may be found in the writings of religious educationists who are interested in developing a more radical posture in teaching/learning.

Conscientization

In chapter 4 of this book consideration was given to the foundational resources for IGRE in several religious fields (biblical studies, church history, etc.). Process theology was a foundational resource discussed. Other theological stances, both historic and current, might have been explored for a broader underpinning of IGRE. One of those theologies inviting elaboration is "liberation theology."

When liberation theology is discussed in conjunction with education, Paulo Friere's name invariably comes up. In working with illiterate poor in South America, Friere, a trained Ph.D. in education, began to see that the imposition of literacy programs on people from without was seldom effective. Even when programs had a modicum of success, they never helped with more fundamental needs, namely, enabling the newly literate to identify basic social and cultural problems and to begin work for worthwhile long-term change. To remedy this no-win situation, Friere and others began doing basic educational programs under the

Spanish label of *conscientizaçao*. This translates into English as "conscientization" or "critical consciousness" (perhaps, most accurately, "critical cognition"). Conscientization suggests a coming to an intellectual grasp of the world in such a way as to understand it, appreciate it (sometimes), and change/improve it. Conscientization differs, obviously, from cultural transmission a la socialization/enculturation in that it is *explicitly* concerned about transformation in society.

The pedagogical principle which guides conscientization is that of "praxis." Praxis, which commonly is misunderstood simply as "practice," is for Friere and others the meeting of theory and action on a middle ground which uses both to foster conscientization, and, ultimately, to emancipate people from oppressive forces. Praxis is "reflective action," a creative blending of abstract and concrete teaching-learning. Friere says that to sacrifice action for reflection alone is to end up with verbalism; to sacrifice reflection for action alone is to end up with activism. Neither by itself is adequate.[29] In North America, generally speaking, we err in educational circles as "too given to theory"—the e-*ther-ea*l—but we need both, even in IGRE.

For IGRE there is an important additional note sounded in the conscientization score. It is the note that teaching-learning at its best is always a "with" activity. Friere says that the pedagogy of the oppressed is "pedagogy which must be forged *with,* not *for,* the oppressed (whether individuals or peoples) in the incessant struggle to regain their humanity."[30] Learning-with is learning that is cointentional between teachers and students. It leads, Friere claims, to committed involvement.

In the learning-with model which Friere espouses, the primary pedagogical technique to use is "in situation" thinking. The teacher helps people become aware of their situation by having them reflect upon various "themes" or concerns and then do "problem-posing" about the world in which they live. This problem-posing stimulates "critical consciousness" leading to action. The action which Friere wants is "Dialogical Cultural Action." Such is quite different from "Antidialogical Actions" taken by ruling elites and oppressors. Consider the two side-by-side:

Antidialogical Actions	*Dialogical Cultural Action*
conquest	cooperation
divide and conquer	unity for liberation
manipulation	organization
cultural invasion	cultural synthesis[31]

Friere wants action (as did Marx) to change the world and not just describe it. For this reason, Friere may be accused of politicizing education, but, lest we forget, education is political already and always. What I want to underscore is that Friere sees the action as "cultural." Religion inescapably and rightly operates at what Talcott Parsons describes as the cultural level in the "systems of action."[32] This is not an inappropriate realm of activity—especially for persons who represent three or more cultural generations.

Following educational leads suggested by Friere are two United States religious educationists: Catholic Thomas Groome and Protestant Malcolm Warford. They have creatively appropriated much of Friere's thought.

One of the things Groome does well is to pick up on the "con"— meaning "with"—emphasis in Friere's *con*scientization thought. Such is seen in his definition of Christian religious education: "A political activity *with* pilgrims in time that deliberately and intentionally attends *with* them to the activity of God in our present, to the Story of the Christian faith community, and to the Vision of God's Kingdom, the seeds of which are already among us."[33] Groome's major book on religious education is an unpacking of the above-mentioned words and phrases. Throughout the pages the "with" (or "shared") emphasis is a constant theme.

A second major emphasis which Groome takes from Friere is that of praxis. Groome takes the idea of praxis as the basis of his so-called pedagogical method of what he terms "shared praxis." For Groome, the shared praxis method of teaching religion has five stages, or what Groome calls "movements": 1) participants name their present action, 2) participants cognitively reflect on why they do what they do and what will be the likely outcomes of this action, 3) the religious educator presents the Christian story and vision; 4) participants relate the Christian story with their own, and 5) participants choose a faith response involving the Christian vision and their own.[34]

Malcolm Warford is a Protestant religious educationist and seminary administrator. He writes: "Let me suggest that Christian education is the continuing praxis of evolving the church's growth as a liberating community and encouraging the development of critical consciousness."[35] With that thought in mind he asks religious educators to look at their faith communities to discover whether their institutions are liberating forces in the culture or bodies promulgating piety, values, and attitudes no longer appropriate or, in fact, destructive of human good. Warford contends that the latter is too often the case. To rectify the situation, he urges Christians to pay less attention to methods in education and more to the milieu or *paideia* of the culture. By *paideia* he means the configuration of ideas and institutions which provides the setting in which individuals learn a community's way of acting, thinking, and feeling. By way of illustration, Warford suggests people take a hard look at what television is doing to people in our culture.[36] That would indeed make for a valuable intergenerational project.

In such ways, then, liberation theology and liberation pedagogy provide help to the work of IGRE. We are not so naive as to suggest that this way of doing religious education is wholly compatible with other pedagogical approaches considered. It is not. Conscientization is open to critique on a couple of fronts. One is that it is overly cognitive. James Michael Lee suggests that Groome, for example, may be labeled as an "ultra-cognitivist."[37] There is virtually no talk about love or forgiveness and other staples of the faith in the writings of Warford and especially of Groome. The educational goal almost seems to be "the development of an angry mind" or, at least, a prophetic posturing, more than anything else.[38] I will say more about the need for holism regarding the learner in the next section and in chapter 9. Suffice it to say here that in the conscientization literature there is a dirth of recognition of the importance of affection and religious lifestyle behavior.

Again, insofar as conscientization is related to liberation theology, we are focused more on social/cultural transformation than on individual faith development. If the truth be told, this writer is vitally interested in the *polis* and most things political too, but as a practical matter I must be reminded that religious institutions of this land are still voluntary associations. Such associations operate of necessity best by consensus, not even majority rule. As a consequence very few congregations take to large socio-economic concerns with alacrity. When religious publishing houses, for example, produce reflection-and-action curricular materials, they are not usually flooded by orders! Congregations are slow to tackle even local social issues. Then too, in terms of IGRE, it is a little hard to imagine children and retirees getting much exercised about "interlocking directorates of the multinational corporations" or some such topic. At this point, then, it is difficult to say how liberation theology and its emphases are going to fit in the life of the North American church, generally, and IGRE, in particular.

Whole Person Focus

The human animal, though able to celebrate rationality, is more than a thinking machine. People are made up of feelings, values, attitudes, hopes, fears, intentions, intuitions, and more. We have physical bodies which move, touch, embrace, ingest, excrete, sit, play, sleep, and die. We are whole beings, and the religious education which accounts men and women of all ages in their totality will be the most successful—for those persons, for the institution, for the faith, for God.

Almost all religious educationists pay homage to a "whole person focus" in their pedagogical prescriptions. Few, though, really work such into their educational programs. I want to single out those who do in this section.

The educationist with whom to begin is Benjamin Bloom, though he is not a religious educator per se. Bloom developed a "taxonomy of educational objectives" which is inclusive of all the aspects of the human. In the taxonomy which he and his colleagues devised, three basic domains of learning are identified: 1) the cognitive domain, 2) the affective domain, and 3) the psychomotor domain.[39] These general classifications are subdivided into more specific categories with the learnings involved for each described. The categories for the affective domain, for example, include 1.00 Receiving (attending), 2.00 Responding, 3.00 Valuing (cf. attitude), 4.00 Organization (of values in order of importance), and 5.00 Characterization by Value or Value Complex. Each of these five is then subdivided with numbers and descriptors (e.g., "2.30 Satisfaction in Response"). This lends greater specificity to the kinds of learning involved for each. By these taxonomies educators are reminded that learning takes place across a wide and often subtle spectrum of areas for a whole person.[40]

A number of religious educators have incorporated Bloom's holistic understanding in their writing. Margaret Sawin, for example, holds that in Family Clusters learning has a 1) cognitive component, 2) an affective or emotional component, and 3) a behavioral component.[41] Charles Melchert in discussing "Understanding" incorporates the same basic taxonomical components—plus one. His components are the 1) sensorimotor, 2) emotional, 3) analytical, and 4) synthetic. The latter has to do with images, metaphors, analogues, and symbols so important in religious god-talk.[42]

While most religious educators nod to the holistic focus, few seem to understand it so well as James Michael Lee. Lee makes clear that teaching/learning involves much more than cerebral activities. Time and again in the 800-plus pages of his *The Content of Religious Instruction,* he underscores that the affective *and* the physical are deeply involved. He identifies nine "molar contents" in the substantive content of learning. They are 1) product content, 2) process content, 3) cognitive content, 4) affective content, 5) verbal content, 6) nonverbal content, 7) conscious content, 8) unconscious content, and 9) lifestyle content. In the book Lee declines to elaborate on conscious content simply because it is implicit in all the other substantive contents and because it is so overemphasized by everyone else. What he comes out for most strongly is *lifestyle content* which is especially physical/psychomotor/behavioral. In effect, lifestyle content incorporates all the other "contents." He writes: "Lifestyle content refers to the overall pattern of a person's activities. Put somewhat personalistically, lifestyle content consists of the way a person organizes his self-esteem and lives out his life. Lifestyle, then, is the all-inclusive shape and operational flow of the totality of a person's behavior."[43] So it is that Lee urges that religious education be lifestyle focused, always aware that the human is *homo integer.* "Translated into the pedagogical realm, *homo integer* means that all the dimensions of the human being, as appropriate, should become actively involved in a personalistic manner in the learning task."[44] Lee wants "holistic functionalism" in the social-scientific approach taken in religious instruction.

Certainly in intergenerational education the holistic way is to be followed. As a way of saying how such might be done, we are not amiss

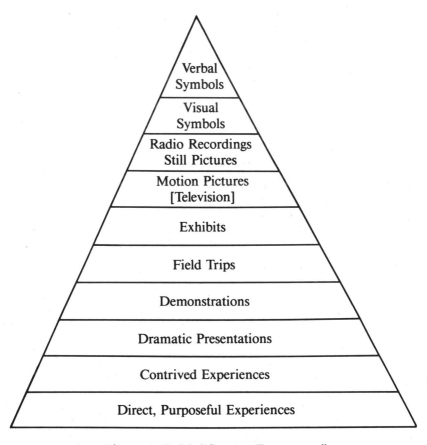

Figure 1. Dale's "CONE OF EXPERIENCE"

in duplicating Edgar Dale's "Cone of Experience."[45] (See Figure 1.) The Cone shows quite well that the base on which the greatest educational gains can be found is that of actual *doing* —doing, which is behavioral and/or lifestyle. "Of course," a critic may say, "everyone knows this!" True. But in the world of educational practice such is all too regularly forgotten. It may be that IGRE can be holistic better than some less global forms of teaching/learning because it involves nonreading and physically active children and youth. Still, the prodding goad needs to be present to keep people of all ages moving toward "direct, purposeful experiences."

Another religious educationist who stresses holism is Mary Wilcox. In her book on moral development, she notes that growth is facilitated by the use of a variety of learning methods employed in complementary ways.[46] A source for Wilcox and for IGRE on this point is George Isaac Brown, chief proponent of *"confluent education . . .* the term for the integration or flow together of the *affective* and *cognitive* elements in individual and group learning—sometimes called humanistic or psychological education."[47] Students in Brown's classes, for example, might be asked to write two essays: one on the subject "Who am I?" (an affective issue) and another on the topic "What is man?" (a cognitive issue) and then compare and discuss the two. Confluent education which joins emotions with intellect is a way of beginning to treat the whole person in a creative way.

An educator who has connected the psychomotor to the process of learning (albeit, especially for cognitive advancement) is Jerome Bruner. He contends that people learn first through physical action or what he calls the *"enactive mood"* or representation. It is physical, concrete, learning-through-doing. It is easier to teach someone how to ski by actually putting them on skis, for example, then to explain verbally or visually how it is done. The visual or *"iconic mood"* is Bruner's second system of representation. It is governed by principles of organization which the eyes, more than anything else, help pull together. In Piagetian terms this is the concrete operational stage of learning. Finally, Bruner says, there is the *"symbolic mood"* which uses signs and symbols, words and language most heavily. The symbolic/linguistic mood is usually the last to be developed in people. In learning people pass through these three moods.[48]

In consideration of people of differing ages learning together, Bruner offers encouragement which is at variance from the cognitive developmentalists. He contends that relative high-order cognitive learning can be taught to people at very early ages: "There is an appropriate version of any skill or knowledge that may be imparted at whatever age one wishes to begin teaching—however preparatory the version may be."[49] Bruner uses examples from mathematics, among others, to describe how learning at an advanced symbolic level can be presented and grasped by children in the early grades. The key to success is to get the mood or language of explanation to the child's level of understanding. Then one can teach practically anything.[50]

Seminal thinker that he is, Bruner offers another insight about people and whole-person learning. This insight goes by the name of "reciprocity." Reciprocity is the desire deep within the human to respond to others and operate jointly toward a common object. "We know precious little about this primitive motive to reciprocate," Bruner says, "but what we do know is that it can furnish a driving force to learn as well."[51] It may be that religious educationist Charles Melchert has reciprocity in mind when he notes the importance of "mutuality" in religious instruction: "Indeed, as the complexity of what is being taught increases (for example, in areas such as religion, or with goals such as understanding) the assurance of success decreases, and greater is the need for mutuality which increasingly approaches equality between teacher and learner."[52] In saying these things, both Melchert and Bruner underscore the possibility for effectiveness in IGRE. We are, it seems, only whole with others.

Finally, Gabriel Moran makes some helpful observations on the issue of holism. Though the goals and processes in Moran's Ideal Religious Education are very cognitive, nonetheless he sees the education of the person as occurring in *all* the important realms of life. Moran believes, rightly, that learning is going on 1) in the family, 2) at school, 3) on the job, and 4) at play. The really determinative learning for persons takes place in terms of *interplay* between and among these four primary forms. He wants that dynamic to be understood and developed. Not surprisingly, given the quotation from Moran which began this chapter, he also argues for "interplay across the generations" with three or more generations in relationship.[53]

Facilitational Environment

In B. F. Skinner's novel, *Walden II,* the protagonist Frazier, while walking through a desolate city, finds a newspaper on a park bench. He recalls:

> I picked up the paper. The president of my university had been in the city, making his most recent version of a standard speech. [It was] an assemblage of cliches . . . "encouraging individual initiative," "ministering to the whole man," "stimulating a spirit of inquiry," [etc.] . . . As usual, I was not sure what any of these utterances mean, though I experienced a nebulous sense of agreement. Insofar as they had meaning at all, they seemed to refer to worthwhile goals. But on one point my reaction was definite: it was obvious that no one, least of all the speaker, had any notion of how to set to work to attain them.[54]

In all candor, it must be admitted that leaders in religious institutions are very like the president of Frazier's university. We have grandeous goals and objectives and almost no idea how to reach them.

A guide on how to get to work to attain religious educational goals is James Michael Lee. He is adamantly opposed to the idea that effectiveness in religious instruction must be left up to the Holy Spirit or some Mysterious Invisible Hand of Benevolent Pedagogy. Lee calls such ethereal notions "Spookification," a "nebulous mass of ineffectualness grounded in the 'Blow Theory' of religious education."[55] He rejects all this kind of nonsense as fraudulent, unreal, and hence ultimately unreligious. He holds that religious educators are responsible for maximizing the learning experience and can do so by attentiveness to the "facilitational environment." "The Spirit does not blow capriciously or in the fashion of a magician, but rather blows in and through the normal antecedent-consequent relationships which exist in the world he [the Spirit] has made and continues to make by his sustaining presence within it."[56] Knowledge of "normal antecedent-consequent relationships," in the teaching/learning act, Lee holds, is not provided by theology but by social science. Religious education, then, is not a branch of theology, not a messenger boy for theology, and not the handmaid of theology. It is, rather, an enactment of social-scientific research into how people communicate and learn. "Religious instruction [is] the intentional process by and through which learning outcomes perceived by the individual and society to be generically related to God are deliberately brought about in an individual in one way or another."[57] Lee's understanding of "one way or another" prompts him to advocate specific structural ideas to improve effectiveness in religious instruction. One should consult *The Flow of Religious Instruction,* the second volume of his comprehensive religious instruction trilogy, for details. For our purposes, there are three instructional ideas to be underscored.

The first key idea from Lee is the *learning environment* emphasis. Effective teaching-learning is facilitated by attention to the "SLS"—the "structured learning situation." The SLS accounts for all of the four major variables involved in all instruction.[58] The environment should be a "facilitation environment" and, as such, purposefully planned, selective, rich in stimuli, evocative of a total response from the learner, reinforcing and warm in climate.[59] Such an environment Lee sometimes calls a "Laboratory for Christian Living." It features 1) concrete here-and-now performance, 2) first-hand experiences, 3) holistic integration of human functioning, 4) controlled conditions, 5) experimentation, 6) performance-based teaching, and 7) an intertwining of theory and practice.[60] Lee states forcefully that the laboratory for Christian living should be characterized by a "personally interactive milieu."[61]

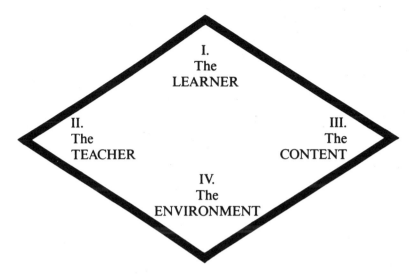

Figure 2. Lee's Critical Variables in Religious Instruction

Though *change in behavior* is central in all teaching and in all faith communities, few religious educationists deal with this critical outcome in a serious or sustained manner. James Michael Lee is the exception. *Change in behavior* is central to Lee's theory and practice of religion teaching for the reason that learning is itself defined by psychologists and students of learning as change in behavior. By behavior Lee means everything the human being does. Thus thinking is a behavior, affect is a behavior, lifestyle conduct is a pattern of behavior. Behavior is central in religious instruction. Because the task of all religious education is to make a person "more religious," the task of the religious educator is fundamentally one of "facilitating the modification of the learner's behavior along religious lines."[62] This kind of facilitation process involves generalized procedures such as structuring the learning situation and specific procedures such as reinforcement and contingency setting. It should be noted that Lee is not a behavior modificationist in the formal sense of that term, and when he uses certain terms they are not meant to borrow from the behavior modification school of social science.[63]

Related to behavior change is a third area in which Lee is boldly willing to venture. That is *evaluation*. Very few religious educationists deal with evaluation, even though evaluation is central to religious education. Lee agrees with Robert Mager about the importance of "specifying instructional objectives" and "measuring instructional intent"[64] when he writes: "A curriculum, if it is to be teachable, should specify which behaviors are involved (for example) in growing in love for God. . . . These behaviors should be expressed in observable performance terms, namely, that level of performance the learner must demonstrate to himself and to the teacher that he has indeed learned the behavior involved."[65] Given this disposition, Lee is willing to talk about "RQ" (religious quotient) and "RA" (religious achievement)! Obviously, his views are congenial to the concept of "mastery learning" which James Block speaks for. Block says that "all or almost all students can master what they are taught."[66]

In subsequent chapters when IGRE planning and programing are discussed, Lee's contributions to our understanding of the learning environment, behavior change, and evaluation will be considered again. He has not addressed directly the topic of interage teaching and learning.

Worship

Religious educationists are persons specializing in teacher-learner dynamics, usually in classroom-like settings. They are not experts on liturgy. Yet almost all have addressed the matter of worship for its learning significance. Here are three selected comments:

"It may be that worship is the most significant factor in a sound Christian education."—Randolph Crump Miller[67]

The proper setting for Christian education is "not the classroom but the chapel."—Michael Warren[68]

"The liturgy is not only an act of worship; it is also fundamentally an act of religious instruction."—James Michael Lee[69]

In discussing worship and religious education, three interlocking ideas emerge in the thought of the religious educationists with regard to people of various ages worshiping together. Much of their commentary revolves around "the place of children in worship." The three ideas to be dealt with in these pages are 1) that ritual and worship are educationally central whatever one's age, 2) that children and adults should worship together for mutual "building up," and 3) that some reform in worship is in order for more effective intergenerational worship.

Centrality of Worship. In Christianity (and to an important degree in Judaism), worship is the central activity of the faithful. It is people's response to God and their source for vision of God. Few dispute this idea, but many wonder, "If that is so for the young, how is it so? Why is it so?" Most pointedly, parents, pastors, layfolk, and the young themselves ask, "Should children attend sanctuary services?" The response regularly forthcoming from religious educators is an unreserved "YES!" They are of a mind that education—even "socialization"—is carried on in large measure by the rites and celebrations of the community. Children should participate. They should be a part of both the *regular rites* of the community (such as the weekly liturgy) and the *life crisis rites* (such as those around birth and death). John Westerhoff puts it this way: "Ritual must always be at the heart of Christian education, for in the community liturgy, story and action merge; in worship we remember and we act in symbolic ways which bring our sacred tradition and our lives together, providing us with both meaning and motivation for daily existence. That is why, if our children are to have faith, they must worship with us."[70]

In his book on Christian nurture, Randolph Crump Miller insists that children can know themselves as members of a worshiping fellowship. Such affiliation enables them to grow and continue growing, nurtured by others in the context of community celebration: "Here is an opportunity for some of the most significant education that a congregation can develop. Here at the center of the church's life, we can be educated to be the church. The only way to learn to worship is through worshiping, and not just talking about it."[71]

In sum, "Yes!" religious educationists are aware that worship is central, and it is central for children as well as for persons of other age groups.

Mutual "Building Up." The second point about children in worship, which is present in the literature, is the notion that people of multiple ages can learn from one another in worship.

One of the most perceptive pieces written on the topic of including the young in worship is by David Ng. Ng focuses on what is likely going on for children of different ages and stages of development when they participate in intergenerational services. He claims that from the time of infancy to age three, for example, the child may associate the service with feelings of warmth, acceptance, comfort, and love. Most of this, of course, comes from the child's parents, but so it is we "build up" one another. What is true for wee children is true for those of older ages too.[72]

In the classic scholarly book on worship, *The Shape of the Liturgy,* Gregory Dix does not address the topic of children-in-worship as a topic per se. About all he says is this: "The apostolic and primitive church regarded the eucharist as primarily an *action,* something 'done,' not something 'said'; and that it had a clear and unhesitating grasp of the fact that this action was *corporate,* the united joint action of the whole church and not just the celebrant only."[73] Taking a lead from this suggestion about corporate action we may suggest that much of the "action" taking place is between and among persons in the pews who model— older-to-younger and younger-to-older—what it means to be a faithful worshiper/person.

Dwayne Huebner, a curriculum theorist with an interest in religious education, identifies part of the interaction of worship. He was asked, "Is it important for children and young people to be in worship together?" He answers in the affirmative and goes on to say that what is needed is special attentiveness to the questions the young ask about the liturgy. In trying to help the questioner understand, it is just as important that *"the teacher also try to understand,* and perhaps move the whole community understandings."[74]

Worship Reform for IGRE. In his usual dramatic way, John Westerhoff says, "If the liturgy of the church isn't relevant to children then it ought to be changed."[75] Modification is certainly in order, but not all the commentators would agree with Westerhoff's sweeping—and perhaps unsophisticated—statement.

David Ng is one who would minimize liturgical change. He is especially mindful of maintaining the integrity of worship. Services need not be diluted for the presence of children. He says there is no need to omit the confession of sin, for example, as children know enough about themselves to rightly kneel. Nor do children need to hear an age-specific sermon. And certainly they should not be excluded from the Lord's Supper.[76]

This note about inclusion of children at communion is, of course, one sounded earlier by Horace Bushnell. Happily, Roman Catholic Christians have allowed younger children (usually around age eight) to receive the sacraments, which may be the reason that the young are more often seen in services as children and young adults. Protestants have not been so open, as Westerhoff and Willimon note: "The involvement of children is a pressing need within many congregations where, even though children are baptized, they are excluded from the Lord's table. This makes no theological or historical sense."[77] It also makes no psychological sense, in that the eucharist is the one part of a service with the most action to appeal to the whole person in terms of sight, sound, smell, touch, and taste. It makes no sociological sense either, as the passing of the peace and the sharing of the elements are dramatic interpersonal events. Most importantly, it makes no religious sense, if the central act of the faithful participation is denied to some very important persons in the community.

Focus on the Lord's Supper brings the discussion back around to consider the Liturgy of the Word as well as Liturgy of the Sacrament. Changes are in order in the whole service if they will enhance the IG faith community's life and learning. Ng says that "within the canons of tradition and scripture" services can be modified and made "as interesting and lively as possible."[78] This might mean that children ages six-to-twelve would take a more active part in services, as by lighting the candles or bringing the offering forward.

Randolph Crump Miller suggests liturgical changes which are greater. He would like to see worship services geared more to "the family"— and, by implication, to intergenerational groupings. The church, he believes, ought to tailor services to meet the family-as-a-unit. The service would be shorter, say thirty-five minutes, with the proper liturgical ingredients (including "sermonette") so that it is "modified but not mutilated." In the service, "we can make use of informality, simplicity, humor, and dignity."[79] *Following* the family service, Miller would then have church school for persons of all ages. I would suggest that those classes be intergenerational. The members in the classes would share a common experience provided by the service.

On this matter of classes vis-á-vis worship, Westerhoff suggests a different ordering. He proposes that the religious education take place *before* worship and, in effect, be used to plan the celebration.[80] The celebrations planned would alter the usual service fare.

There is, though, something to be said simply for having children in worship—almost no matter how gruesome, stodgy, and unimaginative the liturgy may be. Proportionally, over the years, young people attending worship-only become better adult church-goers than their peers attending church-school-only. Perhaps they are not deceived. They know they are participating in the institution's primary activity. Their attendance works to familiarize and acculturate them. If young people are ever to know the music, order of service, liturgical responses, mood, prayers, and pieties of a particular faith tradition, they simply must experience them. These are worship elements that the historic generations in the faith provided. The elements are likely to be around for subsequent generations. People of this age, then, need to feel comfortable with the tradition—if only to change it.

The bottom line to this discourse on worship is that the rites and ceremonies of the community should have positive outcomes with both children and adults. Someone has said that "the crying of a babe is more blessed in the ears of the Lord than the snoring of a saint." The hope is that neither crying nor snoring will prevail, but that lively mutual involvement will be experienced. The service should be lifestyle enriching *for* each, *from* each, *to* each. In the company of other ears—as well as eyes/hands/nose/minds—people of every age may be motivated to re-form their worship act, and so begin to worship in truth, becoming persons of faith together. A story from the life of Albert Schweitzer speaks to the point. He was "convinced that his own experience of worshiping in the sanctuary with his family was crucial in the growth of his own faith. He asserts that the important thing is not that the child understand every word, but that he realize that something *serious and solemn* is taking place and sees his elders full of devotion, worshiping

One who is above them all."[81] I would just hope that interage participants in worship might also realize that something *joyful and celebrative* is taking place with *the One who is beside us all.*

CONCLUSION

In this chapter the thought of more than forty religious educationists and others has been considered. They have provided insights into such topics as relationships in community, socialization, conscientization, whole person learning, the facilitational environment, and worship. It would be untrue to say this has been an easy chapter to write. It has not been easy. Part of the reason for the difficulty is that there is much material to consider and part is because there are differences, some major and some minor, in concepts and emphases among the writers. Some of these differences—or my differences from them—have been highlighted. More often, though, I have sought for common understandings among these thinkers. Differences remain, but the overwhelming testimony from them is that young and old have and can and should be together in life and learning.

Notes

1. Horace Bushnell, *Christian Nurture* (New Haven, Conn.: Yale University Press, 1960), p. 4.
2. Kurt Vonnegut, *Palm Sunday: An Autobiographical Collage* (New York: Delacorte, 1981), pp. 177-78.
3. Gabriel Moran, "Where Now, What Next," in *Foundations of Religious Education,* ed. Padraic O'Hare (New York: Paulist, 1978), pp. 107-8. See also Gabriel Moran, *Interplay: A Theory of Religion and Education* (Winona, Minn.: Saint Mary's College Press, 1981), p. 109, where he says, "The more we can encourage interplay across generations, the richer will be the possibilities of education."
4. Bushnell, *Christian Nurture,* p. 21.
5. Ibid, p. 211.
6. Ana-Marie Rizzuto, *The Birth of the Living God* (Chicago: University of Chicago Press, 1979), p. 134.
7. George Albert Coe, *What Is Christian Education?* (New York: Charles Scribner's Sons, 1929), p. 296 (emphasis added).
8. Ibid., p. 113.
9. Randolph Crump Miller, *The Clue to Christian Education* (New York: Charles Scribner's Sons, 1950), p. 71.
10. Randolph Crump Miller, "Christian Education as a Theological Discipline and Method," in *Who Are We?,* ed. John H. Westerhoff III (Birmingham, Ala.: Religious Education Press, 1978), p. 113. In a recent book the hyphenated phrase has been changed to read "truth-about-God-in-relation-to-*humanity*." See *The Theory of Christian Education Practice* (Birmingham, Ala.: Religious Education Press, 1980), p. 176. The source of the quotation

concluding this paragraph is Reuel L. Howe, *Man's Need and God's Action* (Greenwich, Conn.: Seabury, 1960), p. 75.

11. C. Ellis Nelson, *Where Faith Begins* (Richmond, Va.: Knox, 1967), p. 10.
12. See Nelson, *Where Faith Begins,* p. 95.
13. Ibid., p. 101.
14. Donald E. Miller, *Story and Context: An Introduction to Christian Education* (Nashville: Abingdon, 1987), pp. 20, 91 and 332 for the quoted material in this paragraph.
15. Moran, *Interplay,* p. 173.
16. Randolph Crump Miller, *Christian Nurture and the Church* (New York: Charles Scribner's Sons, 1961), p. 127.
17. See Berard L. Marthaler, "Socialization as a Model for Catechetics," in *Foundations of Education,* pp. 77-88.
18. John H. Westerhoff III and Gwen Kennedy Neville, *Generation to Generation* (Philadelphia: United Church Press, 1974), p. 47.
19. John H. Westerhoff III, *Will Our Children Have Faith?* (New York: Seabury, 1976), p. 80 (emphasis added).
20. Ibid., p. 53.
21. Vern L. Bengston and K. Dean Black, "Intergenerational Relations and Continuities in Socialization," in *Life-Span Developmental Psychology: Personality and Socialization,* ed. Paul B. Baltes and K. Warner Schaie (New York: Academic Press, 1973), p. 208.
22. Quoted in Michael Warren, "Catechesis: An Enriching Category for Religious Education," *Religious Education* 76:2 (March-April, 1981), p. 119.
23. Source: *Family-Centered Catechesis: Guidelines and Resources* (Washington, D.C.: Department of Education, U. S. Catholic Conference, 1979), p. 10.
24. Berard Marthaler, "The Modern Catechetical Movement in Roman Catholicism: Issues and Personalities," in *Sourcebook for Modern Catechetics,* ed. Michael Warren (Winona, Minn.: Saint Mary's College Press, 1983), p. 286.
25. Westerhoff, *Who Are We?* p. 268.
26. Along these lines, see, Gabriel Moran's critique, "Catechetics in Context . . . Later Reflections," in *Sourcebook for Modern Catechetics,* pp. 290-99.
27. See James Michael Lee, *The Content of Religious Instruction: A Social Science Approach* (Birmingham, Ala.: Religious Education Press, 1985), pp. 292-97.
28. Jack L. Seymour and Donald E. Miller, *Contemporary Approaches to Christian Education* (Nashville: Abingdon, 1982), p. 33.
29. Paulo Friere, *Pedagogy of the Oppressed* (New York: Seabury 1970), pp. 75 and 119.
30. Ibid., p. 33.
31. Ibid., pp. 133-186.
32. See James W. White, "The Action University: A New Conceptualization of the Higher Learning," (Master's thesis, Pacific School of Religion, 1969), pp. 212-219, for a discussion of Talcott Parson's and Robert Bellah's notion that religious institutions and higher education both exist "on the upper boundary of the cultural level of action," and, as such, it is here especially we are called to action. In the thesis I make a case for a more active role for colleges and universities in society and culture and with people. Here it is made for churches and synagogues.

33. Thomas H. Groome, *Christian Religious Education: Sharing Our Story and Vision* (San Francisco: Harper & Row, 1980), p. 25 (emphasis added). Groome, of course, is not unique in stressing the "with" character of religious education. Most religious educationists do so—notably James Michael Lee, Randolph Crump Miller, and Leon McKenzie.

34. Groome, *Christian Religious Education,* pp. 207-8 (condensed). See also his "Christian Education for Freedom: A 'Shared Praxis' Approach," in *Foundations of Religious Education,* p. 10.

35. Malcolm L. Warford, *The Necessary Illusion: Church Culture and Educational Change* (Philadelphia: United Church Press, 1976), p. 54.

36. Ibid., pp. 80 ff.

37. He is identified as such by James Michael Lee in *Content of Religious Instruction,* pp. 612, 702, and elsewhere.

38. Illustrative of this, see Allen J. Moore, "Liberation and the Future of Christian Education," in *Contemporary Approaches,* pp. 103-122 and p. 121, in particular.

39. Benjamin Samuel Bloom et al., ed., *Taxonomy of Educational Objectives: The Classification of Educational Goals; Handbook I: Cognitive Domain,* and *Handbook II: Affective Domain* (New York: McKay, 1956 and 1964, respectively). No handbook for the psychomotor domain has been done.

40. To speak of human totality in this threefold way may also be a way to speak of God. When Moses on Mt. Sinai asks the deity to identify him/herself, the name "Yahweh" is given. Yahweh probably means "I AM": "Tell them (the Israelites)," Yahweh says to Moses, "that I AM has sent you" (Exodus 3:14).

It is a linguistic accident, I am sure—but a fortuitous one—that "I AM" can be an acronym for humans as whole persons. Witness: I—Intellect, A—Affections, M—Motor Movements. This alphabetical coincidence suggests that "the holy complete God" and "a whole capable person in learning" are remarkably alike. Process theologians would agree. Witness: "God is like persons, because in him too there is both personality and sociality." Norman Pittenger, *Unbounded Love: God and Man in Process* (New York: Seabury, 1976), p. 64. See also pp. 48-49.

41. Margaret M. Sawin, "A Background Study Paper on the Theoretical Foundations of the Family Cluster Model" (Rochester, N.Y.: a mimeographed publication, 1977), p. 4.

42. Charles F. Melchert, " 'Understanding' as a Purpose of Religious Education," *Religious Education* 76:2 (March-April, 1981), p. 182.

43. Lee, *Content of Religious Instruction,* p. 608.

44. Ibid., p. 705.

45. Edgar Dale, *Audio-Visual Methods in Teaching* (New York: Dryden, 1946), p. 37.

46. Mary Wilcox, *Developmental Journey: A Guide to the Development of Logical and Moral Reasoning and Social Perspective* (Nashville: Abingdon, 1979), p. 194.

47. George Isaac Brown, *Human Teaching for Human Learning: An Introduction to Confluent Education* (New York: Penquin, 1977), p. 3. Many of Brown's "exercises" were originated by Frederick Pearls. American youth have been involved with confluent education exercises in some of the *Serendipity* books developed by Lyman Coleman.

48. Jerome S. Bruner, *Toward a Theory of Instruction* (Cambridge, Mass.: Belknap Press, 1978), pp. 1-12.

49. Ibid., p. 35.
50. This is the contention of Joel Macht, educational psychologist at the University of Denver, shared in a personal conversation in the Spring of 1981.
51. Bruner, *Toward a Theory of Instruction,* p. 125.
52. Charles F. Melchert, "What is Religious Education?" *Living Light* 14:3 (Fall, 1977), p. 343.
53. Moran, *Interplay,* p. 109.
54. B. F. Skinner, *Walden II* (New York: Macmillan, 1970), pp. 311-12.
55. Lee's description is found in a personal letter dated April 8, 1986.
56. James Michael Lee, "Roman Catholic Religious Education," in *Foundations for Christian Education in an Era of Change,* ed. Marvin J. Taylor (Nashville: Abingdon, 1976), p. 256. See also, James Michael Lee, *The Flow of Religious Instruction: A Social Science Approach* (Birmingham, Ala.: Religious Education Press, 1973), p. 275. The rest of the statement in this paragraph is the thesis of Lee's first book in a trilogy of books on religious instruction. See *The Shape of Religious Instruction* (Birmingham, Ala.: Religious Education Press, 1971), pp. 2, 182-224, 246, throughout this volume and others.
57. James Michael Lee, "Key Issues in the Development of a Workable Foundation for Religious Instruction," in *Foundations of Religious Education,* pp. 41-42.
58. Lee, *Flow of Religious Instruction,* pp. 196-205 and 233-248. See, especially, p. 234, for a fully nuanced flow-diagram model on this.
59. Ibid., p. 243.
60. Lee, *Content of Religious Instruction,* pp. 619-26. Obviously, Lee writes as a thoughtful teacher, not as a speculative theologian. He is joined by others in his emphasis on the importance of the environmental setting for education: "The environment itself conveys the critical and dominant messages by controlling the perceptions and attitudes of those who participate in it." So write Neil Postman and Charles Weingartner in *Teaching as a Subversive Activity* (New York: Delta Book, 1969), p. 17.
61. Lee, *Shape of Religious Instruction,* p. 81.
62. Ibid., p. 56.
63. Someone who does talk this way is Joel Macht in his book, *Teaching Our Children* (New York: John Wiley & Sons, 1975). Behavior modification language used in this sentence is borrowed from Macht's writings, as in the glossary, pp. 134-137.
64. See both of Robert F. Mager's books: *Preparing Instructional Objectives* and *Measuring Instructional Intent: or, Got a Match?* (Belmont, Calif.: Fearon, 1975 and 1972).
65. Lee, "Toward" in *The Religious Education We Need,* p. 127.
66. James H. Block, ed. *Mastery Learning: Theory and Practice* (New York: Holt, Rinehart and Winston, 1971), p. 3.
67. Miller, *Theory,* p. 284.
68. Warren, "Catechesis," *Religious Education,* p. 123.
69. Lee, *Content of Religious Instruction,* p. 640. See also his statement, "The liturgy is fundamentally an affective and lifestyle event, a focused *Gott mit uns."* James Michael Lee, Curriculum Response Statement, *Religious Education* 77:4 (July-August, 1982), p. 393.
70. John H. Westerhoff III, *Will Our Children Have Faith?* (New York: Seabury, 1976), p. 60.

71. Miller, *Christian Nurture,* p. 104. And see also Randolph Crump Miller, "Religious Education Today and Tomorrow," *Reflection* (a Yale Divinity School publication) 78:3 (April, 1981), p. 8.
72. David Ng, "What Children Bring to Worship," *Austin Seminary Bulletin* (October, 1978), pp. 11-19; also, David Ng and Virginia Thomas, *Children In the Worshiping Community* (Atlanta: Knox, 1981), pp. 327-41.
73. Gregory Dix, *The Shape of the Liturgy* (London: Dacre, 1964), p. 15.
74. Dwayne E. Huebner, "From Theory to Practice: Curriculum," *Religious Education* 77:4 (July-August, 1982), p. 367.
75. John H. Westerhoff III, *Values for Tomorrow's Children: An Alternative Future for Education in the Church* (Philadelphia: Pilgrim Press, 1971), pp. 77. For Westerhoff, at that time, the change included excluding the sermon!
76. See Ng and Thomas, *Children in the Worshipping Community,* pp. 41-47.
77. John H. Westerhoff III, and William H. Willimon, *Liturgy and Learning Through the Life Cycle* (New York: Seabury, 1980), p. 51.
78. Ng, "What Children Bring to Worship," p. 21.
79. Miller, *Christian Nurture,* pp. 107 and 108. These themes are also found in "Continuity and Change in the Future of Religious Education," in *The Religious Education We Need,* p. 32, and in Miller's *Theory,* pp. 182-189.
80. Westerhoff, *Will Our Children Have Faith?,* p. 57.
81. Roy W. Fairchild, *Christians in Families: An Inquiry into the Nature and Mission of the Christian Home,* (Richmond, Va.: The Covenant Life Curriculum Press, 1964), p. 20, referencing, Albert Schwietzer, *Memoirs of Childhood and Youth* (New York: Macmillan, 1949), p. 45 (emphasis added.)

PART III

PRESCRIPTION

Chapter 8

The Total Parish Paradigm

No church or synagogue has put together an intentional and comprehensive program for intergenerational religious life and learning that really does the quality job which needs to be done. Some faith communities have done a laudable job in the field, sometimes almost unknowingly. They just found IGRE to be the "natural" way to order their life together. On the other hand, some congregations have been more self-conscious in their development. Whatever may be the case, what religious leaders and religious educators can use are assists, enabling them to do better what they do best. Facilitating that possibility is the purpose of this book.

In this chapter I present a Total Parish Paradigm for IGRE. By the word "paradigm" I mean to suggest something stronger than a model, something that approaches the ideal, "paradise" almost. It is an ideal-type construction. The Total Parish Paradigm is a holistic integration of the six basic models of IGRE presented in the first section of this book, enriching these known practices with the theoretical insights presented in the middle section of this volume. So, "what we do" (chapters 1-3) and "what we know" (chapters 4-7) are brought together to help the ongoing "being" and the "becoming" of IGRE in faith communities. At the end of the present volume (chapters 9-11) there is further prescriptive detailing of the Paradigm based on the theory and practice of IGRE.

In-ter-gen-er-a-tion-al re-li-gious ed-u-ca-tion, our fourteen syllable, three word phrase, is fleshed out for practical embodiment in these later chapters. There is increasing specificity regarding with whom, by what, just how, and to what effect IGRE life and learning should be done. This chapter especially considers *who* will be creating the IGRE facilitational environment and *what* are the major pieces in the picture puzzle which is the Total Parish IGRE Paradigm.

As people consider this Parish Paradigm for new embodiment, it may

159

be they will actually pick and choose among parts of it as their own starting route into IGRE. Such a response is not necessarily undesirable. The hope is that as religious institutions experience success with the parts (or even with a particular model program), they will be reinforced for further ventures leading toward the fullness of comprehensive inter-age life and learning.

Our paradigm, happily, has empirical supports: All the models, programs and parts have been tried. They are known to function effectively in churches and synagogues, as reported in the text and notes presented in chapter 3. Many have been operationalized in one place, reported upon, read about by others, and then recapitulated. In this chapter I borrow illustrative material from the many enactments but rely most heavily on the worship-education model, especially as it has been shaped by the All-Saints Church experience. (See chapter 3 and the Appendix on this.) Even though All-Saints is a fictitious name, the experiences are of a real institution.

THE FACILITATION COMMITTEE—The Who

In his book *A Rumor of Angels,* Peter Berger tells of a mother who awakens in the night to the cry of her infant who is frightened by dreams. Entering the nursery, the mother picks up the child and gives comfort saying, "Don't be afraid—everything is in order, *everything is all right.*" With that assurance, the child soon returns to sleep.

Berger then turns to ask the reader, "Is the mother lying to the child?"[1] Is *every*thing all right?"

The *thought*-full person living in this day and age certainly knows that everything is not all right. The thought-full person knows what a dangerous edge the world is on. Among many things, the thought-full person is aware that isolation and insulation of individuals is all too real. The thought-full person is sensitive to the changed realities of our society as discussed in chapter 1: numerically smaller nuclear families, geographical mobility, single-parenting, age-specific social formations, the separations caused by various institutions, and more. These factors work to pull generations apart. The thought-full person knows all is not right. That person might answer Berger saying, "The mother is lying."

A *faith*-full person (who may also be thought-full) will tend to reply to Berger's question affirming the mother. In God's time and care, we believe, all is well. In the face of surrounding chaos (not unlike the child's bad dreams) the faith-full person projects a canopy of meaning and creates a ground of connectedness under or upon which "everything is all right" for sleeping and waking.

Such is the stance of religious leaders who understand the society's bad dreams and who are willing to work to effect a world more in keeping with faith's all-right canopy of meaning and ground of connectedness. In practice it may take only one sensitive person to bring a religious institution into a plan and program of intergenerational development. That person can initiate the creative process by beginning to talk with others about the issue of separation and the possibility of relatedness for generations through the church/synagogue.[2]

Ultimately and ideally in the Total Parish IGRE Paradigm, leadership will be vested with a *body of religious leaders who assume overall IGRE responsibility*. I call this body the Facilitation Committee. This body would see that 1) the goals of the church/synagogue are directed toward the building up of an intergenerational religious lifestyle, 2) the whole congregation in its programs and operations is working toward the achievement of these goals, 3) the *people* who are responsible for specific IGRE domains in the community are supported (and held accountable), and 4) the *evaluation* of goals, people, programs, and the whole church/synagogue is done with findings used for improved ongoing IGRE. In essence the Facilitation Committee continually would be asking the questions: What are we doing now? Where do we want to go? What do we need to do? How can we help the process? Who do we need to support? When shall we begin (or end) a project? What has been the result of our efforts?

The Facilitation Committee which oversees a faith community's IGRE total program needs to be composed of people who are able to influence goal selection, set or suggest congregational policy, make plans, see that plans are implemented, and support the plans with resources both physical and peopled. Such a committee, then, should *not* be an "ad hoc group of the parish education commission." Instead, its members need to be influential parish leaders. At a minimum the Committee should have good access to the decision makers and major program people of the institution. Better, though, the Committee should be some of the ranking officers of the congregation and key professional staff. Such leadership would be able to influence worship, music, teaching, special events, the calendars, social action, publicity, expenditures, custodians, secretaries, and trustees. All such elements and people help shape "the total parish," thus reminding us: "The whole church/synagogue educates by all it does or fails to do."[3]

The last line of the paragraph above underscores one of the primary duties of the Facilitation Committee. That duty is to continually consider how the whole institution is doing in its faithing/teaching responsibility. Obviously this means attentiveness to formal programs of the congregation (which subject is the focus of the next sections). It also means attentiveness to *informal* actions and interactions taking place among people in—and beyond—the life of the faith community. An astute Facilitation Committee knows what religious educationist Craig Dykstra states, namely, that "our faith is formed in our primary communities through day-to-day interactions with the people who surround us."[4] Those interactions include consideration of the things taking place in the church/synagogue *and* on the job, at play, in the family, at school, and in the interplay of them all.[5] This group of people, in other words, has holistic education as its everpresent concern.

Part of the wholeness of outlook will be determined by the interage wholeness of the Committee itself. Our paradigm calls for a committee not only of parish leaders but also people of various ages, thus modeling what is sought. This age-inclusive compositional criterion presents a practical problem on when to meet. For children and grandparent-age persons serving on the Facilitation Committee, late-into-the-evening midweek meetings are out. The most feasible time to meet may be right after school or a weekend afternoon. If on the other hand the IGRE Committee is composed mostly of middle-aged adults who can gather in the evenings, these persons will need to get input from younger and older persons. That can be arranged by doing pre- and post-meeting consultation with children and with seniors.

Ongoing *self*-education would be of great importance to the Facilitation Committee. The members would strive to understand the religious lifestyle they want to facilitate and what is needed to realize it. So they would become acquainted with intergenerational action theory, pedagogical methods in IGRE, personality and development theory, alternative models of IG learning, and so forth. Religious educationists David and Margaret Steward say, "The intergenerational educator must have accurate and sensitive awareness of age-group characteristics and interage match, because responsive education happens not just among children but along the entire life span."[6]

A word about the "leadership style" of the Facilitation Committee and other IGRE actors is in order. In a study of intergenerational programs, James Call found four different styles of leadership present: the directive, the nondirective, the consultative, and the collaborative. Call found the last to be most compatible with the various IGRE programs. He describes it as follows:

> *The Collaborative.* Mutuality is the most characteristic factor in this style. Leader and participant, trainer and trainee, instructor and student, counselor and client are working together on mutually identified interests and needs, cooperatively established goals and plans, with specific roles, functions and tasks being assigned to individual, subgroup, or group endeavors and actions. The designated leader's or leaders' concerns and goals are as legitimate a consideration in this style as are those of the participants.[7]

In the IGRE practices which Call observed, the collaborative style was the one most often used. Actually, though, he prefers a style called "corroborative" which combines all four styles—even the directive, which, he feels, is called for at certain times when large numbers of people are involved. The corroborative would be most appropriate for the Facilitation Committee to adopt, as its members would be involved in a broad range of IGRE investments, each of which needs special leadership tailoring.

In general, a *with*-people, rather than a *for-* or *to*-others approach would be taken by the primary leaders.

If IGRE life and learning is initiated at the highest levels of an institution's organizational structure, before much conscious programing has developed, it would be incumbent upon the members of the Facilitation Committee to consider the models, variations, and operations in IGRE open to them for implementation. Specifically, they would profit from familiarity with the six models described in chapter 3. Familiarity would also make planners aware of what written and other resource materials are available for their use.

Having reviewed IGRE options and materials, the Facilitation Committee may either elect to borrow heavily from what others have done or decide to birth programs and devise curriculum themselves. One church in North Dakota found that in designing its own curriculum they did so cheaper, better, and with a resultant high sense of ownership of the program by both leaders and participants.[8] I shall return to this theme in discussing "creating curriculum," chapter 10. Suffice it to say here, getting the generative juices flowing is developmentally significant (a la Erikson) for adult persons.

Finally in this section on the *who* of IGRE, I want to indicate that the Facilitation Committee requires special people, but they need not be superhuman. They mostly need to be folk—again, hopefully, of multiple ages—who are faith-full/thought-full, willing to learn, and committed to seeing that faith growth occurs through wholeness in the church/synagogue's intergenerational life. Such special people are in our faith communities already. Working together on an IGRE Facilitation Committee, at the same time they are "building up" the faith community, these persons will be growing personally and addressing creatively the larger societal problem of isolation/insulation which prompted concern to move in this direction in the first place.

THE *WHAT* FOR THE COMMITTEE

Now we turn to the *what* of IGRE in Total Parish IGRE Paradigm. That "what" may be classified in three categories of general charge for which particular members will take shepherding responsibility. The three areas are 1) worship-education life, 2) community life, and 3) institutional life.

We may in this chapter consider IGRE as a kind of picture, but a picture in a picture puzzle. There are a number of pieces which can be examined separately. We shall do that. Finally, though, these pieces need to be joined together so that the total IGRE composition is visual. In that united picture, one may then discern the picture's foreground, midground, and background.

I. Worship-Education Life

In the foreground of the whole intergenerational picture is worship-education. Some persons on the Facilitation Committee would concentrate their IGRE-enhancement efforts on this dimension of the institution's life. That dimension has several component pieces.

The Worship Piece. In the Total Parish IGRE Paradigm worship is decidedly inclusive of all generations. Young children and the eldest adults will worship together. There will be times, though, when all-age inclusiveness is not observed in worship, but to err is to err on the side of keeping people together. Inclusiveness will be observed in both the *regular* rites of the parish or congregation (Sabbath/Sunday, midweek, Ash Wednesday, Rosh Hashana services, etc.) and the *life passage* rites of the institution (baptisms, bar/bat mitzvahs, weddings, funerals, etc.). In regard to the life-passage rites, it might be that the Facilitation Committee would work to see that "god parenting" is taken seriously at a baptism or a *B'rit Banot*. Upon the occasion of a funeral for one in the faith community, the leadership might well encourage parents to allow children to skip school to attend.

Some of the elements, timing, and form of worship services would be changed or at least affected by IG inclusiveness. The basic integrity of worship need not be compromised. What persons in charge of the liturgy would do, though, is pay greater attention to the language, action, pace, and so on, of services so that they communicate and resonate with as broad an age spectrum as possible. Responsive litanies, for example, might include lines to be spoken by children-under-twelve, parents, single persons, retirees, and so on, thus recognizing congregational distinctions while being one body. There would be time built in during services for sharing between and among people of all generations. Taking clues from Virginia Satir, such might include questions or topics to be considered more than just saying, "Hello . . . nice to meet you." There certainly should be more drama in the ritual, and there would be visual, audible, and kinetic dimensions which take the "whole person" into account. In the heretofore low Mass/free worship parishes of the Christian religion, Holy Communion likely would become a more frequent action, perhaps a weekly event, as we know it can be an action important for all ages.

These and other liturgical modifications have been discussed in several places in this book, but especially in the "Worship" section of the previous chapter where the particular issue of including children in services was considered. The worship planners on the Facilitation Committee certainly would want to consider what David Ng, James F. White, Will Willimon, Jerry Jordan, and others say about age-inclusive worship. Since communal worship is such a central activity—especially in the Christian community—it is the place I recommend the Facilitation Committee first focus attention for IGRE. Beginning IGRE at the traditional center of a congregation's life would be a positive signal to all regarding oncoming generational inclusiveness.

The Classroom Education Piece. It is most likely, though, that the starting place for IGRE in the typical church or synagogue will be in programs related to education per se. "E"—standing for "education"—is the most obvious characteristic of "IGR*E*." Formal learning settings have been where IGRE concentration most often has been given. We are operating in this book, of course, with a more holistic understanding of education, but the classroom is one area of importance in the whole collage. We treat it here.

As noted in chapter 3, IGRE weekly classes of one sort or another have been tried in many congregations. Considerable experimentation has been done with classes. Sufficient curriculum material is available to help persons moving in this direction of IGRE programing. Greater development—especially in new and potentially more significant areas, as suggested by the macro-theorists—is possible in various IG classes. A class, for example, might focus around "Life Developmental Tasks" (a la Erikson) and the generations help one another with everything from acquiring a sense of basic trust in infancy to overcoming a sense of despair in old age. Perhaps an IGRE class would work with moral dilemmas as means to help people move in stages of moral reasoning (Kohlberg); here educators could facilitate "stage modeling" which would provide decalage for learners in ways not possible in same-age classes. Indeed, the educational possibilities are not limited.

The Facilitation Committee also would see to it that strong new educative actions are taken with families having young children. Perhaps too much educational effort has been vested in religious "schooling" for persons six to eighteen years old. In the Total Parish there might be increased focus on the mother-child intergenerational dynamic by which the "face of God" is nonverbally communicated to infants and young children, as Ana-Maria Rizzuto suggests.[9] If, in this faithing process a surrogate face/smile/touch/wisdom/presence/caring by an older parishioner is resourced, then so much the better for the parents and the child. At the older age range it is likely that in the both-parents-working shape of modern society, the religious community will rely more heavily on older active retirees as the IG teachers. They may be the freest to teach, even as "home-maker" mothers were in earlier eras.

In general, the formation of cognitive beliefs, verbal practices, non-verbal signals, affective dispositions, and explicit behaviors which are faith-full to self/others/world/God by parishioners of all ages would be under consideration in the faith community's educational offering and work.

Indeed, such would be more than just "under consideration." There would be educational action to facilitate this holistic lifestyle.

Worship-Education Piece Joining. The particular model for IGRE with which I have greatest working familiarity is the one which integrates worship and education. Previously we noted that religion educationists Randolph Crump Miller and John Westerhoff commend the concept in general, and William Abernethy, Maureen Gallagher, and others have put such elements together in practice. Abernethy's way is particularly commendable because it 1) brings all ages together for worship, then 2) sends them with mutual instruction into various educational settings (which may and/or may not be age-integrated), and finally 3) brings everyone back together at the end for a common celebration.[10]

One of the things to note as a positive development coming out of the joining of worship and education is that people of all ages focus on the same scriptural texts, subject themes, or calendar events. That focusing provides common grist for a sharing that energizes. With this model there is also the strong likelihood of the faith community enacting all the "Patterns for IGRE Relationship" commended earlier, namely, those of 1) in-common experiences, 2) parallel learnings, 3) contributive occasions, and 4) interactive sharing. In truth, the Facilitation Committee would want these patterns lived out in all the formal and informal dimensions of the congregation's life.

II. Community Life

The second major part of the picture in the Total Parish Paridigm concerns the building up of intergenerational community and/or fellowship. Here concentration is on more non-Sabbath/Sunday life and learning experiences and programs.

It may be that contemporary social and cultural realties will not allow for full-fledged "community," meaning biblical *koinonia* or the sociologists' *gemeinschaft* of living in intimate, daily face-to-face relationship. At least, though, we can have significantly improved "communal relations" (Moran's phrase) which move people of all ages beyond superficial association and toward closer acquaintance, friendship, and caring. Such would be a major goal (see the next chapter) which members of the Facilitation Committee would work toward with various community-enhancing pieces.

The Informal/Extramural Piece. Building IG community requires looking at the informal activities of an institution's life: what is going on at the front door, during the wedding reception, at choir rehearsal, and beside the bulletin board. Not only that, Facilitation Committee members will consider beyond-the-church-walls interchange: in the supermarket, at the factory, on the athletic field. From consideration of these interactions, leaders may devise means to improve the quality of interage activities, including something so simple as the institution of nametags—or, nametag replacement by floating-*human*-namedroppers.

Let us consider some of the things which might come to pass. For one thing there can be the promotion of new informal interaction mechanisms such as "play groups," which could be for drama, recreation, or socializing. Maybe a church will set up a Godparents-Godchildren's Night (no doubt entailing considerable new "matchings") to revitalize baptismal vows. A synagogue might have a Dreidls-Plus Games Afternoon where young and old would teach and enjoy old and new games and activities.

Reflection on what could transpire in music, arts, and crafts suggests IG programs and actions of a nonverbal sort. There can be an all-age orchestra, a painting workshop, a Chrismon crafting day or *sukkah*-building Sunday, or something else. Again, the possibilities are many.

The Family Groupings Piece. The Facilitation Committee would not fail to enact some form or forms of the Family Grouping Model described in chapter 3. The small group form of family clustering, for example, would be a prime candidate for institutionalization. The congregation would be assured that leaders were trained to work in this or other small group forms.

In addition to family clusters, the parish-in-a-parish structure might be worked up. This structuring enables people of sundry ages to come together on occasions where good interpersonal happenings in smaller community are possible. One such sub-parish in Moline, Illinois, went on an overnight on a Mississippi River houseboat. The sub-parishioners discovered they were engaged in significant learning and care and fun, even *homo integer* development.

The Pastoral Care Piece. All the social/educational analysts who were quoted earlier (e.g., Parsons, Duvall, Scanzoni, G. H. Mead, J. Nelson, Bronfenbrenner, etc.) are convinced that family qua family, though changing, is still of utmost importance in modern society. Taking our bearings from their shared perspective, in the Total Parish Paradigm the most effective ways to do *individual* pastoral care will be through conjugal and extended church/synagogue families.

Virginia Satir, Carl Whitaker, and David Friedman say that in counseling, if any "identified patient" is to be helped, the whole family must be involved in the therapeutic process. Clergy who conduct their ministry in the context of the IGRE paradigm, then, would become more skilled in conjoint family counseling—more so than individual therapy. They would be increasingly sensitive to family context in both home and hospital calling. More importantly, they might better understand how the congregation can be a dynamic extended family. Elise Boulding, mother and peace activist, says in this regard, "For the family to fulfill all its potentialities for nurturing open loving persons free to carry out a mission in an aching society, some equivalent of extended family is necessary. No family can do this alone."[11] The faith communities will know this in their bones and come to act so in the world.

There is reason to believe that churches and synagogues can make themselves more like extended families for their members. As we have seen, a number of congregations have moved in that direction. Care for individual persons is possible because "more people are one's own." Charlotte Sickbert, a clergywoman in Sydney, Montana, illustrates how such can be so. She notes that an "adopt-a-grandparent" for church school classes was set up there. On one occasion after the program was going, a child said to her, "I know this church really cares for me."

"How do you know this?" Sickbert asked.

"Well, last week my grandfather died, and when I came to Sunday School today, the church got me a new Grandpa."[12]

Sickbert's illustrative example is joined by Stanley Hauerwas' statement that "parenting is an office of the whole community and not just those who have children," and "it is assumed that the whole community is ready to support those who have children by relieving them of total and exclusive responsibility."[13]

In general, the ministry to individuals in the Total Parish Paradigm is advanced by the development of cross-age relations.

Advancing-through-Retreat Piece. Remembering the truism that more time is spent in community on a single weekend retreat than most people gain in a year of ordinary ecclesial activities, the Camp-Retreat Model should be on the Total Parish Paradigm's plate. In my experience this most-holistic experience provides community-building relationships with much positive after-effect in the life of congregations.

If a congregation does travel caravans, work projects, overseas pilgrimages, and so on there is the possibility that these could become more intergenerational.

These many possibilities for enriching congregational life, then, are some of the IGRE activities that the Facilitation Committee would put on the calendar and then into life, confident of good consequence.

III. Institutional Life

Some persons on the Facilitation Committee will keep their eye on institutional maintenance and outreach operations of the congregation, searching for ways to make ordinary organizational functions contribute to IG lifestyle wholeness. Here too are separate, identifiable pieces to be examined.

The Administration Piece. The Facilitation Committee is itself an administrative device to reach IGRE goals. To set up and activate new rituals, inclusive classes, parishes-in-a-parish, and so on, requires administrative work. Up and down the IGRE line, it is always so. One place where good administration along IGRE lines may be considered is in the religious institution's own organizational structure. Working committees of a congregation can be age-integrated for mutual benefit. It may be possible, for example, to enlist some youth to serve and function happily in the committee structures of a church/synagogue. That is certainly intergenerational and desirable. Where I suggest more development in institutional life take place, however, is in getting a wider age span among adults on the committees. That can be most stimulating and has the further positive potential of effecting good "interplay" with regard to job and leisure-related concerns.

Administration can facilitate IGRE in congregational celebrations, official occasions, and meetings of various kinds. The Annual Meeting of the congregation or a Futures Planning Retreat are two ostensible "business" occasions where greater intergenerational inclusiveness can be instituted.

In terms of pieces in the IGRE total picture puzzle, the administrative piece may be the shortest in descriptive prose but is by no means the least important. Good administration is the table on which the congregation's IGRE puzzle is assembled.

The Special Event and Seasonal Pieces. Occasional gatherings also are present in an institution's life. They can use directed attention. Leaders need to look at one-time events (e.g., an anniversary or an ordination or a community-related festival), annual happenings (e.g., a *cursillo* or an officers' training day), and focused workshops (e.g., on planned giving or on developing a Stephens Ministry). These are all writ large with teaching/learning/growing opportunities for mixed-age participants.

In chapter 3 the Workshop and Special Event Model of IGRE was discussed. Almost any group in a parish might sponsor such a happening—and should be encouraged to do so. What members of the Facilitation Committee would do is to help such events be as inclusive as possible. Seasonal workshops on Chanukah/Christmas, Pesach/Easter, Pentecost, and so on, are usually IG already; they are rich with expansive possibility.

The Mission, Action, and Evangelism Pieces. The *mission* or outreach dimensions of a faith community's life are natural arenas for multi-age involvement. Not a few congregations have discovered, for example, that the sponsoring of refugee families is an activity which has brought young and old together in contributive relationship. Such united efforts resemble James Michael Lee's project technique of religious education. The project is one which typically is whole-person involving, appealing to a wide spectrum of interests, abilities, and ages.[14] In terms of projects, one can think of an inner-city service effort (which activity is important in itself) which is remembered by participants as much for the life-shaping friendships established across or within generations as for the event's results.

Reflection-Action activities for *social action* have been recommended for religious communities generally. One such activity suggested earlier is that of doing "television analysis"—and doing it across a wide age range of viewers. Joint analysis might affect both personal viewing behavior *and* the media. A delegation of preschoolers and nursing home residents going to a FCC hearing or a local TV station's program-review committee, for example, would have an impact! It would be newsworthy. Too often we think that social action is a middle-aged or young-adult thing, but these can involve persons of many ages, and with good influence. One illustration may suffice. In the spring and summer of 1985 four or five generations of women (mostly) across the length and breadth of the United States in their homes/churches/synagogues/work places made flag-banners on the theme "What I Would Not Want to Lose to a Nuclear Holocaust." These sewings/stitchings/paintings/tie-dyings/etc., were then collected and sewn together into a miles-long Peace Banner. The final ribbon was used "to wrap the Pentagon." So we are reminded of how the generations may effectively act together and, perhaps, the world made better for it.

Just like mission and social action, *evangelism* takes on an intergenerational cast in the Total Parish Paradigm. We have known for some time that people affiliate with a church/synagogue primarily on the basis of friendship—more so than on the basis of the quality of the music, preaching, educational classes, or something else. This suggests a new and potentially powerful way to promote membership growth by using multiple-age teams for calling and cultivation. If it takes, on average, six "friendship associations" to bring someone into the life of a congregation successfully, a faith community might be half-way there with a three-generation visitation call. Evangelism would be forwarded as friendships-for-sharing-the-faith are several generations deep.

The Evaluation Piece. Concerned that the church/synagogue actually realize its institutional IG goals, the Facilitation Committee will engage in congregational testing and evaluation. They will take the lead here and help others make critical appraisals. In the final chapter of the current volume, I suggest some ways to discover if, in fact, IG-enhancing things actually are occurring in the faith community.

CONCLUSION

Now someone might ask, "To what end is the Total Parish IGRE Paradigm directed?" This question, regarding ends/goals/purpose/objectives, is pursued in detail in the next chapter. Suffice it to say here, the end being sought by the Facilitation Committee in assembling the various "pieces" is not inconsequential. When the proverbial "visitor-from-another-planet" enters the porous circle of the Total Parish, observing and participating in it, that intergalactic visitor will beam back home a message similar to one conveyed about a previous body of believers: "Behold, how they love one another!"

Notes

1. Peter L. Berger, *A Rumor of Angels: Modern Society and the Rediscovery of the Supernatural* (Garden City, N.Y.: Doubleday, 1970), p. 55 (emphasis added).
2. At All-Saints Church, four concerned parents wanted to "do something" educationally worthwhile in the summer with and for their children. The four were the impetus behind what became the full-blown IGRE program in the whole church. Similarly, in Farmington, Connecticut, a minister found an ally in the Christian Education Director. The two moved together to devise a significant IGRE program in the Congregational Church there. See Bob Stowe, "All-Age Church Planning," *New Forms Exchange* (New York: United Church of Christ, 1978), pp. 1-2.
3. Quotation by John Westerhoff from personal notes, St. Louis, Mo., November, 1976.
4. Craig Dykstra, "Faith Development Issues," in *Changing Patterns of Religious Education,* ed. Marvin J. Taylor (Nashville: Abingdon, 1984), p. 86.
5. Gabriel Moran, *Interplay: A Theory of Religion and Education* (Winona, Minn.: St. Mary's College Press, 1981), p. 45.
6. David and Margaret Steward, "What Does the Church Need to Know to Do Intergenerational Education?" *JED SHARE* 7:3 (Fall, 1979), p. 9.
7. James Michael Call, "An Exploration of Leadership Styles in Four Intergenerational Programs Designed for the Local Church. (Master's thesis, George Peabody College for Teachers, August, 1975), p. 23.

8. Sandi Dewald et al., "Our Romance with Intergenerational Christian Education," *New Forms Exchange* (Fall, 1980).
9. Ana-Maria Rizzuto, *The Birth of the Living God: A Psychoanalytic Study* (Chicago: University of Chicago Press, 1979), pp. 41ff.
10. See chapters 3 and 7 of this present volume, as well as Randolph Crump Miller, *Christian Nurture and the Church* (New York: Charles Scribner's Sons, 1961), pp. 107 and 188; John Westerhoff III, *Will Our Children Have Faith?* (New York: Seabury, 1976), p. 57; William Beaven Abernethy, *A New Look for Sunday Morning* (Nashville: Abingdon, 1975), pp. 20 and 34; and Maureen Gallagher, "Introduction to Family Parish Religious Education," *FAMILY: Parish Religious Education Program* (Paramus, N.J.: Paulist, 1974), throughout.
11. Elise Boulding, "The Church as Extended Family," *Families* 3:4 (Autumn, 1982), p. 2.
12. Charlotte Sickbert, Minister of the United Churches of Christ in Sydney and Savage, Montana, personal conversation, May 15, 1982.
13. Stanley Hauerwas, "The Family as School for Character," *Religious Education* 80:2 (Spring, 1985), p. 279.
14. James Michael Lee, *The Content of Religious Education: A Social Science Approach* (Birmingham, Ala.: Religious Education Press, 1985), p. 699.

Chapter 9

Toward Goals and Objectives

In this and the next two chapters prescription is given on how to design and implement intergenerational life and learning in the religious community. The *starting line* of the enterprise of building good IGRE begins in consideration of the *end.*

The ancient philosopher Aristotle provides a key idea for thinking about the end, relative to how something (such as an IGRE program) comes into being. In Aristotle's thought there are four types of causality: there is a *material* cause which is the substance of which something is made; there is a *formal* cause which is the internal structure and organization of the thing; and there is an *efficient* or moving cause which gives impetus to the shaping of the material into its structure. We will get into these three "causes" while discussing curriculum building in the next chapter. Here, though, I want to deal with Aristotle's fourth or *final* cause—the *telos*—for something. Robert Calhoun, the great historian of philosophy at Yale Divinity School, described Aristotle's final cause as "the end with respect to which the whole process goes on, a process which is determined not merely by the constituent stuffs, but also by the outcome, which in the case of a living human being is resident in itself."[1] It is about the end/*telos*/final cause that we think at the start of intergenerational programing.

THE VISION

IGRE in itself is not the end of a religious community's striving so much as IGRE is the means of attaining other ends. "The end" sought by a people of faith worshiping, witnessing, and working together will be related to their ultimate commitment. Such a commitment has been spoken of in phrases, such as: "The Day of the Lord" . . . "The Kingdom of God and All God's Righteousness" . . . The Eschaton or Second

173

Coming . . . "That Time When Everyone Shall Know the Lord" . . . A
World at Peace with Love and Justice . . . "The Glorious Fulfillment of
the Earth." These ultimate/high/cosmological/beautific commitments
are more nearly related to what religion educationist Mary Elizabeth
Moore calls "visions" for faith communities.[2] Visions refer to our largest, most sublime, grandiloquent hopes and ideal outcomes.

A generation or three ago, it may have been believed by well-meaning
Christians that the Kingdom of God could be ushered in by human
effort. Two world wars, a M.A.D. [Mutually Assured Destruction] international nuclear arms race, and a planet courting ecological disaster
have disillusioned most thoughtful people of a bootstraps kingdom-
creating effort. Today, even a Christian theologian of hope, such as
Jürgen Moltmann, who advocates an assertive stance toward the future,
still insists that it is Christ who comes toward the world from the
future—and in Christ's own time. "Thy Kingdom come" comes under
Divine grace, finally, and not by our efforts—though, in hope, we *work*
toward that coming reign.[3]

In this study, then, I do not want to presume to inform God when/
where/how the Holy's ultimate reign of righteousness is to be. Even so, I
think we need to say that the vision is important as a kind of Holy Grail
that lures us to a brighter tomorrow.

INSTITUTIONAL PURPOSE

For education to take place, it is necessary to be more modest in aim
than the above-stated macrovisions go. We need to speak in terms closer
to the humanly realizable, perhaps even in terms of the observable, if
not the measurable. We need to talk about *what a religious institution,
as human institution, might set forth for itself to attain in time with its
own constituency.* At this point, the definition which H. Richard Niebuhr put forth as "the purpose of the church and its ministry" may be
recalled. Niebuhr said such purpose is "the increase among men of the
love of God and neighbor."[4] Niebuhr's statement might serve for purposes of IGRE, but a little different one for IGRE is offered. It says,

"THE PURPOSE OF THE RELIGIOUS COMMUNITY IS TO FA-
CILITATE THE MOVEMENT OF PERSONS IN HOLISTIC LIFE-
STYLE TOWARD THE FULFILLMENT OF GOD, THE WORLD,
AND THEMSELVES."

Within such a purpose (or, teleological conceptualization) for the institution, IGRE can work quite well.

Purpose is here used as the largest overall conception for what realisti-
cally might be sought in an institutional setting. *Vision,* of course, may
stand behind this purpose. After this section we consider *goals* related to

purpose and, later, discuss measurable *objectives* pursued in attainment of goals. In the next chapter, as we move toward curricular planning, we consider operational *procedures*.

The religious community spoken of in the purpose statement means to include, at least, churches, temples, synagogues, and other institutional religious bodies, primarily in the Judaeo-Christian heritage. These are the religious forms I know best, but the definition is not meant to exclude other major faith traditions if what is written is applicable. In actual fact—and in most illustrative instances—the religious community spoken of is primarily the Christian church in its Protestant and Catholic manifestations in the United States and Canada. "Religious community" in these pages also means local faith community more than denomination or universal institution.

By stating that the purpose of the religious community is "to facilitate movement . . . toward," I am trying not to claim too much for what might be realized or hoped for, but certainly something. The great statement by Niebuhr noted above, on institutional purpose, is similarly modest in what it looks for. He said that the purpose of the church and its ministry is "the *increase*." "Increase" is not realization. The reminder is again that people in religious communities are called to be faithful, not necessarily successful. Faithfulness does call, however, for some process—if not progress—toward the good envisioned. So it is that we speak of "movement . . . toward" and its facilitation by the body of believers.

Even as the words "facilitate movement . . . toward" suggest modest realism, some other ideas in the statement are decidedly more idealistic, participating in The Vision. Especially I am thinking of the conclusion to the purpose statement. It speaks of the pilgrimage of persons *toward* "the fulfillment of God, the world, and themselves." The grounding of IGRE in process thought is here seen most clearly. As noted in chapter 4, process theologians speak of the "primordial" and "consequential" nature of God. The primordial nature of God is that which begins all and aims the world and humanity into a future fulfillment. That fulfillment, however, is not totally controlled by God; the world and humanity constitute independent forces. If, however, they/we develop toward fulfillment of God-visioned primordial potential, that helps determine the future of God. Who God will be is, in part, a consequence of what the world and humanity become. Likewise, the consequent nature of the world is not unrelated to God and humanity, both of whom continue to participate in the creating enterprise. And, similarly, with humanity vis-á-vis the world and God. The three are in a dynamic relationship, and the three are not so dissimilar. The growing fruition of all occurs through loving, relating, becoming, creating, and enjoying, which the religious community in this mix can model and do.

In talking about *fulfillment,* I am suggesting a teleological—more than a deontological—orientation, borrowing ideas also from various theologies of hope. As noted, *telos* means end, goal, ultimate purpose, or *omega* point toward which we are directed. It is future-directed activity, and, theologically understood, it emphasizes the idea that God calls to/beckons us from the future. Deontological activity, on the other hand, is motivated more by the past in which the "Thus says the Lord" was spoken and "so we obey the command of yore" is primary.

The religious community has its greatest direct influence on the fulfillment of God/world/humanity through its adherents, its pilgrim people. So the heart of the IGRE purpose statement has to do with the movement or pilgrimage "of persons in holistic lifestyle." The *big philosophical question, then, is, "How do you educate?"* ("How to educate" is always the big philosophical question.) How do you educate persons so that they become more fully human (as God intended) and thus contribute not only to their own growth but that of the world and God too? I think the answer will be found in education concerned with promoting and enacting a faith-full HOLISTIC LIFESTYLE among adherents. James Michael Lee speaks of such "lifestyle"—or "lifestyle content"—in his book *The Content of Religious Instruction.* It

> refers to the overall pattern of a person's activities . . . consists of the way in which a person organizes his self-system and lives out his life . . . is the all-inclusive shape and operational flow of the totality of a person's behavior . . . and has at least two fundamental and interrelated characteristics, namely, totality and integrativeness.[5]

In IGRE, education takes place in the context of multiple-age persons and thus is already on a holistic road. With "lifestyle" emphasis in teaching we are making sure that what is learned is not just giving a learner cognitive knowledge. Being holistic is to include the physical and emotional as well as the noetic. We are concerned about affective content, psychomotor content, *and* contents having to do with product, process, verbal and nonverbal characteristics, and the unconscious. The *whole* person, then, is what the religious community is working with and for, the whole person whose coming together with others and moving with others in the community facilitates the movement toward the faith vision itself. That whole person might be called "disciple" or "saint" by Christians or "the righteous one" *(tsedek)* by Jews.

MAJOR GOALS

Being the rational—and sometimes irrational—creatures that we are, it happens that people "try on" programs and practices in religious education before they have articulated teaching/learning goals for them. That is not to say that some goals are not operating implicitly. They are. They always are. From my own entry into IGRE I know that the almost blind doing of IG programing preceded thoughtful specification of what we thought we were accomplishing. Later though, reflection upon the action generated articulated and written program goals.[6]

Further study, reflection, and action, especially in light of the *purpose* presented above, prompt me to present the four *goals* most often embodied in and important to effective IGRE. They are 1) quality intergenerational relations, 2) significant cognitive learning, 3) positive subjective impact, and 4) sound lifestyle consequence. Each of these goals needs to be considered separately and in relation to the others.

1. Quality Intergenerational Relations

The "problem of society" which piques interest in IGRE is that of people's isolation and insulation. We live, so it appears, without enough cross-age human contact. The relations which people do have tend to be unigenerational—youngsters in day schools, young adults in bars, oldsters in retirement villages. *The first major program goal of IGRE, then is to respond creatively to this problem by helping people relate to one another in qualitative ways across generations.* This goal seeks to bring persons of various ages, stages of development, and other diversities into relationships of consequence.

At this point in societal time, almost *any* subject matter or *any* activity which would enable people of various ages to talk and do things together would be helpful. Some of the IG activities reported in the literature (e.g., egg coloring) seem to be focused on matter of minor learning import. Nevertheless, mundane egg decorating activities are valuable. If the content matter in the program or activity is of some cognitive substance, that is simply a plus to this goal of intergenerational human relations.

People of different ages have things to offer one another, things of life-sustaining value. To use a dramatic biblical example, consider 1 Kings, first chapter. It says that when King David was a very old man he was given a young woman, Abishag, to keep him warm. Literally, Abishag may have tried to nurse the aging monarch. It was believed that a woman's milk was a "vital force" for the sustaining of life—even of the old by the young. In the Bible the transferring of vital force worked in the other-age direction too, as when the infant Samuel was "lent" to the old priest, Eli, to receive the elder's tutelage.

In any case, it is the contention here that young and old have gifts to offer one another which help both. As matters now stand, religious institutions often prevent vital-force blessings because the CCD and Sunday/Sabbath schools are so much modeled after the public schools which cut off generations one from another. IGRE can reestablish the vital life-force sharings.

The macro benefits from developing quality IG human relations were described in the theory chapters of this book. Beginning with George Herbert Mead, we learned how mind itself and the sense of self are given through interchange with others. Insofar as primary interpersonal interchanges are attenuated in our time, then mind and self of many persons are the poorer for it. Mead's point, that we *build* human beings by humans interacting with others, was also underscored by Virginia Satir. Similarly, Erik Erikson held that the human developmental tasks of industry, identity, generativity, or integrity are fulfilled primarily by and through relations with others. We also heard from Kohlberg, Wilcox, and Fowler that development in moral reasoning and in faith stages is helped or hindered by the kinds of human interactions individuals have. The better the quality of these, the more apt the person is to advance in stages and successfully master the developmental tasks of his or her life journey.

The goal of quality intergenerational relations is put within reach— or, at least, facilitated—by a number of specific actions and practices that can be built into various models of IGRE. Talking, working, drawing, charading, listening, and so on, across generations have the promise of enabling good things to happen with and for people. This is part of being holistic in approach and thus leading to fulfillment of God/world/ persons. Such activities fit in the four patterns of IGRE learning relationships[7] which people have 1) in common, 2) in tandem, 3) in mutual contribution, and 4) in active sharing. *It is especially in active sharing that significance in relationship will appear,* for here there is greater depth and "crossing over" into one another's world. In active sharing an "I-Thou" relationship is made in which God is also party.

2. Significant Cognitive Learning

Living in the modern world, we know that knowledge has exploded exponentially, that is, by powers of three and four every ten years. A Renaissance man/woman can no longer be. One can hardly get the rudiments in all the sciences and humanities, much less the basics, to say nothing of "knowing everything worth knowing." So, today in education we have to be selective about what cognitive content is taught. This is certainly true in religious institutions where the educational *moment* too often is no more than sixty a week! What we can put into the time available by way of cognitive data had best be of consequence. *The second program goal of intergenerational religious education is to achieve significant conceptual learning outcomes related to the faith.*

What one learns with and from other people is important. Four criteria for determining "significance" in the cognitive learning area are that the topics be faithful, truthful, broadening, and relevant.

First, consider: *IGRE learning should be faithful.* What people learn in the context of the church or synagogue should be related to that institution's sacred canon, historic tradition, and ecclesiastical concerns and values. Learning needs to be of/by/for/about/in/etc., the faith. World religions like Christianity and Judaism have tremendous historical wisdom and experience to share. That wisdom of the ages is worth calling to mind for contemporary persons in that tradition. So, part of significant learning has to do with keeping faith with the faith.

Equally important is that *what is taught should be truthful.* Subject matter should reflect what the best of modern scholarship knows about the Bible, the world, human beings, whatever. I don't know how to say this gently, but as a matter of fact a lot that come with "the tradition" are lies. Some of the stuff which passes as "Gospel truth" would not stand up to elemental tests of veracity. I think we ought to temper whatever is taught with what we know to be *new* good news, such as, that the world is round, there's more than one Isaiah, angels probably aren't, there were inquisitions and witch trials, God is not a "he," and so on. In the year 1520 Pastor John Robinson in Holland told the departing Pilgrims that "God has yet more light and truth to break forth from his holy word." That's important to remember, and we might update Robinson's counsel to say, "God has yet more light and truth to break forth from the holy *world.*" That truth makes for significance too.

IGRE life and learning should be broadening for the participants. If our contemporary social setting is as suggested, namely, given to insulation and isolation, then significance in learning will be found by opening people up to the world in width and heighth and depth. Let me illustrate. The programs of the IGRE Church/Church School Model of All Saints Church were, I think, faithful/truthful/relevant, but especially they were broadening. They opened up doors to learn important things that adults and children had not known before. Note the following regarding those nine programs:

PROGRAM NAME	CONTENT CONCERN
1. Universe Man	All of God's Children
2. Fabulous Time Machine	Our Judaeo-Christian Heritage
3. Wizard of OT	Lesser Known Biblical Characters
4. Saints Go Marchin'	Saints/Seasons of the Church
5. Plymouth, USA	United States Religious History
6. The Good News Times	Jesus as a Loving Human Being
7. Holy Earth Log	Meeting Other World Religions
8. F P Barnum Ethical Show	Making Moral Decisions
9. The Music Machine	Inner Spiritual Development

Without going into detail, let me note that each of these topics was chosen for reasons such as to expose people to different cultures and religions, to meet biblical and historical characters not usually met in regular church school classes, and to cover topics hard to teach and so usually neglected. I can add too that with these programs, which spanned nine years, there was also growing sensitivity to sexism and to national/international issues. The programs, then, focused on learnings which broadened participants' knowledge and experience of the world, their religion, and themselves.

The fourth criteria for significance is this: *IGRE learning needs to be relevant,* that is, perceived by participants as important. Kierkegaard is right to suggest, in essence, that "little is true unless it is true for me."[8] The learning that folks do together needs to be existential, real, important to each person's life. In working with illiterate peasants in South America, Friere and his colleagues learned that they needed to find issues that interest, involve, even trouble people. So must we in IGRE. In Christian education some content topics may be worth knowing. "Patristic theology" is one topic, for example, that I personally think is exceedingly important . . . but such knowledge very likely will not appear to be of much value to "the average person in the pew." Crass as it is to say, "significance" is determined in part by whether the topic will "sell."

(Having made a statement advocating relevance, a counter statement is in order: Fadism in IGRE should be avoided. The topic of "cults," for example, might be a "simply fascinating subject" for some, but in reality is more of a digression from more important educational themes. If we are to have significant learning it must be substantive.)

The largest problem in selecting significant cognitive learning topics in IGRE is to know how to make the topic worthwhile to persons of all ages. The concerns of adults, teenagers, and children may not coalesce on one subject, or, more often, a subject will be of unequal interest among participants. There are ways to handle this, but the reality of the problem should not be forgotten. The positive corollary of the warning, then, is this: *Focus on a topic around which all participants likely will have something to share.* Find common topical ground. In one intergenerational worship service at All Saints Church, the focus of the service was on "the fish." During the discussion part of the service, people of all ages shared "fish stories." Then, for the scripture lesson(s), they recalled "fish stories in the New Testament" and eventually focused on the name and symbol.

Later in the service, worshipers served smoked fish to one another as part of the communion service—all somewhat reconstructive of what happened with the disciples on the Sea of Galilee in Jesus's postresurrec-

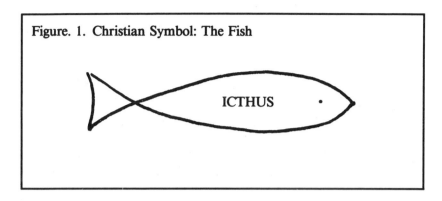

Figure. 1. Christian Symbol: The Fish

ICTHUS

tion appearance. All participants stayed highly involved throughout the hour.

Finally on this topic of significant learning, let me just record two points which I will later underline more boldly: One is that *any specific learning topic should be accompanied by stated learning objectives.* It is important to know where any program and its sessions are headed. So if, for example, there is an IGRE workshop on the topic of "Decision Making in the Family," then let the planners specify as clearly as possible the learning outcomes which they look for. Designers of IGRE programs will find their greatest success when they are able to articulate learning objectives in a simple sentence or two.

Running right alongside this counsel on stating objectives is a second: *Verify learning outcomes by testing.* Much more will be said on "evaluation" in chapter 11, but suffice it to say here that at the beginning of IG life and learning events a plan should be established to determine at the end if, in fact, significant learning did transpire. It will be necessary, then, to inventory participants *before* and *after* a major program. People who plan on testing will also discover that this is exceedingly helpful in gaining clarity about the learning objectives.

3. Positive Subjective Impact

After a sabbatical year in Great Britain, Randolph Crump Miller reported to his students at Yale Divinity School that one difference between English and American youth was that the former possessed formidable religious knowledge but had almost no commitment to the church. American youth, on the other hand, were amazingly involved in the church but were almost illiterate in religious knowledge. Miller indicated he preferred the latter situation. Learning of cognitive facts, he felt, was more likely to follow from positive emotional feelings and attachment, rather than the other way around.[9]

It is "in our guts"—at the core of being—where faith begins and is maintained, not just through cerebral acquisition. *In intergenerational life and learning we want people to be affected positively.* I described the sentiments-sought in a paper delivered several years ago: "We want children to *want* to come to church, to look forward to a good time and learning experience, and to have it! As far as that goes, we want the same thing for adults. Let people enjoy their worship experience and be glad they came."[10] Intergenerational programs are aimed at hitting the heart and emotions of people, maybe more than the head. At least by comparison with much traditional religious education it would seem so.

Alfred North Whitehead once said, "The mode for self-development is enjoyment."[11] I believe he is right. Which is not to say that the life of faith has no solemn or rigorous dimensions to it. It can be so. David is the "teacher of grieving" and Jesus "the man acquainted with sorrows." Certainly sin, guilt, penance, hell, and serious-mindedness are on the Christian and Jewish table, but so are joy, novelty, forgiveness, love, and thankfulness. These are good food too! In life we "learn lessons" from hard times, but usually those lessons are about what to avoid. We also learn from good-time experiences, and these tend to be alluring rather than aversive. So positive emotional experiences in education can lead us into deeper levels of learning, trusting, and loving. Perhaps this is what Whitehead means in saying that there needs to be a "stage of romance" in education prior to the "stage of precision."[12] We need to love learning, first. Such love is possible by enjoyable life and learning experiences which involve us with other people. These are the people who laugh with us, give love with their eyes, pat our back, send "atta-boy" nonverbal messages, work alongside, sensitively share their feelings, empathize with us, and invitingly say, "Tell me about it." It is these kinds of things which we want to happen in IGRE so that the a person's affections are affirmatively quickened.

In religious education there has long been a polar tension between the folks who emphasize cognitive content (often meaning Bible knowledge) in curriculum and the folks who emphasize starting where the learner is in his/her life experiences and working from there. Both emphases must be maintained, but I do believe that the experiential pole has a priority. In fact, I believe that total lifestyle consideration has the highest demand in IGRE. I talk about that under the fourth program goal. Because cognition and experience are so distinct in people's thoughts, we need to treat them separately, recognizing difference and priority, before joining them.

One important aspect of the positive subjective impact goal is consideration of the innerlife of each person. In developing his "hypothetical structures" of personality, Sigmund Freud suggested that there is the superego, the ego, and the id in the mind of each person. These we often call the conscience, the rationality, and the animal impulses. Thomas Harris has described the three inner-concepts as the parent, the adult, and the child within each of us. Sometimes one or two of these inner-persons gets locked up inside, operating to the detriment of an individual's functional wholeness. IGRE experiences may provide a freeing function, even as Margaret Sawin suggests: "When all ages are together, the childhood ego states of persons of all ages are more easily activated. This is the state within each of us from which creativity, spontaneity, and trust are elicited. Therefore, all persons in an intergenerational community are more apt to be more whole together."[13] The idea is that IG life awakens latent parts of personality, including the child in the octogenarian and (who knows?) the wise conscience of the grandparent in the eight-year-old.

Positive, growthful, subjective gains are enabled by life and learning that involve affirming interactions with other people. That participants say one to another "You are very important!" is essential. Such can touch the soul. That message is almost always conveyed by another—hopefully, a significant other—someone who cups a child's cheeks in her hands and, looking into the eyes, says, "I like you, Amy Garcia!" A positive subjective impact is made in the other direction of ages too, as when some youngster clumsily but lovingly pins a flower on a widower seated alone in the sanctuary on Father's Day.

Hey, sometimes it is enough to make a body cry—from inside—for joy.

In IGRE we want individual persons to be affirmed and inwardly empowered for their life pilgrimage.

4. Sound Lifestyle Consequence

One of the most intriguing notions I have run across in recent years is a thought of Rubem Alves, Brazilian theologian. It is:

> "What do you want to be when you grow up?"—that's what we say to children. If, without irreverence, we could ask God the same thing, he would say, "But you still don't know? Haven't I told you? I told you and you didn't listen. You thought I was joking. Yes, I want to be Jesus of Nazareth. I am Jesus of Nazareth. I am an ordinary man. I am all ordinary people. . . . There is nothing better than to be a man, a woman, a child. No, I don't want fleshless human beings. Let the bodies be resurrected."[14]

Interesting thought that . . . that what God wants is a human body just like ours!

The fourth goal for IGRE has to do with *making sound the body—the body and all that is of a person.* If cognition (in goal two) has to do with the mind and affect (in goal three) with the spirit, then "lifestyle" refers to the whole person—with all one's psychic, cognitive, affective, and psychomotor dimensions. Lifestyle initially refers to physical actions, to behavior, to conduct, to what people do with their bodies; but these bodies are neither decapitated or spiritless. Lifestyle includes the previously discussed mental and emotional sides of a person and goes on to be quite holistic.

For some readers "lifestyle" seems to refer to something contrived or artificial, such as, "California lifestyle" or "Yuppie lifestyle." What religious writers mean by the word, though, is the basic way we live out our lives. The major religious education theorist who has advocated lifestyle goals and processes is James Michael Lee whose definition of this we discussed in terms of overall institutional purpose. "Surely," Lee says, "Christianity is a way of life, not a set of words."[15] The key chapter in his monumental book the *Content of Religious Instruction* is on lifestyle. There are, to quickly repeat his argument, nine "molar" learnings which comprise substantive content:

Product Content	Process Content
Cognitive Content	Affective Content
Verbal Content	Nonverbal Content
(Conscious Content)	Unconscious Content

and
Lifestyle Content

"Lifestyle," he says, "not verbal content, should be the *terminus ad quo* and the *terminus ad quem* for all religious teaching."[16] Lifestyle content, he affirms, contains all the other substantive contents and leads to holistic living by *homo integer* (the integrated and total human being.) "Lifestyle is the integrated living out in behavioral form all the molar contents."[17]

With a goal of Sound Lifestyle Consequence in IGRE, we have the possibility of looking at psychomotor behavior which is observable, even measurable. Religious educators should be able to specify behaviors sought in teaching. I talk about behavioral objectives in the next section. It is enough to say now: With this goal we are not just dealing with the "black box" of the mind or the nebulus world of feelings but with observable behavior which can be assessed as "Christian" or "Jewish" or whatever.

More than that, though, with lifestyle we are talking about wholeness which one man described as follows:

> The point is that we all need to experience a glimpse of wholeness even if the only way to find it is to lift your bowed head during the prayer in Sunday

worship, and staring you straight in the eyes, are the sparkling, bright, curious warm eyes of a 2 1/2-year old child. A glimpse of wholeness and a little insight toward your place in the whole picture goes a long way toward bringing you peace.[18]

OBJECTIVES—PROGRAMATIC AND BEHAVIORAL

"Goal analysis is not for every goal. Only for those that are important."[19] So says Robert Mager in his book *Goal Analysis*. Believing that the four goals described above are important in the doing of IGRE, I want to do goal analysis and elaboration on the goals in this last section. We moved from *vision* to *purpose* to *goals* and now go on to *objectives*. Objectives are both for programs envisioned by the faith community and for participants in them. We move toward "behavioral" or "performance objectives." In the next chapter on Creating Curriculum we consider *procedures* for realizing goals and objectives.

The institutional goals for IGRE programs discussed in the previous pages are still rather large, unspecific, and not always measurable. The goals need specificity in order to ascertain whether they are reached or not. Consider the most inclusive of the goals, the Sound Lifestyle Consequence goal: How would one know if this was happening?

On the one hand, a respondent might say, "Well, we have this *program* which was designed to meet that goal."

A program *aimed* at something, though, does not necessarily mean the target has been hit. We need to be more rigorous in our evaluation. Goals should be established in education and religion in terms of "lives changed." Effecting change in persons is what education and religion are all about, anyway. Beyond that, the change sought needs to be specified. Please consider the four goals as program-goals-moving-toward-attainable-objectives as described on the next page.

From time to time in the previous section I talked about assessing "quality," determining "significance," doing the "positive," and being "sound" in regard to the four program goals. Without repeating information, let me simply say that *adjectival evaluation is best made by knowing what happens with individuals* inside any activity of the faith community. Religious leaders would be well-advised to hold a workshop on "IGRE Goal Planning," perhaps using one or more of Robert Mager's books in this field. In quick review, here are the steps to good goal articulation which Mager recommends:

Step One: Write down the goal.
Step Two: Jot down the performances that, if achieved, would cause you to agree the goal is achieved.
Step Three: Sort out the jottings.

**CHART 1. MOVING FROM INSTITUTIONAL GOALS
TO PROGRAM OBJECTIVES**

GOAL	PROGRAM OBJECTIVE
1. QUALITY INTERGENERATIONAL RELATIONS	To realize more than "the usual" age-group inter-changes because intentional IG activities and programing have been initiated and developed in the church/synagogue. (NOTE: stating the objective this way begs the question of "quality" in IG relations.)
2. SIGNIFICANT COGNITIVE LEARNING	To decide that people together are going to study X subject or do Y things so that they will learn about this matter which the leadership sees as important. (NOTE: this begs the question of whether such learning actually occurs and it specifies nothing about what constitutes "significance.")
3. POSITIVE SUBJECTIVE IMPACT	To build into the IGRE program experiences and learning that not only "inform" participants but also move/touch/affect their lives at a psychic or emotional level. (NOTE: this begs the question of whether the do-ings *really* had "positive" impact—or, for that matter, any effect.)
4. SOUND LIFESTYLE CONSEQUENCE	To influence people in a holistic way, program enactors will build in life and learning elements which are more in the psychomotor and behav-ioral realm. (NOTE: this begs the question of how one would know if the program had "sound" lifestyle conse-quence.)

Step Four: Write a complete statement for each performance, de-scribing the nature, quality, or amount you will consider acceptable.

Step Five: Test the statements with the question, "If someone achieved or demonstrated each of these performances, would I be willing to say he has achieved the goal?"[20]

Taking a lead from Mager we can illustrate what spelling out objective or performance behaviors might look like in IGRE under each of the four goals. Please consult Chart No. 2.

It will be observed in the chart that it would be hard to know if the "General Objectives" were being attained or not. To know/appreciate/feel/commit/love/ and so on, are vague statements, however desirable. So it is that under "Indicative Performance Objectives," I have listed possible concrete behaviors which, if met, likely would indicate that a

CHART 2. SPECIFYING IGRE GOALS INTO OBJECTIVES

PROGRAM GOAL	OBJECTIVES	
	General	Indicative Performance: "The person will be able to . . ."
1. QUALITY INTERGENERATIONAL RELATIONS	Know other older/younger people Appreciate young adults Better understand elderly Several ages work together	Greet X number people/make introductions Interview/write-up profile for newsletter Deliver Valentines in nursing home Present original IG cast playlet
2. SIGNIFICANT COGNITIVE LEARNING	Be familiar with local resources Know books of the Bible Know way around the building Learn Apostle's Creed	Draw map showing social services agencies In "Swords" game find passages in <10 seconds Lead guests on complete tour of building Memorize and recite
3. POSITIVE SUBJECTIVE IMPACT	Feel adoration for God Want to come to church Have better self-image Become more imaginative	Meditate with Holy Name for 20 minutes Attend 3 out of 4 times per month Talk animatedly about events of one's week Do fantasy trip and tell others about it
4. SOUND LIFESTYLE CONSEQUENCE	Be at peace and calm Commit to peace Love others better Worship more sincerely	Practice Jacobson Relaxation Exercise Write letter to Congressperson on subject Do "secret pal" gift-giving for a month Increase church pledge/pray for gift given

portion of the General Outcome Objective has, in fact, been attained and, thus, the Program Goal is being fulfilled.

Since we are especially concerned about Lifestyle Outcomes, one way to proceed in becoming specific about performance outcomes is to raise a question such as,

WHAT DOES A PRACTICING CATHOLIC LOOK LIKE—THAT IS, "DO"? WHEN SOMEONE IS BEING A "GOOD JEW," HOW WILL HE/SHE DEMONSTRATE IT?

Once when devising a confirmation class curriculum in terms of behavioral outcomes, I asked parents to consider: "If you were following a Christian around with a motion picture camera and tried to 'catch' him or her being Christian, what are you likely to get on film?" The responses to the question generated such notions as observing the person

praying	reading the Bible	worshiping
saying grace	giving money	singing a hymn
volunteering	witnessing	doing merciful acts
teaching another	forgiving an offender	visiting a prisoner
marching for peace	confessing one's sin	reading devotions
receiving communion	fasting in Lent	memorizing a creed

. . . and so on. The thing about these things is that we *can* describe many important dimensions of the faith lifestyle, and we can work to recapitulate these behaviors in ourselves and in other generations. Such becomings may be facilitated by IGRE. We do better on all these demonstrable lifestyle characteristics in the company of others, younger and older.

CONCLUSION

From visions to performance objectives, we have gone from considering very global, even extraterrestial, outcomes to specification of very particular individual behaviors. With clarity about goals and objectives, we are in a position to move into consideration of design and implementation of such ends in life and learning along intergenerational lines.

Notes

1. Robert Lowry Calhoun, *Lectures on the History of Philosophy* (New Haven, Conn.: Yale Divinity School, 1958), p. 92.
2. See Mary Elizabeth Moore, *Education for Continuity and Change: A New Model for Christian Religious Education* (Nashville: Abingdon, 1983), pp. 154-5.
3. Jürgen Moltmann, *Theology of Hope: On the Ground and the Implications of a Christian Eschatology* (New York: Harper & Row, 1967), p. 329.
4. H. Richard Niebuhr, *The Purpose of the Church and Its Ministry: Reflec-*

tions on the Aims of Theological Education (New York: Harper Brothers, 1956), pp. 34-35.

5. See James Michael Lee, *The Content of Religious Instruction: A Social Science Approach* (Birmingham, Ala.: Religious Education Press, 1985), p. 608.
6. See the Appendix of this book and various write-ups on IG programs by James W. White in, for example, *New Forms Exchange* (December, 1978).
7. See chapter 2 of this book, pp. -.
8. Søren Kierkegaard, *Concluding Unscientific Postscript* (Princeton, N.J.: Princeton University Press, 1960), p. 71, or p. 176: "All essential knowledge relates to existence, or only such knowledge as has an essential relationship to existence is essential knowledge."
9. Randolph Crump Miller, from comment in class, Yale Divinity School, New Haven, Conn., 1961.
10. James W. White, "Interage/Intergenerational Education: A Six Summers' Case Study." (Paper delivered at the Meeting of the Association of Professors and Researchers in Religious Education, St. Louis, Mo., November 20, 1977, pp. 6-7.)
11. Alfred North Whitehead, *The Aims of Education and Other Essays* (New York: Free Press, 1967), p. 31.
12. Ibid., pp. 17-19.
13. Margaret Sawin, "Intergenerational Ministries" (Paper delivered at Rochester, N.Y., September, 1980.)
14. Rubem Alves, *I Believe in the Resurrection of the Body* (Philadelphia: Fortress, 1986), p. 34.
15. Lee, *Content of Religious Instruction,* p. 348.
16. Ibid., p. 296.
17. Ibid., p. 614. In his book, *The Flow of Religious Instruction,* Lee talks about "The Integralist Position," which regards "The primary purpose of religious instruction as the fusion of one's personal experience of Christianally understanding, action, and love coequally," p. 11.
18. Harvey H. Pinyoun, "Guest Commentary: One Brief Glimpse of Wholeness," *United Church News* (New York Conference edition, March, 1987), p. 2.
19. Robert F. Mager, *Goal Analysis* (Belmont, Calif.: Lear Siegler/Fearon, 1972), p. 132.
20. Ibid., p. 72.

Chapter 10

Creating Curriculum

So grade- and age-consciousness are we in educational planning, there has not been much curricular material that is age-inclusive. Most IGRE curricula generated is usually location-specific, that is, the product of some creative people working in a local setting, putting a program together. Sometime later they may write it up.[1] This chapter speaks to the IGRE curriculum lacuna, laying out guidelines for good design and implementation.

In building IGRE curriculum there are six components.

First of all, there is the *context*. As the first determinate in *IG*RE curriculum-shaping, context for curriculum is discussed initially in this chapter. Then there are *goals* (and *evaluation*). These are treated only briefly, in the second section, as goals were discussed in detail in the previous chapter, and evaluation will be in the forthcoming chapter. Third, there is *scope* in the curriculum to be considered. Scope is closely related to the fourth component, *content*. The fifth section covers *design* (or format) for programs, and the sixth concerns *implementation* of IGRE in the faith community. A postscript on *"do-it"* enacting procedures concludes the chapter.

A double duty is being attempted in these pages. On the one hand, macro-designers (curriculum publishers/denominational planners/educational writers) need help in the pursuit of their large-scale, mostly written, curricular work. On the other hand, micro-designers, persons operating in a local faith community on an IGRE project also are looking for help. This chapter seeks to speak to both curriculum makers.

(Before proceeding directly, though, let me insert an extended parenthetical word about the *curriculum design thicket*. There is simply no simple way to organize thought and work in this area. Curriculum theorists are widely divergent in their language regarding components involved in curriculum development. Historically, Ralph Tyler says there are *"four* central questions" needing answering in design. The questions have to do with 1) purpose, 2) experiences, 3) organizing experiences, and 4) evaluation.[2] Tyler's highly influential fourfold schema can be followed by a *five* point program forwarded by D. Campbell Wyckoff. He speaks of 1) context, 2) scope, 3) purpose, 4) process, and 5) design in the construction of curricula.[3] In the book accompanying the Protestant Joint Education Development (JED) project, a similar five-component design program is described which includes consideration of 1) the objective, 2) the scope, 3) the context, 4) the learning tasks, and 5) the organizing principle. The authors note that these components are "interdependent and interactive."[4] It is precisely because curricular components are interactive that there are wide differences arising in deciding just how many "discrete" parts there are. Two persons come up with *six* point curricular design models. James Michael Lee says that the classic considerations are 1) design, 2) scope, 3) sequence, 4) continuity, 5) balance or range, and 6) integration. These he calls the "structural elements of the curriculum."[5] The other sixfold curriculum organizer is Iris Cully, who speaks of "components" for development being 1) basic design, 2) goals and evaluation, 3) theological and educational assumptions, 4) teaching/learning opportunities, 5) resources, and 6) leadership development.[6] Just to make matters more complex, let me note that a seven-, an eight-, and a ten-point schema are forwarded. Colson and Rigdon suggest that a good curriculum "has at least *seven* characteristics": 1) biblical and theological soundness, 2) relevance, 3) comprehensiveness, 4) balance, 5) sequence, 6) flexibility, and 7) correlation.[7] In discussing curriculum preparation Donald Miller observes that *eight* "decisions" have to be made, decisions having to do with 1) objective, 2) concept, 3) learning task, 4) organizing principle, 5) format, 6) content and style, 7) production of materials, and 8) marketing of materials in curriculum.[8] Finally, there is a *ten*-point program put forward by Smith and Moss who work in vocational education curriculum development. Their program includes "1) specifying the role for which training is to be provided, 2) identifying the specific tasks that comprise the role, 3) selecting the tasks to be taught, 4) analyzing each of the tasks, 5) stating performance objectives, 6) specifying the instructional sequence, 7) identifying conditions of learning, 8) designing an instructional strategy, 9) developing instructional events, and 10) creating student and curriculum evaluative procedures and devices."[9] I could go on. It may be that the most truthful word about curriculum development has been delivered by Mary Jo Osterman:

No comprehensive curriculum theory is available today for Protestant religious education in spite of the fact that curriculum theorizing has been engaged in for the past two hundred years. The theorizing process thus far has resulted in suggestions of various components of curriculum such as aim, content, scope, experiences, learnings, learning models, grouping, context, organizing principle, evaluative scheme, learning tasks, curriculum development processes, and implementation processes. However, *no agreement exists about which of these components belong in the phenomenon called curriculum.*[10]

This extended paragraph is offered as introduction to the presentation of what follows on the creation of curriculum for IGRE. My conclusion is *there simply is no simple way to proceed descriptively/prescriptively into IGRE curriculum development, AND yet there are recurring concepts and procedures—described variously—that have to be treated in curriculum development.* The basic concepts and procedures are covered in this presentation. They go by the names *context, goals* [and *evaluation],* *scope, content, design,* and *implementation.* They are the components of IGRE curriculum.)

COMPONENT I: The Context

In his book on curriculum development, Paul Dressel holds that "the desired learning environment [should] be determined in detail before methods are selected to achieve it."[11] It is the "Intergenerational Faith Community" which is the environment, the context, for planning and implementing IGRE curriculum. This community is both goal (actually Goal 1 outlined in the previous chapter) and means to the goal. IGRE curriculum is distinct from other religious education curricula precisely because it begins with context—the context of religious people of multiple ages being in relationship to live and learn with/from/beside each other in the faith.

As observed in the opening situational analysis of chapter 1, the church/synagogue is the one institution in contemporary society which has people of all ages in its natural constituency. That is one thing that sets religious groups apart from other collectivities. We should capitalize on this situation and make positive things happen for and among these people who are in the communities of faith.

It is *the faith community,* then, which provides the context for curriculum building. There could be other starting places or contexts for doing religious education. As Jack Seymour and Donald Miller note, there are several models: a religious instruction model, a spiritual development model, one that stresses liberation motifs, another emphasizing religious resource interpretation, and a faith community model. I intentionally want to focus on the faith community model, the goals of which are "to build the congregation into a community where persons encounter the faith and learn its lifestyle."[12] Discussing this approach in his own monograph, Miller speaks of "the faith community as teacher" and notes that "the individual faith pilgrimage occurs within a network of relationships that make up the community context of life. In these relationships the primary meaning of life is carried."[13] Such a pilgrimage occurs, of course, in families, but Miller argues that today *the church is needed to help families do their work.* "The whole ecology of education," he says, "is quite different than it was a half century ago. . . . The church is now in a position of nurturing family life, including that of single parent families and many single persons. The congregation has become the stabilizing force for the family, not the other way around."[14] What Miller is saying echoes what was noted earlier by C. Ellis Nelson, namely, that "faith is communicated by a community of believers and that the meaning of faith is developed by its members out of their history, by their interaction with each other, and in relation to events that take place in their lives."[15]

So it is that in approaching the task of developing IGRE we think first about the faith community—all the people from infancy to infirmary—as the context in which whatever we do takes place. Whatever happens happens there.

This contextual prerequisite calls for curriculum designers who have an inclusive vision of learning. We need writers and doers who are sensitive to life-span growth and development issues, people who appreciate continuity among the ages groups and the need for people to learn from different-age others. We want planners who understand that an individual's "course of development depends largely on what happens *throughout* the life of the organism, not only what happens in early life."[16] At the denominational or publishing house level, curriculum planners need to be people who are familiar with developmental and life-span thinking, among other things. At the local level it means that planners should appreciate the differences *and alikenesses* of children, youth, and adults.

At whatever level of curriculum design, the *patterns of* IGRE *relationship* should be consulted regularly. Designers would be asking how the various-aged people can worship/learn/act together in "common experiences, parallel learning, contributive occasions, and interactive sharing." People of sundry ages in a congregation are within close physical proximity of one another on a sabbath day. They even may interrelate on a day-by-day basis. What IGRE curriculum planners would be thinking of is how to capitalize on these normal interactional patterns, enhancing them for greater benefit of all involved.

Consideration of the faith-community-as-a-whole is the first and ever-present component of successful IGRE curriculum development.

COMPONENT II: Goals (and Evaluation)

I need not add more here on goals and evaluation except that, given the context of a wide range of ages in the faith community, it behooves persons doing curriculum planning to achieve clarity about purpose, goals, objectives, and behavioral outcomes. These we discussed in the previous chapter. It is enough to repeat that the major goals in IGRE are 1) quality intergenerational life, 2) significant cognitive learning, 3) positive subjective impact, and 4) sound lifestyle outcomes. For any-one approaching curriculum design or selection, it is well to recall Iris Cully's counsel: "A serious study of goals by each congregation is a funda-mental necessity before any curriculum materials may be chosen."[17]

In working out the objectives and performance criteria for attainment of IGRE goals, there is wisdom in inventorying participants to deter-mine if, in fact, the positive changes anticipated are happening for people. We come to the matter of evaluation in greater detail in the final chapter. Right now I only underscore the idea that planners need to build evaluative moments into their design at the beginning and at the end to ascertain whether what is sought for actually occurs for partici-pants.

COMPONENT III: Scope

D. Campbell Wyckoff says, "The scope of Christian education is *the whole field of relationships* in the light of the gospel."[18] Designers of curriculum for IGRE should feel comfortable with such a definition, in that the whole church or every dimension of a faith community's life might be included in the scope of concern for programing.

In truth not everything can be intentionally programed for IGRE. Much must be left to operate on its own according to ways that have been. I like to think of the faith community (whether in national/inter-national dimension or in storefront size) as a *sailing ship.*[19] Such a ship has many sails, but not all can or should be raised at once. Selectivity in just which sails should be put into service at which time needs to be exercised. Which is to say, a number of intergenerational programs could be hoisted in a church, but prioritization needs to occur. This counsel was offered earlier in discussing the Total Parish Paradigm. Concerning selectivity, Iris Cully suggests that a listing be made of "all learning situations" and then in planning, selecting for use those that are key to a group's educational plans.[20]

In describing the whole field of IGRE, I identified six basic models: 1) the family group, 2) the weekly class, 3) the workshop or event, 4) the worship service, 5) the worship-education program, and 6) the all-church camp. One of these might be selected by curriculum planners as the model by which to proceed. In so choosing, a congregation is thereby deciding on a particular setting for IGRE, such as the home, a sub-parish neighborhood, the sanctuary, work-service area, or other.

Whatever model-with-setting is chosen, planners also have to deal with the matter of "time available" for the program. That too is consideration of curriculum scope. "Two hours and fifteen minutes on Saturday mornings from Passover to Shevouth" may be the time parameter established. Such a parameter setting helps decide just how much activity/learning can be scheduled. As such, this too is a scope decision.

Since scope is particularly concerned with relationships (as IGRE is), we must consider which relationships to emphasize in the curriculum. Please note: *It is the individual who is in relationship.* I see that individual needing to "run the course" (follow a curriculum) which has relationships according to learning arenas suggested in Figure 1.

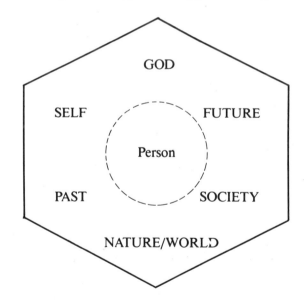

Figure 1. Hexagon of "Right Relationships" for IGRE
Curriculum Development

The hexagon of right relationships for IGRE is inclusive but also exclusive enough to give distinctive direction to curriculum builders. It indicates that the "person" is in relationship to *God*. That means here "the things that are of God," such as holy rituals, symbols, and concepts, not to exclude prayer. The relationship to the past means to include familiarity with the basic story and stories of the faith, especially as those are told in sacred scripture but also in sacred history. The *self* that is spoken of is in recognition that there is an intra-individual dynamic relationship going on. That internal dialogue needs facilitation. The self dimension takes account of the importance of experiences for the learner. In speaking of one's relationship with *nature* and/or *world,* I want to call attention to the notion that lifestyle learning is physical and involves us with real things. We are not dismembered cerebral cortexes or disembodied spirits but flesh and blood beings who do not leave the earth. We need to stay in touch with what is going on around us in the real world. *Society* includes family, all friendship associations, extended acquaintanceships, and life in the many societal roles that the human must play. In IGRE we are especially attentive to the quality of relationships among people in the community. Finally, I have noted that the person has relationship to the *future.* It is at this point that I see curriculum of the future looking more toward shaping that future. Here the influence of both process and liberation theologies with their hope themes make an impact. The person in right relationship needs to be open to the future to help shape a better tomorrow. The curriculum may be, in John Gilbert's word, "proactive," aimed at changing the world, not just in recapitulating it.[21]

If one discerned in the relationship hexagon some polarities, that is intentional. The scope of education needs to keep competing forces for the individual in some tension, not neglecting any one. What needs to be said is that in the best of curriculum situations, these polarities do not stand so much in opposition as they do in complementary relationship. Mary Elizabeth Moore's thesis is that religious education should encompass opposites, such as "continuity" (here, read: the *past* or history) and "change" (and here, read: the *future*).[22] She says that emphasizing both poles should take place in a "traditioning community." With Moore, the traditioning community would be quite intentional about bringing up the best of the differences in the faith. "Traditioning," she says, "requires passing on the past and looking forward toward the future, for the sake of transforming our praxis in the present."[23]

In talking about scope it is important to recall that "context" is still the first of the curriculum components. The individual person on a lifestyle faith pilgrimage is accompanied in relationships by others in the faith community. Note, then, the dash-circle in the hexagon around the "person." The dashes represent the faith community. These others are with the individual relating to God, self, past, and so on. All move together.

Scope, then, asks of the many things, "What . . .?" So *content* can ask, "What specifically?"

COMPONENT IV: Content

In the discussion of "purpose" regarding IGRE I said that "life-style"—one's whole way of being in the world in terms of religious faith—is to be the communicated "content" of religious education. Conveying cognitive information is not our only concern. We are rather interested in the wholeness of life, its affective, psychomotor, unconscious, nonverbal, etc., aspects, as James Michael Lee always reminds us. Mary Elizabeth Moore speaks to the point: "The debates among cognitive-, affective-, and action-oriented education models have worn thin by now, but they continue. The mark of traditioning education is that persons are formed and transformed in all these dimensions of existence."[24] In talking to religious groups, I sometimes use a graphic to make the point that the curriculum needs to relate to the wholeness of a learner. Please see Figure 2.

Ears-per   Hol-per

Figure 2. *Per*-sons Learning Through Limited or Full Senses

The first caricature, I usually say, is "the typical religious person at worship." He/she is whole but usually invited only to be active with his or her ears—listening, taking in cognitive facts or ideas. Hol-per, on the other hand, would be a person in the faith community who is encouraged to use his or her eyes, nose, mouth, hands, feelings, as well as ears in worshiping and learning.

The point for curriculum builders is obvious: People need to be allowed to be full-sense involved when communicating with one another. The life of faith is made up of mind, spirit, body. So, consideration of that fullness goes into curriculum design and lesson plans.

Another way to consider the whole person in worship and learning is to recall the variety of ways people learn. Jerome Bruner, it may be recalled from chapter 8, speaks of three learning modes. They are the enactive (physical), the iconic (visual), and the symbolic (language).[25] While Bruner may advocate movement toward the third and most abstract of these three, all three should be incorporated in IGRE programing. Especially the enactive needs to be present as it is the one most often slighted in curriculum development and yet the one closest to lifestyle learning.

The more we build curriculum around lifestyle concerns, the more mutual faithing becomes possible. Figure 3 is a supportive illustration of this point. In this swirling cone there are expanding modalities for learning.

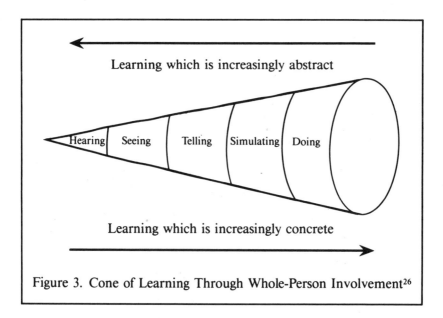

Figure 3. Cone of Learning Through Whole-Person Involvement[26]

The expanding cone of experiences suggested by the figure will be present in the planning of persons doing better intergenerational programs. The expanding swirl of the figure suggests that as people move from hearing to seeing to telling to simulating to doing they are apt to be more fully involved. So they remember, articulate, feel, and do more that is lifestyle faith-full on their pilgrimage.

These Hol-per involvements are also related to "right brain" learning with its moral, gestural, spacial, artistic, synthetic, holistic, mystical dimensions, in addition to the left hemisphere learning with its verbal, mathematical, logical, analytical characteristics.[27] The use of the whole mind (and everything else about the human) is important if the whole person is to grow.

All the above is said preparatory to consideration of "content" traditionally understood, namely as cognitive acquisition. To devalue conscious content is something I will not do for long. To do so would belie this book itself. What is *in* a person's head is important, as it so strongly influences how he or she responds to events and how one lives. I even agree with the cognitist views of Dwayne Huebner on the importance of communicating curriculum "content," that is, "knowledge and other forms of cultural wealth."[28] There really are things worth knowing, mental/verbal/conceptual things that can make a real difference in individual lives and in the world. This content ought to be in motion with IGRE programs.

In consideration of cognitive subject matter *and* all lifestyle content, it is well to re-recognize that decisions on content here are based on consideration of three agendas: 1) that of the tradition and wider faith community, 2) that of the people for whom you write or with whom you will be involved, and 3) that of the world.

1. *The agenda of the inherited faith* is first considered. In its teaching ministry, the church/synagogue is concerned to replicate the faith. It has both a historic faith to speak of and faith-full vision for the earth to speak for. The Christian church, for one, seeks in all things "the increase among people of the love of God and neighbor" (H. Richard Niebuhr). Toward that end, it strives to transfer its basic beliefs, practices, folkways, hopes. Included in the agenda of the Christian church are belief in a triune God, confession of Christ as Lord, attentiveness to the Bible, the practice of prayer, maintaining community, service to others, and knowledge of—with support for—the institution of the church itself. In terms of specific content or topics, we might offer "courses" not unlike those in a theological seminary. So that the prophets, reformation ideas, denominational polity, worship planning, spiritual formation, social ethics, and so on, would be possible offerings. Such concerns are not necessarily the burning issues of a local congregation, but they are part of a world religion's living heritage and as such need to be factored in for inclusion when considering educational curriculum.

2. *The agenda of the people in the faith community* (ecumenical/denominational/local) are not to be forgotten in program consideration. It is never wrong to begin by asking people, "What would you like to learn?" The answer to this question may not be a content idea related to the historic agenda of the religion. I know of churches, for example, which offer cooking classes and aerobic dancing (even, "Jogging with Jesus"!). I myself have taught fly-tying to people at a family camp. Curriculum composers want to be attentive to folks' expressed interests,

issues, and perceived personal needs. When asked their preference, though, individuals also will have concerns that are deeply significant—faith essential, of God. Stated dramatically, in Paul Tillich's language, persons have "ontological anxiety, even unto death" on which they would like assistance. Their agenda—whether practical, mundane, or profound—should be considered in deciding curriculum content.

3. *The world has an agenda too.* There is need to ask more broadly and objectively, "What is going on in the world, for weal or woe, to which faithful people should be attentive?" Beyond meeting-house doors and personal concerns, there are needs/possibilities/happenings in the society and culture which can inform decisions regarding educational subject matter.[29] Not the least of these goings-on in the world is the increasing insulation/isolation of people which IGRE itself is trying to address. Some of this focusing on the wider world can be a form of conscientization in a base community. To serve the world we want to raise critical consciousness among people, exercising relevance in wider circles of concern.

Much of what has been said above about the three agenda applies to curricula that is nonintergenerational. There are, though, some unique factors regarding IGRE curriculum. The topic/concern/activity/focus which is selected for programing should be one to which people of every age can relate. It is best that it be one on which people have a modicum of common interest and perhaps a little experience, so they can share. One of the ways this can be done is to focus the topic on "people" more than on abstract topics or concerns. So that participants are dealing with Old Testament Characters (more than "the history books"), Jesus' Disciples (rather than "The Synoptic Gospels"), Great Rabbis (rather than "Evolution of the Talmud"), and so on. Multidimensional persons appeal to persons of multiple ages.

In addition to the three agendas and cross-age considerations in curriculum building, three other questions can be helpfully asked in determining specific content. One is, *"What has been neglected* in regular or usual offerings to the congregation?" The "Lesser Known Old Testament Personalities" or "Saints of the Church" may be two neglected areas inviting attention on which participants of every age start out on equal footing. A second question is, *"What is hard to teach* —and thus neglected—to which we might give special attention?" One such topic in this category—pop-culture stereotypes of "Sunday School" and CCD notwithstanding—is "Ethics and Morality." In IGRE curriculum, rightly developed, there can be some interpersonal ethical modeling *and* idealizing from one generation to another. A third question is, *"What is a hot or current topic* of religious interest?" From year to year interest peaks on certain concerns that can be picked up on. Such topics as

"Middle Eastern Religions" or "The Centennial of Our Church" or "TV Evangelism" are three of possible interest. With regard to TV Evangelism, the very young and the very old may know more about this than people in their middle years.

Finally, a helpful rule of thumb in deciding curriculum content is to inquire of the writers or program planners if the projected content is something in which *they* are interested. Is this a subject you would like to have preached on and have people respond to? Is this Lenten midweek series on "Our Neighbors" something in which you would like your family to participate? And so on. If the answer is in the affirmative, then that topic has possibility. Hopefully too, the curriculum content decision makers are persons who 1) appreciate the roots of their faith, 2) sense their own needs and those of their family, 3) are attentive to the world generally, and 4) have a feel for the peculiar nature of intergenerational learning.

Consideration of these many things, then, will determine the specific content for IGRE.

COMPONENT V: Design

If, after deciding "what" is to be the subject matter, curriculum creators then simply assign the topic to a lecturer or knowledgeable writer and assume it will be communicated *they are mistaken.* As important as is the content decision, no less important is that regarding format, structure, and design for that content's presentation. We are talking about *how* we communicate the lifestyle content concerns. Specifically, we are talking about "the sequence of activities and experiences by which the learning tasks may be effectively undertaken by individuals and groups."[30]

Decisions about educational content and format may be likened to decisions on form and function in architecture. For the curriculum to really take shape, the designers need to go to the drawing board—perhaps literally. Especially needed is a design structure where the overall purpose/theme/content of a program is carried well by the units or individual sessions of that program. See Figure 4 for a visual idea of what is involved.

Figure 4 is presented to make several important points about curriculum building. One is that there needs to be a central theme for whatever is attempted. This theme is related to the general purpose and the program goals for which it is envisioned, and it needs to run across the program from beginning to end. Second, each session must touch that theme and uphold it.

The reader will note in the graphic that each designated session is in

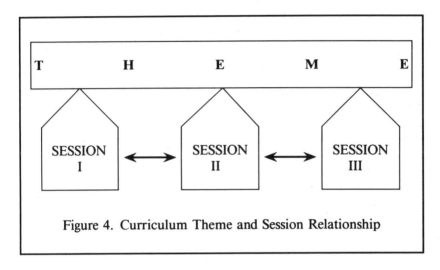

Figure 4. Curriculum Theme and Session Relationship

the shape of a house. The idea is that each unit is a self-contained event, complete in and of itself. This understanding is one of the overlooked necessities required for more and more religious educational curriculum today. As a rule, curriculum writers presuppose too much prior and/or subsequent learning in their lesson designs. Unless we are talking about devising curriculum for a most unusual and particularly faithful-in-attendance target population, curriculum design counting on continuity of attendance is self-defeating. "Irregularity" is the prevailing condition. Iris Cully says, "Most courses of study assume regular class attendance, yet attendance records in local churches do not bear out this confident assumption."[31] Participants enter a session with unequal readiness every time. Moreover, they do not remember well from week-to-week, especially when their presence is quite often month-to-month. It would be wonderful to think that sequencing works in such a way as to build one lesson on top of another, as with building blocks. It cannot. In some situations such may be possible, but in most instances full understanding of the coherence of the curriculum will be known only to the creators. So, as much as possible, let each session stand on its own.

Yet, each session is in relation to others and to the theme.

Note: There are two-way arrows between the session blocks. That is to suggest that sessions stand in a similar way to each other, each one supporting the theme. Moreover, the arrows suggest that each session should have a "Review and Preview" of other sessions. (More on this later.) Leaders in each session should *review* what happened in previous meetings for the sake of both newcomers and former attendees, and they should *preview* what is coming, both to whet appetites for a return but also to give people who may not complete the program a feel for the whole. In this way, all participants are made aware of what is going on generally and can enter in more fully to the activities of any given event.

In curriculum design there are several additional things which, if done, will make IGRE life and learning better. Perhaps the most helpful is to urge the planners to *specify session objectives.* As in sermon preparation, so in lifestyle session it is exceedingly helpful "to say in one sentence what the thing is about." If an education committee decided to do an intergenerational class on the life of Jesus, for example, it would be wise to decide just how they wanted to portray him, perhaps as "a real, interesting, and loving human being." That would be their program goal. Each session would take a part of that overall goal, one session setting out the objective to show Jesus' forgiving side and another Jesus' righteous indignation. In program design the "K.I.S.S. Rule" is always in order: *K*eep *I*t *S*imple, *S*tupid! Too often educators try to "cover" too much and end up "hiding" the truth they would convey. They/we should *un*cover just one or two things of importance in a given session.

In specifying objectives, one of the best ways to do so is to *state cognitive, affective, and lifestyle objectives for participants.* In the aforementioned session on Jesus the Forgiver, we might want people to know that Jesus forgave particular people, e.g., Zaccheus. This cognitive objective can be formulated in behavioral terms to say, "The participants will be able to identify Zaccheus as a man Jesus forgave and write down one thing about the encounter between these two men." The affective goal for this session might say, "Each participant will be able to recall verbally to someone of another age an incident of personally forgiving or being forgiven." And in terms of lifestyle (which also includes the above): "The participants will simulate a situation of estrangement and practice asking forgiveness and forgiving." In such way we may enable people to experience forgiveness or knowing how to forgive—which would be wonderfully behavioral, wonderfully faithful! The session might conclude with a brief worship service which has a meaningful and just-created confession of sin and absolution. That is lifestyle content for the pilgrimage.

The design of IGRE facilitates the learning outcomes planned for.

COMPONENT VI: Implementation (or, IGRE Guide-Ideas)

It is customary in a chapter on curriculum to end with a discussion on "Resources." Here that is simple enough to do by referring the reader to the notes of this chapter, and of chapter 3 especially. In these two sections much of the available written resource material is listed, along with audio-visual and other resources. The various curricula related to the various models point to additional resource materials.

The one resource I would want to identify as being of inestimable value is not in print. It is *persons* —persons in the faith communities who are concerned "to do something to bring generations together for growth in faith." Such persons have within themselves the capacity to envision and enact significant IGRE life and learning activities. They are the ones who create the curriculum. To quote C. Ellis Nelson, "The finest curriculum is that which is created locally."[32] Such "finest curriculum" is regularly "homegrown" by these persons—homegrown being "the process of developing and carrying out the educational ministry in a local congregation. It is 'grown at home' as opposed to a purchased package. Externally produced materials can serve a valuable function in the Christian education process; but for many, the most authentic and most usable approaches are those that are developed in the local community itself."[33] In truth most of the literature generated in IGRE has come and "continues to come from those who have participated in intergenerational activities in the local church."[34] The people in the faith communities have the ability to generate significant multi-age programs for others. May their tribe increase! In asking what is the most important element in planning for IG learning, George Koehler says, "The crucial element is leadership. It is people—the real, live human beings who will guide others in this experience—that spell out the difference between effective Christian ministry and just another program."[35]

It is on the basis of a decade-plus of working with some very generative people in a local faith community doing IGRE that I now offer some *guide-ideas for implementation and enactment of IGRE programs.* The baker's dozen of ideas proved to be especially relevant in terms of the Worship-Education Model of IGRE and will be instrumental in development of the IGRE Total Parish Paradigm.

1. *Coordinate the program to fit into the whole life of the congregation.* If the religious education theorists who talk about socialization have anything to teach, it is that instructional programing cannot be isolated. The whole church/synagogue teaches by everything it does or fails to do. So let the IGRE program tie in with the whole life of the congregation. At All-Saints Church, for example, the summer IGRE program harmonized the worship service and educational hour of the church. It also worked in with other facets of the church's life: carrying over into all-church camp, neighborhood dinners, evangelism efforts,

new member picnics, outreach projects, stewardship, business management, and even staff work assignments. The church secretary, for example, taught youngsters and grandmothers to run the ditto machine, and the custodian was recruited to take a role in an IG playlet. This reflects a holism in the institution. Curricular designers and implementors should consider whatever program they focus upon as part of the whole community's effort to edify (build up) its own.

2. At all stages of IGRE curriculum enactment, *involve people of all ages as much as possible.* IG educators must confess not doing as good a job in practice of involving all ages in the learning process as we publicize doing. Even so, facilitating cross-age relationships should be done from the initial shaping of the curriculum to the final evaluating. Pastor-educator Douglas Tracy of Delphi, Indiana, says, "Everyone — adult and child—must have the opportunity to share his or her insights with others. It's in the sharing at the end that we participate in one another's growth."[36] The place where all models of IGRE run the greatest danger of failing in their purpose is with regard to "interactive sharing." One of my highest recommendations to persons doing program design, then, is to *build into each session at least one major child-adult interactive sharing time.* The may be so simple as "getting acquainted and sharing something verbally" in an IGRE setting; or, it could be more significant, as collaborating on a postcard message to mission partners overseas; it could be as extensive as together visiting someone in a children's home. Whatever it is, such interage activity has to be planned explicitly to guarantee the possibility of effecting a significant, more than a casual, exchange.

3. *Employ symbols, songs, and rituals.* Quality relationships are best built on the ground of shared experience. Visual symbols which attract, songs sung with gusto, meaningful litanies recited together can provide in-common experiences for all. Such signs/symbols/songs/shared sayings hit the right-hemisphere side of the brain in ways that only now are we beginning to appreciate fully. So use these less verbal contents. They go deeper into the psyche and stay with folks much longer. After the cognitive content is lost, the visual image and melody linger on.

4. *Consider using dramatis personae often.* Since its third IGRE program, All-Saints has had a "central character" in its worship-education program. The character—usually a colorful figure at that—in some way typifies the program. He/she/they, for another thing, provide continuity from week to week. This person also may become a "significant other" for the children with whom he/she interacts, especially if that character is a warm, likable, and believable personality. It works in the other age direction too, with adults. By the central character's costumed

playfulness, the "child" in the adult is freed to come out, thus facilitating possibilities of greater IG interplay. In our experience, dramatic role playing gave "permission by example" for adults to drop inhibitions and take on a teaching-acting role—even in costume—for others. Thus a wonderful Elijah, St. Clare, Dr. Spock, and Herbert the Snail emerged. One excellent thing that personifying does is let historical figures of the faith come alive. The "cloud of witnesses" becomes real, and the witnesses serve as models of faith for lifestyle emulation. Social-psychological "identification" can occur. The roleplaying can also have a long-term effect: For two years after my debut as "The Wizard of OT," one little boy always addressed me as "Mister OT." Jeff has since learned my real name, but I always felt the role created a special and valuable interage relationship.

5. *Keep timing, action, and movement going.* Too often "schooling" means the student sits passively to absorb seemingly arbitrary stuff which is thrown at him or her. If "churching" is like that too, people should be turned off. Certainly IGRE programing cannot be of such a genre. If we are talking about IG worship or a one-shot special event, it needs to be well-timed and lively paced. If we are talking about family group meetings, these need room-in-and-out, carpet-to-table movements—and not just because the attention span of children is limited but because older learners need fresh starts in special settings to facilitate their learning too. Most adult education is too sedant and boring already. I like to *think of an IGRE session as a piece of art, albeit dance art,* which calls forth various movements and steps in tempo with music which is likely to have varying rhythms. Such art needs both visual and physical action. At regular intervals in a total program, "big-muscle activities" should be devised to get people moving vigorously. Marching around the synagogue, for example, and then storming a Box-City of Jericho is a big-muscle thing to do. Playing run/chase/hide/escape at all-church camp reenacting the Underground Railroad is another. Not all sessions can be drama-filled or big-muscle. Quieter, even meditative, IGRE times can be programed. Regardless of what, for any given session there should be consideration of the physical movement of participants from pew to chancel, classroom to fellowship hall or corner to corner. Such movements are for a learning purpose in a new space — to *do something,* such as take a trust walk, make musical instruments, practice a skit, interview someone, center down in meditation. Attention to the order of the agenda, timing of it, varied pacing, movement, and so on, will help keep interest up. One measure of success will be if no child asks to be excused to go the bathroom!

6. *Be full-sense involving.* In IG lifestyle education, the whole person

is present, so let all the senses be utilized in learning. Folks have *ears* not just to receive prosaic utterances but also to enjoy lyrical poetry, music from a sitar, and birds chirping. Folks have *eyes* to see symbols of world religions, pantomimes of the Elisha stories, slide shows of an IG work camp, and reflections of one's self in the eyes of another. They have *fingers* to paint a Shadrach/Meshach/Abednego mural, to touch the simple things that St. Francis loved, to shake hands with a newest member, to massage the shoulders of a friend. They have *feet* with which to crush grapes or—on another occasion—to get dirty so Mary Magdalene can wash them. They have *vocal chords* to sing "Prepare Ye the Way of the Lord," to speak the lines of Ruth, to chant "OMMMMMMM." They have *noses* to smell their communion loaves baking or identify perfume—which people put on for a reason. And they have *taste buds* to enjoy the Seder Meal or "chicken on the ground" with a saddlebag preacher or Space Sticks with Captain Kirk. Such whole-person/full-sense involvements help realize the goal of a positive subjective impact on learners.

7. *Do review and preview ("R n P") regularly.* Every session needs to give a feel for the whole program, as discussed previously. That is done by recounting what went on in earlier sessions and describing what will be happening in future occasions. R n P establishes the overall theme and indicates session relationships. He helps with sequencing for both participants and planners/doers. If the R n P is done with symbols or visuals, that is all to the good. The review portion can be helped by using previous session artifacts.

8. *Have "R n R"—restating and reciting—in the sessions.* The R's in this formula can stand for a number of words: repeat, rehearse, remember, re-present, review, recreate, and more. R n R points to repeating the story/message/theme/lesson in a variety of ways, that it may be received. Participants can then exclaim: "I see . . . I know . . . I hear . . . I feel . . . I think . . . I agree with what we are trying to realize." The recitation side of this is akin to restating, but here the emphasis is on the participants giving back the story/message/theme/lesson to others by themselves reciting it, acting it out, singing it, painting it, or writing it up. If an artifact can be generated and taken by participants from the session, that piece will serve to facilitate R n R at home—and in the office!

9. *Ask "Where's the party?"* For the most part, programs should be enjoyable for each and all. (I will make a major point of this directly.) "Enjoying" in the perspective of process thought is more than acceptable. It is positively of God. I think God would value the monk's prayer in the accompanying cartoon.

"ONCE AGAIN, LORD, I COME TO YOU WITH THIS
CRAZY, OVERWHELMING DESIRE TO PARTY."

Figure 5. Cartoon on "En-joying."

(Used by permission of Ed Sullivan)

In our own culture "having fun" is a significant value—perhaps rightly
so. Allen Breck, professor of history at the University of Denver, put me
onto this in his lively teaching of *ancient* history. Regularly he would say,
"Isn't this fun?"[37] And it was! He made it so. So might we. Let me say
with a few *words* and illustrative examples what might be involved in
en-joyable IGRE. Consider *"fun."* It is fun for children to sing as loud as
they can, even yell in church! It is fun for older adults to dance in a big
circle with teenagers and children. It is fun to share childhood-home
floor plans with others. Consider enjoyment created by *surprises.* In the
All-Saints Church program there were lots of surprises, such as the day
worshipers learned about Daniel and two "lions" (Golden Retrievers
with black cardboard manes) came down the sanctuary aisle or the day
the sprinklers came on in the courtyard just as Elijah's enacted proph-

ecy of rain came true! Enjoyment occurs by using *imagination* as much as possible. Through the media of "pretend" IGRE participants can be Romans and Christians in 250 B.C. under the Emperor Decius' reign and play the simulation game "Persecution." With a simple headband and feather, participants are with Father Junipero Serro establishing the Franciscan missions in California. It is imaginatively enjoyable to be transported to the twenty-first century and consider old problems in the New World together. Enjoyment comes by *playfulness* too, such as making the Esther story into a melodrama at the Festival Night of Purim and getting out all the bells and whistles. Finally, let me say that en-joyment is frequently accompanied by *food*. Rabbi Zwerin says, "There is no Jewish celebration which is not accompanied by eating together."[38] IGRE pioneers, Sharee and Jack Rogers say regarding their interage church school, "We sometimes omitted one item or another, but we never forgot the food."[39] Food makes events special. There is something special about filling the platter at a family night supper and about napkins and sheet cake in the post-worship coffee and punch hour. These food-and-fellowship times bind people to one another in sound ways.

10. *Affirm people one-by-one.* Though there is hoopla suggested in much of the above, in IG programing there is need to keep a human face on it all. Persons as individuals should be encouraged to speak and act. In so doing they need to know that they are appreciated. Writing down people's buzz-session ideas, recording comments on cassettes, making a video for playback, and reprinting stories offered are ways to let participants know that their responses are registered, their presence valued. The message is simply, *"You are very important!"* Through the session, leaders can be rightly attentive to individual persons. At the time of registration for an IGRE workshop, for example, the nametag can be given with human touch and naming. James Michael Lee says that nonverbal communications such as touch, smiling, nodding, and so forth, all contribute to the substantive content part of lifestyle learning.[40] In teaching, in preaching, in the conduct of the liturgy, or in the simple act of serving refreshments, hundreds of personal, nonverbal signals are sent out. Let those signals convey "Attaboy... Yes M'am ... Right on . . . Keep it together . . . For Sure!"

11. *Factor in physical/material dimensions.* The whole *physical plant* of an institution and its surrounding environs are potential settings for IGRE events. They might be used to enhance a program, remembering, of course, to be sensitive to handicap accessibility. Planners must be realistic in program design to keep implementation costs within reasonable bounds. *Weather* is another factor not to be forgotten. Snow, thunderstorms, overly hot days, wind, and so on, can spoil a perfectly de-

signed session, unless alternative activities are planned. Part of the last notation includes counsel to remain flexible in the face of malfunctioning projectors, locked doors, disappearing supplies, and the unexpected things that make teaching such a challenge.

12. *Exercise quality control.* From beginning to end in curriculum design and implementation there needs to be double-checking to ascertain if the things being planned and done continue to work toward fulfillment of the overall program goals. A litmus test or quality control procedure is called for. The thing I recommend doing is mentally to place whatever is being considered for program inside a "Design Diamond," such as suggested by Figure 6.

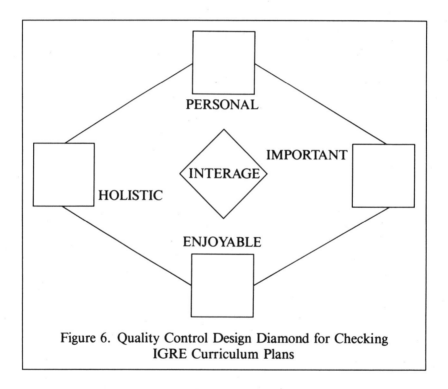

Figure 6. Quality Control Design Diamond for Checking
IGRE Curriculum Plans

In this baseball diamond for IGRE, the idea is to keep running the four bases around the pitcher's mound, asking questions about what is being developed: 1) Is it worth knowing? 2) Is it existentially relevant? 3) Is it whole-person involving? 4) Is it spunky? *and* . . . 5) Is it multiple-age inclusive?

The first-base question asks about content: Is this lesson of faithful religious substance? Is it *important?* The second-base question is concerned with affective meaning to persons: Is this activity going to have a positive subjective impact? Is it *personal?* The third inquires about lifestyle learning. Is what we're doing physical, full-sense related, behavioral in consequence? Is it holistic? Then there's the base which really is not related directly to any heretofore mentioned goal: Is this program going to be fun, well paced, lively? Is it *enjoyable?* Finally, there is the pitcher's-mound question which makes IGRE life and learning unique: Is what we are doing involving persons of varying ages in learning with/from each other? Is it *interage?* If these questions are asked of the curriculum both in large design *and* by individual sessions, and if affirmative answers are given, planners may be assured they are creating a quality IGRE curriculum.

13. *Allow angels to enter.* While the rule is to have a carefully constructed, precisely timed, well-controlled program, a rule-breaking rule is in order: Unexpected interruptions, spontaneous responses, comedies of error, serendipitous happenings, and surprise guests may be considered unexpected blessings. Unplanned incidents occurring within a well-conceived and orchestrated schedule can occur and work for the good. In the All-Saints experience, unscheduled time for children to pat the saddlebag preacher's horse was time well spent. The slow rising communion bread (because of a faulty oven) generated a great lesson in patience. Answering pertinent-impertinent questions of junior-high youth in front of their younger siblings proved to be a "best thing that happened" one Sunday. Hearing from an eighty-one-year-old matron who just "popped in to thank somebody for their thoughtful card," turned out to be the blessing of the day. A missioner on furlough, traveling through, telling stories of Africa was the presence of an enrapturer. And so on. Obviously I am at least talking about the *need for flexibility* in the curriculum, but it is fun to think maybe "something more" is going on. When some of these things happen, the best response may be just to speculate that "divine beings" have entered. Who knows? The beings may be facilitating a new intergenerational relationship— that between contemporaries and the saints who from their labors rest. We certainly sing about "heavenly hosts" enough. It is pleasing to think that occasionally generations of people in the twentieth century receive grace and edification from a venerable guardian angel! "Angels fly," someone said, "because they take themselves lightly." So might we.

CONCLUDING DO-IT POSTSCRIPT

All the preceding pages on curriculum are offered to help persons plan both comprehensive programs and individual sessions of IGRE. Once the curriculum is shaped there are many, many, many things which have to be done to complete it, that is, to *do it*. I have written down some eighty-plus verb-direct object statements related to program enactment. Such DO-ITS are the task assignments of successful operations. The DO-ITS include the following:

act roles	invite participants	rejoice in community
anticipate emergencies		r n p the sessions
arrange rugs	join in whenever	r n r stories
assign responsibilities		repeat litanies
	know people's names	respond to crises
be on time	know the rap	
build sets		schedule movements
buy refreshments	listen to one another	select music
	look to fill gaps	serve refreshments
check the weather	love one another	set timing
clean up		sing songs
commend people	make announcements	sit down in circles
coordinate efforts	make costumes	stay flexible
		stay with schedule
dance to the music	orient youth helpers	
deliver the sermon	order worship	take offering
display artifacts		train teachers
double check	paint pictures	tune instruments
	pass offering plates	
enjoy colleagues	phone requests	use maps & charts
evaluate program	photograph people	use pins
	plug in record player	
find prayers	practice songs	videotape action
find props	pray for help	
	preview films	write litanies
gather art supplies	print bulletin	write scripts
get crazy	print materials	write up learnings
get nametags	publicize the events	
go to bathroom		xerox materials
greet folks	quiz for responses	
		yell when necessary
hand out crayons	recruit helpers	
have fun	rehearse presentation	zero-in on goals
hold meetings	reimburse expenses	

This long list of DO-ITS is only partial. What is suggests is the immense amount of active doing needed in successful program implementation. The extent of the doing/enacting should not be forgotten in the design process, if only to temper enthusiasm with reality. Such doing, though, can be a fun/holistic/personal/important intergenerational learning event in itself. IGRE curriculum composers and enactors should consider that design and implementation are not so much a production-for as a pilgrimage-with others in which we all learn by this doing together.

Notes

1. So observes Charles Foster reporting on IGRE, in *Changing Patterns of Religious Education,* ed. Marvin J. Taylor (Nashville: Abingdon, 1984), p. 278. In this same volume, p. 232, Iris Cully suggests this pattern of parish level initiative will continue. With minor exceptions, I share their evaluation of the situation.
2. See Herbert M. Kliebard, "Reappraisal: The Tyler Rationale," in *Curriculum Theorizing: The Reconceptualists,* ed. William Pinar (Berkeley: McCutchan, 1975), p. 71.
3. D. Campbell Wyckoff, *Theory and Design of Christian Education Curriculum* (Philadelphia: Westminster, 1961), p. 79. His schema may also be fourfold, as he will omit number five and insert for the whole an "Organizing Principle." See p. 114.
4. Cooperative Curriculum Project, *The Church's Ministry: A Curriculum Plan* (St. Louis: Bethany, 1965), p. 4.
5. James Michael Lee, *Principles and Methods of Secondary Education* (New York: McGraw-Hill, 1963), p. 190 and ff.
6. Iris V. Cully, *Planning and Selecting Curriculum for Christian Education* (Valley Forge, Pa.: Judson, 1983), p. 95.
7. Howard P. Colson and Raymond M. Rigdon, *Understanding Your Church's Curriculum* (Nashville: Broadman, 1981), p. 50.
8. Donald E. Miller, *Story and Context; An Introduction to Christian Education* (Nashville: Abingdon, 1987), pp. 302-06.
9. James B. MacDonald, "Curriculum Theory," in *Curriculum Theorizing,* p. 7.
10. Mary Jo Osterman, "The Two Hundred Year Struggle for Protestant Religious Education Curriculum Theory," *Religious Education* 75:5 (October, 1980), p. 528 (emphasis added).
11. Paul Dressel, *College and University Curriculum* (Berkeley: McCuthan, 1971), p. 31.
12. Jack L. Seymour and Donald E. Miller, *Contemporary Approaches to Christian Education* (Nashville: Abingdon, 1984), p. 32. Further elaboration on the faith community model is provided by Charles Foster in a chapter in the Seymour/Miller book entitled, "The Faith Community as a Guiding Image for Christian Education," pp. 53-71. He says, "The life of the community is the content of Christian education," p. 64.
13. Miller, *Story and Context,* p. 214.
14. Ibid., pp. 31-32.
15. C. Ellis Nelson, *Where Faith Begins* (Richmond, N.C.: Knox, 1978), p. 10.
16. Paul B. Baltes and Hayne W. Reese, "The Life-Span Perspective in Developmental Psychology," in *Developmental Psychology: An Advanced Textbook,*

ed. Marc H. Bornstein and Michael E. Lamb (Hillsdale, N.J.: Erlbaum, 1984), p. 497.

17. Cully, *Planning and Selecting*, p. 70.
18. Wyckoff, *Theory and Design*, p. 79 (emphasis added).
19. An image of an *umbrella* under which are many programs, a select few of which are actually worked with, is used by Colson and Rigdon in *Understanding*, p. 41.
20. Cully, *Planning and Selecting*, p. 96.
21. John P. Gilbert, "Curriculum Planning in the Proactive Mode," *Religious Education* 71:5 (September-October, 1976), p. 542. Don Miller is similarly persuaded in contending that Christian education should be "education for global community," *Story and Context*, p. 88.
22. Mary Elizabeth Moore, *Continuity and Change: A New Model for Christian Religious Education* (Nashville: Abingdon, 1983), p. 17.
23. Ibid., p. 121.
24. Ibid., p. 145.
25. Jerome S. Bruner, *Toward a Theory of Instruction* (Cambridge: Belknap, 1978), pp. 11-12.
26. Please compare this figure with Dale's Cone of Experiences presented in chapter 7 of this volume. For two variations on the pyramid learning model, see R. Ted Nutting, *Family Cluster Programs: Resources for Intergenerational Bible Study* (Valley Forge, Pa.: Judson, 1977), p. 13, and Donald and Patricia Griggs, *Generations Learning Together: Learning Activities for Intergenerational Groups in the Church* (Livermore, Calif.: Griggs Educational Service, 1976), p. 18.
27. Robert Ornstein's idea of right and left hemispheres of the brain as applied in religious education is discussed insightfully in Charles Melchert's "What Is Education?" *Living Light* 14:3 (Fall, 1977), p. 349. See also James Michael Lee, *The Content of Religious Instruction: A Social Science Approach* (Birmingham: Ala.: Religious Education Press, 1985), pp. 496-499.
28. Dwayne Huebner (interviewed by William B. Kennedy), "From Theory to Practice: Curriculum," *Religious Education* 78:4 (July-August, 1982), p. 363.
29. See D. Campbell Wyckoff's "Foreword" in *Understanding Your Church's Curriculum*, p. 10, for a discussion on the importance of the "context of the culture."
30. Wyckoff, *Theory and Design*, p. 161. For an excellent guide into design for IGRE, see George E. Koehler, *Learning Together: A Guide for Intergenerational Education in the Church* (Nashville: Abingdon, 1976), pp. 49-72. Also consult the Grigg's *Generations Learning Together*, pp. 16-22.
31. Cully, *Planning and Selecting*, p. 56.
32. Nelson, *Where Faith Begins*, p. 204.
33. David W. Perry, ed., *Homegrown Christian Education: Planning and Programming for Christian Education in the Local Congregation* (New York: Seabury, 1978), p. 1. One contributor to this volume, Jane Hilyard, has a chapter on the creation of a specific IGRE program.
34. Charles R. Foster, "Intergenerational Religious Education," in *Changing Patterns*, p. 278.
35. Koehler, *Learning Together*, p. 58.
36. Douglas J. Tracy, "New Approaches to an Old Problem: Church School in Summer," *Church Teachers* (April, 1979), p. 36.

37. Allen Breck, class notes and conversation, University of Denver, 1972-73.
38. Rabbi Ray Zwerin, from a talk at Temple Sinai, Denver, Colorado, March 22, 1987.
39. Sharee and Jack Rogers, *The Family Together: Intergenerational Education in the Church School* (Los Angeles: Acton House, 1976), p. 18.
40. Lee, *Content,* pp. 378-474.

Chapter 11

Evaluating

Amid memorabilia for past IGRE programs at All Saints Church is a picture of a tall grade-school girl. She is shown role-playing Queen Esther. In my travels I called on "Queen Esther" at Ripon College in Wisconsin. We had dinner and a wonderful conversation during which time she spoke fondly of her "many church friends back home." A little to my surprise I found that the friends of Sally Sharer—that's her real name—included not just youth group peers but people my age, young children, grandparent types. She spoke of them by name. They were all folks she had gotten to know over the years in the church.

Sally's words were thrilling. It made me glad to think that here, anyway, with this one lovely person, the intergenerational dimensions of church life at All-Saints had done what we hoped might happen. A young person with a real sense of community existed!

When it comes to evaluating IGRE there are countless stories to be told such as Sally's. Their telling needs to be figured into the overall appraisal of things. Alongside such episodic and subjective testimony, I also want to place more objective measure and test findings—where they are available. We come, then, to *EVALUATING* IGRE.

Evaluation is seemingly something done most appropriately "at the end." In truth, it is continuous, from beginning to end in curriculum development and implementation. The point can be made graphically. See Figure 1.[1] I use this graphic to show visually, what Iris Cully says verbally, namely, that evaluation "is a continuous process."[2] We have been evaluating IGRE all along in this book, but in this chapter I want to look at IGRE *outcomes* as directly as possible.

Several things need to be considered in doing terminal evaluation. One consideration is the outcomes/results/consequences in terms of *individual participants*. Did anything positive happen to persons because they were involved? "Did the learners attain the objectives?"— that is the question, not "Did the instructor cover the material?" And

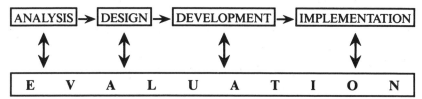

Figure 1. The Basic Instructional Systems Design Model
(Used by permission)

yet we are concerned about how things were done. So, a second arena for evaluation is that of *sessions or units* of programs. Educators want to know, "Did our efforts succeed or not?"—meaning, usually, "Was our attempt with teaching/preaching/gaming/and so on, completed-with-appreciation by those who participated?" Much "evaluation" which one reads about in the IGRE literature concerns this level of appraisal. There is a third level to consider. It has to do with *overall programs and the curriculum as a whole.* We are at a rather high level here. Unfortunately, we are not thereby at a high level of good evaluation. The record of curriculum writers, publishers, and denominational educators for testing and validating programs in the field of IGRE—or anything in religious education—is very limited. I remember well a conversation on this point with religion educationist Maria Harris. She indicated that the vast majority of curricula used in schools and churches for "moral education" had *never* been field tested.[3] In truth, there is not much done in the way of significant evaluation in the field of religious education. IGRE programs are no exception. This chapter may be considered a start to remedy our poverty. Finally, there is evaluation of *church/synagogue life and efforts generally.* This evaluative scene is even more barren. Religious leaders invariably talk a great game of "changing people's lives," but very little empirical verification of such change is ever done. Mostly there is assertion. In this book, considering as we do "lifestyle impact," I hope to indicate how testing for such change in individual and corporate life might be made.

In these pages, then, I am talking about individual, session, program, and faith community evaluation. It is very broad. What we shall do is move from 1) "soft" data indices in evaluation to 2) "harder" data findings and finally 3) consider evaluation of IGRE goal and objective outcomes.

"SOFT" DATA EVALUATING

With an eye only toward evaluation of programs, I reviewed the literature in the field of intergenerational life and learning. In general, people are positive about what they dreamed up and enacted. They are positive about it, I observe, because participants were affirmative about what occurred. Personal commendations to the writers convinced them that the programs had "succeeded" in their intended IGRE efforts. Below is a collection of evaluative statements from the literature. It is arranged according to the Six Basic Models of IGRE. The statements indicate favorable appraisals of what people did. More than that, they promise success to readers who might attempt similar programs.

Evaluation from Various IGRE Models

Speaking of the Family Grouping model of IGRE, reporters said: "We believe this intergenerational experience has *great* value for today's families." After comments like Terry's, age eight, "I had fun with my family at family education evenings," the evaluators say, "Everyone is saying the experiences were worth the time and effort and that they resulted in growth for themselves and as a family." . . . "Given the opportunity, it works." . . . "It was special."[4]

Speaking of the Weekly IGRE Class: "The results can be exciting and rewarding." . . . Adults "were able to develop personal relationships with a number of children who they grew to like and appreciate as people." . . . "We have discovered that in learning together we can have fun." . . . "It helped our church become more of a community."[5]

Speaking of the Workshop or Event: "The closeness of the members of the different age groups has been a boon to the *whole church* feeling." . . . "We felt that real Christian education did take place for all who participated." . . . "We became 'connected' as a church family that evening in a new way." . . . "When it was over . . . you could sense the awe and wonder." . . . "The response at the end of the evening was overwhelmingly positive."[6]

Speaking of the Worship model: "This [anointing service] event had a tremendous impact on the participating families." . . . "The response to the program (of baptism and eucharist preparation) was very positive." . . . An older adult said, "This is what worship is 'pozed to be—all of us together praising God." . . . "The norm for understanding Christian life is expressed in the celebration of the Eucharist . . . It is a celebration that unites all ages and provides us with a sense of community."[7]

Speaking of the Worship-Education model of IGRE: "We feel that the theme and beauty of multigenerational events did take root." . . . "The children (and the adults) have been quite intrigued." . . . "This summer was the first time my seven-year-old even *wanted* to come to church in three years. During this time she *insists* on coming. Hooray!" . . . "One church member has told me [concerning the worship-education-cele-bration program that it] gives him a sense of peace and understanding and excitement as he obtains in no other way."[8]

Speaking of the All-Church Camp or Weekend form of IGRE: "The lab proved . . . that generations can learn together . . . (and) . . . can create a caring Christian Community." . . . " 'This is the best thing the conference has going!' said a seventy-six-year-old grandmother. . . . Families and individual persons grew in their relationship to God and one another." . . . "The majority have rated each retreat in the very good-excellent range. . . . One of our senior citizens said that for him, the retreat is the high point of the church year." . . . "The results of the weekends have been a greater sense of community in the whole church." . . . "People can, in short, take home from camp lifestyles of faithfulness."[9]

So it is that the reporters of the various models of IGRE have "evaluated" their programs. These are all rather "soft" indices of effectiveness but, nevertheless, indices.

Evaluation by IGRE Leadership

In a more systematic effort at evaluation of programs, Franklin Dotts did a study of "Benefits, Results or Outcomes of Intergenerational Education" using survey findings from 529 United Methodist churches. Respondents self-described the following beneficial outcomes for their churches: 1) togetherness/fellowship/sharing (30%), 2) spiritual attitude/growth (14%), 3) increased understanding/knowledge/ study (21%), 4) communication between the ages (18%).[10] When asked about the *difficulties* encountered in planning and carrying out various IG learning events, Dotts reports, "Respondents in the random sample mentioned most often the following (in order): getting people involved, lack of teachers and leaders, difficulty of finding meeting times, irregular attendance."[11]

When I tried to recall the difficulties of IG programing according to the Worship-Education model at All Saints Church, I reviewed the write-up evaluations which were done over the years. A balancing of plus and minus aspects is discernible in the write-ups, to wit:

POSITIVE ASPECTS	NEGATIVE ASPECTS
General idea of an integrated church/church school	Unfamiliarity of the new model to most parishioners
Value in designing/doing our own curriculum	Long hours, grueling planning sessions
Excitement of creativity, props, characters, "machines"	Too much hype? Not enough attention paid to traditional?
Teenager and older adult involvements	How to involve teenagers and older members
Take-home materials to continue learnings	Question as to how well the home material was used

Evangelistic value of program to church	Difficulty in explaining the program to visitors
Coordination of music around a theme song	Getting song leader/piano player/ guitarist to help

The balancing of the above might suggest that program evaluators were evenly divided in their appraisal of the various programs. Such was not the case. As programs concluded, the All Saints Church leadership teams were annually enthusiastic about what was done. "Proof" for that can be inferred by the large number of leaders who came back to do two, three, and more years of programs.

After a decade of programing at All Saints, I called together twenty people who had been most involved in IG efforts over the years. I asked for their long-term evaluative comments. From what they said, three things came through clearly. The first was that the *programs were educative*. Especially they were educative for program doers themselves, but also, the evaluators insisted, for the membership generally. The second and freshest insight was that the *programs were integrative.* They integrated the various age people attending *and,* in the summer IG programs, they integrated all parts of the Sunday morning offering and the season. So that worship, education, music, prayers, and so on, hung together and all this fit with the church's life of camp, choir, discussion groups, and so on. Third, the evaluators said, the *programs were celebratory.* These folk recalled the programs as occasions when the church was especially en-joying being the church together. In reflecting on these three analyses, the interesting thing about them is that they echo the primary program goals which were envisioned during these years. (More on this below.)

Not all observers of the IG scene are so enthusiastic as those at All Saints. Religious educationist Charles Foster contends the purposes of IGRE "are essentially conservative, at times defensive or protective in nature." IGRE encourages, he says, "withdrawal from the world into 'oases' [albeit] for renewal and revitalization." What Foster finds most impressive is that "children and youth are recognized officially as making a necessary contribution to the nurture of their elders."[12]

Evaluation by IGRE Program Participants

It could be that IG program designers and enactors—who often are also reporters of the same—are too generous in their self-appraisals. One would like to know, of course, what the participants themselves conclude. In querying participants at All Saints we asked for and received their views through regular surveys. Here is what was concluded in one write-up:

The comments—to be candid—were glowing. The word "excellent" to describe the programs showed up on about every third questionnaire of the 74 completed. Eighteen parents and 56 non-parents recorded their comments—all anonymously. Other words frequently mentioned were "fantastic," "super," "very good," "novel," "terrific," "creative," "superb," and "how can you top this?"[13]

Respondents were also given opportunity to register negative criticism by saying where improvement could be made. Some criticisms of parts of the program were made but none were registered which indicated a pattern of general or recurring disapproval. One needs to exercise some caution at this point, though: Those who did not like what was happening may have not been present for the evaluation exercise.

One excellent way to get relevant feedback is suggested in the booklet, *To All Generations.* The author suggests that at program's end participants be asked to list the "ten most positive things," as well as "five negative things," that were happening in the intergenerational program. When those are collected, the evaluators then need to ask themselves how many of these "positive and negative things" are *related to the objectives* that were set for the learning experience.[14] This becomes almost a "trick" on the planners themselves, forcing assessment on how well they really did in attaining the goals set forth!

Even as evaluation needs to be done of total programs, so should it be done of individual sessions. In the family cluster programs, Ted Nutting says he asks participants for evaluation at the end of *each* session.[15] Howard Colson and Raymond Rigdon join that counsel, saying that "PMR"—*Post Meeting Reaction*—should be registered for proper assessment of educational efforts.[16] More or less, such evaluation is done by most IGRE enactors, as evidenced by the reported reactions to programs. So they should. Thus planners may get helpful feedback to improve their efforts. George Koehler says that the youngest persons in an IG event can input if the questions of evaluation are framed correctly. He says, most people can respond by saying, "What I enjoyed . . . What I learned . . . How I would change things."[17] I use Koehler's suggestion in an evaluation form (shown later in Table 7). The point for the moment, though, is that all persons should participate in the evaluation of IG program efforts.

"HARDER" DATA INDICES FOR EVALUATING

An empirical researcher, while not rejecting "soft" data indices such as unsolicited comments, findings from questionnaires, and programers' self-appraisals, would ask for something more substantive. Are there any evaluative efforts which are more objective?

There are some. They should be factored in. The first is the traditional one which church leaders have used most 'often to gauge "success or not," namely, one of the three B's—*Buildings, Budgets*, and *Bodies*. Consider *bodies* in educational programs. One may look at *attendance figures* for indication of how people are, in fact, responding to IG offerings and by so doing one will get an idea of whether it sold in Peoria.

Table 1 is a report on worship and church school attendance for ten summers of IG programing at All Saints Church. The main thing to notice on the table is that with the advent of proto-intergenerational programs, a major pick-up in Sunday service attendance occurred. In the year prior to the start of the first program, average attendance at worship was 164 persons per Sunday. In the first summer of IG programing, average attendance jumped per Sunday by thirty. Then it went up another fifty each of the next two summers to the range of 275 per Sunday where it stayed. For nine weeks of summer, total averaged attendance increased by almost a thousand attendances. To have had attendance increases of over a hundred persons per Sunday for the months of June and July can only be interpreted as a positive response to the IG offering of the church.

Attendance data on children's and youth participation, as shown in Table 1, follows a similar pattern. In Year Zero there was no church school and, so, zero attendance. Attendance during the first summer of programing was just below thirty per Sunday. By the second year it was approaching forty per week, and by the third summer it exceeded fifty per Sunday. There it stayed in the years following. These attendance figures are not high by comparison to the potential enrollment or by comparison with regular church school (September-May) year averages. It is just that they are so much better than no attendances and, for summertime, very good.

These figures are positive too in the sense that during the ten-year period under consideration the congregation experienced a total membership loss of 100, going from 1410 down to 1295. The number of children and youth registered in the church school for these years dropped 175, going from 721 to 542. Yet sanctuary attendance and church school attendance in the summer months stayed constant once the programs were in operation.

One positive note about summer programs, such as the one enacted at All Saints or just the usual vacation church/Bible school, is that these attract people. In a survey-study of local churches, researcher William McKinney discovered that vacation church school was *the* church pro-

TABLE 1

TEN YEAR SUMMARY OF ATTENDANCE DATA FOR WORSHIP SERVICES AND RELIGIOUS EDUCATION FOR THE SUMMERS AT ALL SAINTS CHURCH.

Year and Program	Adult Sanctuary Service Attendances					Children/Youth Attendance		
	June	July	Aug 1st Sun	9-Week Summer Totals	Average per Sunday	Number of Enrollees	Weeks in Program	Average per Sunday
Yr 0—None	666	615	200	1481	165	0	0	0
Yr 1—U Man	810	932*	—	1742	194	294	10	29
Yr 2—Time M	776	1112*	—	1888	210	377	10	38
Yr 3—Wiz OT	1292	1198*	—	2490	277	555	10	56
Yr 4—Saints	1385	861	265	2511	279	606	10	61
Yr 5—Ply USA	1137	1067	258	2462	274	462	9	51
Yr 6—Good NT	1121	1372*	—	2493	277	571	10	57
Yr 7—Holy E	1144	1324*	—	2468	274	561	10	56
Yr 8—Ethic'l	1212	1298*	—	2510	279	531	9	59
Yr 9—Music	1368*	964	—	2332	259	476	9	53
OVERALL AVERAGES				2322	258	493	9.6	51

*Indicates five Sundays in the month.

gram of fifteen possible programs with the highest correlation for numerical church growth.[18]

I have not seen attendance figures for other congregations who have tried IG programs. I suspect similar results, but not necessarily. One evaluator remarked about an IGRE class, "Although there was a slight drop in church attendance, perhaps by those who missed the usual format, evaluation for the most part was positive."[19] Such a "drop in church attendance" also may be because IG programs mandate fewer teachers and there is "The PTA Rule Reversed." The PTA Rule is "to get one parent at a PTA Meeting you need 1 and 1/2 children on the program." The reverse here may be that with fewer parent-teachers involved, it could decrease the number of children brought to participate. Doubtless too, some adults may bow out if they think they are going "to be asked to do childish things." Some adults really want nothing to do with children, we know, and are critical of the children's sermons, for example.[20]

Beside consideration of attendance data, one other way to make some objective evaluation of an intergenerational program is through "Assessment of Ripple Effect." Did the program seem to affect constructively other portions of the church/synagogue's life afterwards? Did people involved in one IG program shape other programs to be more age inclusive? In the Appendix case study of All Saints Church the "ripple effect" of IG programs is tracked: IGRE-involved members later developed intergenerational art shows, mother-daughter-friends banquets, and more.

In such manner, with such statistical and observable data, we infer "success" or "shortcomings" with IGRE in evaluation. With future enactments of IGRE, persons will rely on such yardsticks and others for assessment of effort.

DATA ON IGRE GOALS/OUTCOMES

In discussing outcomes I have managed so far not to talk about the outcomes which are really central, namely, the outcomes in terms of changed individual lives. It is time. As the writers on the Cooperative Curriculum Project put the matter: "The curriculum is designed for the learner. The curriculum is projected in the last analysis so that the learner may be aware of God and respond to him in faith and love."[21] The curriculum, in other words, is useless unless it comes alive in the learner.

So it is that we have spoken in this book about learning outcomes for *vision, purpose, goals, objectives,* even *performance behaviors.* We need to consider if, in fact, any of these have been realized—or, at least, how in projection we are to evaluate outcomes. Did expected developments for the participants actually occur? And how would we know or not?

Too many religious educators, if we can judge by the report record, are reluctant to engage in testing. "Tests smack too much of schooling," they say. Such a protestation may, in fact, have more to do with uncertainty about how to make valid assessment (or, worse, to do with general laziness). I know that in years of working in adult, children's, youth, confirmation, and intergenerational education, there are very few colleagues interested in inventorying learners to determine teaching outcomes. We seldom test for results, and when we do, we so poorly. Even in the examples and studies I am about to present, the evaluative efforts are not nearly as strong as ought to be. We are back with the problem mentioned earlier that most curriculum is never field tested, validated, or evaluated. James Michael Lee says, "A lack of evaluation . . . is ruining the cutting edge of educational innovation."[22] This is no less true with intergenerational efforts. In all my reading I have yet to come across a report (except my own) which tried to ascertain anything more about results other than whether what was offered was liked or not. We do very unscientific kinds of evaluation—and that usually of *programs* rather than of *individual* growth and learning.

People may avoid the question by saying, "Religious learnings cannot be measured," "faith education is too personal," too much "up to the Holy Spirit," "too subjective," and so on. We need to hear Robert Havighurst's words: "Religion does bear fruit in a person's life—that fruit can be seen, described, evaluated."[23] Especially I want us to consider Havighurst's assertion in terms of lifestyle outcomes, but his truth applies to other IGRE goal outcomes as well.

What is especially needed in religious education programs is testing with a pre-program assessment (or, what some call a "baseline inventory"), and then at the end of the teaching-learning period test with a post-program assessment (or, what is called a "terminal" or "summary inventory"). Along the way there might be what James Block calls "formative evaluations"[24] to help shape the learning environment for persons. All these are needed because far too little measurement of outcomes ever happens. Baseline inventories are needed to prevent instruction starting out too far behind or ahead of where learners really are. By ascertaining position, program planners can hook up with participants knowledge/feelings/behavior and build from there. The baseline inventory also provides a measure against which terminal inventory findings can be compared. Joining in this call is James Michael Lee. He urges use of quantification to provide "some measure of precision as to the degree and extent to which the desired learning outcomes are being achieved."[25] Thus religious educators may determine what learning gains—if any—transpired.

Verbal Content Outcomes

Early on in the programs at All Saints Church we began to make assessment of cognitive teaching/learning outcomes. We wanted to specify program outcomes with participants—or, at least, with our younger participants with whom we could exercise some testing controls. In the goals talk, we spoke often of "significant *and verified* learning." Getting the verification was then a program focus.

It may be that the most unique feature of the All Saints IG worship-education model and program was the attempt with pre- and post-program inventories to assess knowledge gains. Before each program began we specified what verbal content we wanted participants to know by program's end. For each discrete session within the nine or ten week format we identified learning objectives. Whenever possible those objectives were specified in behavioral or performance outcome terms. Results were to be demonstrable, for example: "At the end of the hour, in singing a memorized song, each student will be able to *name the nine fruits* of the Spirit."

What one hopes for in religious education is that people learn important things, about life in the faith, things of the Spirit, of moral consequence, concerning one's heritage, related to the scriptures, essential to ongoing practice, that are motivational, and so on. That is the hope. The next questions, though, are, "Did they?" and "How can we be sure?" On the whole and with a greater degree of objectivity than is yet available with affective and lifestyle learning, I can say, "Yes, there is good evidence that substantial cognitive learning gains were achieved in the All Saints programs." The evidence of this assertion will be found in Tables 2, 3, 4, and 5. These show the results of inventory tests administered in conjunction with four IGRE programs. (Please consult the accompanying tables.)

The first useful assessment instrument was administered during the Wizard of OT program, Year III. See Table 2. There we did a pre- and post-program inventory. The aim of these tests was to assess participants' "level of familiarity" with important but lesser-known personalities in the Old Testament. By the end of ten weeks, children recognized the names of Gideon, Elisha, Esther, and others whom they apparently had not known before. They usually could tell one thing about each character.

A similar pre- and post-program testing was done two years later in the Plymouth, U.S.A. program. See Table 3. In those inventories chil-

TABLE 2

"WIZARD OF OT" PROGRAM. COMPARISON OF PARTICIPANTS' PERCENTAGE RECOGNITION SCORES ON OLD TESTAMENT PERSONALITIES ALL SAINTS CHURCH, YEAR III.

Percentage of Participants Indicating Acquaintance

Grade:	K-1		2		3		4/5		6/7		Total Group	
Test:	Pre	Post	Pre	Post	Pre	Post	Pre	Post	Pre	Post	Pre	Post
Number:	(6)	(8)	(11)	(7)	(16)	(8)	(17)	(14)	(9)	(11)	(61)	(48)
Joshua	83%	75%	55%	100%	88%	100%	59%	100%	100%	100%	72%	95%
Gideon	0	63	9	100	13	100	35	100	11	73	16	88
Samson	33	75	9	86	31	100	0	100	44	91	20	93
Ruth	0	75	9	100	25	100	0	64	0	64	8	77
David/Jon'n	17	75	18	100	63	87	100	71	66	55	62	75
Elijah	0	50	0	71	0	63	12	38	0	55	3	52
Elisha	0	50	0	43	25	50	0	64	0	55	7	54
Esther	0	63	0	57	19	87	12	79	0	45	8	67
Shad/Mes/Abed	0	50	9	86	13	63	24	93	22	73	15	75
Daniel	17	63	0	100	68	100	100	100	88	100	61	94
Averages:												
Post-Test		64%		84%		85%		81%		71%		76.87%
Pre-Test	-15%		-11%		-35%		-34%		-33%		-27.04%	
IMPROVEMENTS	49%		73%		50%		47%		38%		49.83%	

TABLE 3
"PLYMOUTH U.S.A." PROGRAM. COMPARISON OF PARTICIPANTS' SCORES AND PERCENTAGE ON RECOGNITION OF HISTORICALLY IMPORTANT RELIGIOUS PERSONS ALL SAINTS CHURCH, YEAR V.

Children's Recognition Scores

	Pre-Test			Post-Test	
	Grades 1-8, Number: 62 TOTAL RECOGNITIONS			Grades1-8 Number: 62 TOTAL RECOGNITIONS	
	Raw Score	% Score		Raw Score	% Score
Hutchinson	40	65		34	55
Eliot	2	3		43	69
Edwards	2	3		30	48
Muhlenberg	4	6		23	37
Madison	24	39		43	69
Tubman	15	24		41	66
Lazarus	2	3		13	21
Carnegie	2	3		33	53
Scopes	6	10		35	56
King	38	61		57	95
Kirk/Spock	42	68		62	100
	177	25.9		414	60.8

IMPROVEMENTS IN
Raw Scores . . . . +237
% Difference . . . . +143%

dren were queried on name recognition of persons important in the religious history of the United States. Participants seemed to have heard of James Madison and Martin Luther King as the program began. By the end of the ten weeks they were also familiar with Johns Eliot, Edwards, and Scopes. An improvement in recognition scores of 143 percent is shown on the table.

A different and exciting test was created for the Good News Times program. In this all-grades course, we wanted "to present Jesus as a loving, interesting, and real person." To know if we had any success in achieving the learning goal we asked children at the beginning of the program to "say what kind of person Jesus was." Usually they could provide about three predicate nominatives or adjectives. When the same question was asked at the end the program, four such words per child on the average could be called forth. See Table 4. Not only were

TABLE 4
"GOOD NEW TIMES" PROGRAM. LANGUAGE DESCRIPTORS FOR "JESUS" USED BY PARTICIPANTS IN PRE- AND POST-PROGRAM INVENTORIES, ALL SAINTS CHURCH, YEAR VI.

	Inventories	
	Pre-Program	Post-Program
	May 29	July 21
Number of Children	66	50
Grades of Children	1 thru 9	1 thru 9
TOTAL WORDS REGISTERED BY ALL	204	212
Average Number Words Per Child	3.09	4.25
Most used words . . . . and Frequencies		
"JESUS WAS . . ."		
Love, loving, lover	28	29
Helpful, helping, helper	29	28
Kind	29	24
Nice	18	24
Good	16	6
Caring	4	10
Teacher	10	6
Healer	10	11
Understanding	6	4
Thoughtful	6	1
Forgiving	3	7
Friendly	2	7
Gentle	4	6
Unique Words:	Gutsy, Believer, Son of God, Holy, King, Sinless, Spirit, Intelligent	Storyteller (4), Trusting (4), Calm, Playful, Jewish, Liked Children, Bright, "Far Out"
Variety of Descriptors Used	41	49

more words given by more children but the variety of words was greater, more earthy/less transcendent and along the lines by which the program leaders tried to portray Jesus.

For the year of the Holy Earth Log program we did pre- and post-program inventories too. These were aimed at assessing what was known about religions of the world. Not only were children in grades one through eight asked if they recognized the *name* of the world religion but also if they could say in what *country* that religion might be found and what some of the *characteristics* of that religion were. The more the children recalled out loud, the higher were the scores regis-

TABLE 5

"HOLY EARTH LOG" PROGRAM. COMPARISON OF PRE- AND POST-PROGRAM INVENTORY SCORES OF PARTICIPANTS ON RECOGNITION* OF WORLD RELIGIONS ALL SAINTS CHURCH, YEAR VII.

	Pre-Test May 29 N:62	Post-Test July 30 N:61+1#	TOTAL SCORES Children Grades 1-8 DIFFERENCES Raw Score	Percentage
Tribal	56	79	+ 23	+ 41%
Hindu	27	91	+ 64	+238%
Jewish	124	126	+ 2	+ 1%
Confucian	22	85	+ 63	+286%
Orthodox	49	82	+ 33	+ 67%
Shinto	22	84	+ 62	+282%
Islam	17	57	+ 40	+229%
Catholic	107	108	+ 1	+ 1%
Buddhist	74	72	− 2	− 2%
Protestant	79	110	+ 31	+ 39%
TOTALS	577	894	+317	+ 55%

*"Recognition" includes scores for (1) having heard of the religion before, (2) being able to name a country where the religion is practiced, and (3) tell of a feature of that religion. Scores on all three were totaled to get a single composite score for each category.

#To simplify comparisons, one averaged score from the 61 persons who actually took the test was added to the totals in this column.

tered. Children in every grade and with every religion but one (Buddhism) showed increases in scores. Overall, a better than 50 percent familiarity gain was recorded. See Table 5. Especially were Hinduism, Confucianism, Shintoism, and Islam better known.

The main thing the inventories do is verify that cognitive learnings took place. Most importantly, we believed, it was *worthwhile knowledge:* Christians should be familiar with biblical characters who are male and female "pioneers and perfecters of the faith." Peter Muhlenberg and Harriet Tubman are important people in understanding of who we are as religious citizens in the United States. Becoming articulate about "Jesus" is no mean concern. Being cognizant of other world religions is needed for making one's way into the future. And so on. We know these cognitive transmittals occurred because there was evaluation which evidenced it.

Looking back it would have been better if testings had included *older* participants in the programs as well. We have to infer cognitive gains for adults, as signaled for example by the purchase of eighty of Huston Smith's book, *Religions of the World,* during the Holy Earth Log program.

Affective Outcomes

"A Positive Subjective Impact" on learners is one of the major goals spoken of throughout these pages for intergenerational life and learning. It is much harder to evaluate this phenomenon, but it can be done. One of the ways to do so is by attributional inquiries. You simply ask people how they feel they may be changing or think they have changed in attitudes, feeling, values, sensitivity, spirit, and so on, on the basis of what has been offered in the way of an event, program, or class.

Unhappily, there are not many studies keyed to evaluate IG *religious* education effects on the affections. Happily, though, there are some studies from the world of *secular* (often school-related) intergenerational education from which we can make importance inference. Working with a multi-age group of children, combined in one classroom setting, and a control group of multi-age children in a traditionally graded arrangement, and testing them all with a Piers-Harris self-concept scale, Dennis Milburn found no differences in basic skill achievement between the children, but discovered that *children in the multi-age structure were decidedly more positive in their attitude toward school.*[26] For the children involved in cross-age education there is positive reverberation in their attitude toward the institution. Reporting on other studies, Kaye Parnell found that for older people, too, there is good internal consequence flowing from their cross-age association with younger people. Reviewing the literature on intergenerational programs, Parnell found several sources which reported that, because of interaction between young people and older people in nursing homes, "the self esteem of the elderly was significantly improved." One nurse observed that mixing with younger people "gave life when some [elderly] had almost given up the spirit." When older adults went into schools to be with young people, those elders gave a 98 percent positive response regarding their experience. The positive effects of IG go in the other direction too. Parnell reports a study which found positive change in young people's perception of the elderly after they had visited retirement/nursing homes.[27] Parnell's report is supplemented by other secular studies done at the Center for Generations Together at the University of Pittsburgh. Reported data reveals that both children and youth attribute improvements in self-esteem to various IG programs in public schools. It was found that seniors discovered "the special joy of working with children, and, in some cases, (the work) increased their ability to cope with trauma.[28]

These reports all suggest positive subjective impact on persons by and through the several secular IG programs. Though basically attributional studies themselves, they support the more impressionistic IGRE reports which also assert that good things were happening at the affective level with people. In those IGRE studies, participants reported they *enjoyed* their IG time together, *felt better* about the church/synagogue, *liked* getting to know multi-age others, *appreciated* the growing *sense* of community, etc.

What people say voluntarily is not unimportant. Attributional claims may be considered in evaluation. The thought here is that people do stay in touch with their feelings and, if asked in the right way, they will share what is going on inside. We need to do more systematic asking. Asking questions of people and doing interviews of them are, according to theorists Virginia Satir and William Perry, two of the keys to personal growth.[29]

In lieu of tightly controlled studies, what we must then point to are things which give inferential evidence of positive subjective impact. Three follow:

1. In the affective domain, we believe that people grow through enjoyable and rewarding experiences. We are "built up internally" by a willing involvement with people we trust, doing something which feels special, getting excited, having a good time, opening ourselves to the world/others/God. The royal road to emotional advancement is through imagination, the senses, involvement, extension, other people—the very things which were described as essential ingredients of a quality IG curriculum. So if someone says, "I really enjoyed that!" (as many do regarding IGRE), it may be interpreted as an indication of positive subjective impact.

2. What educators hope happens is that IG congregational offerings hook-up with the existential issues of people's lives. We are open for growth in areas where we are also vulnerable. Preachers know this. They try to sermonize close to real concerns of individuals. Leaders do this in IGRE by tying the program theme and content concerns in with personal development concerns, such as the ever-important issue: "What does it mean to be a 'boy' or 'girl' or 'man' or 'woman' in a family? among friends? at school? in my work?" In looking at the family grouping model of IGRE, for example, one sees that such existential foci are in the curriculum regularly.

3. Healthy subjective influence and growth may be seen over time. One benefit of being a part of a faith community for over a decade is the chance to see people mature, to observe youngsters become young adults who seem "to have their heads screwed on right" (that is, "have their interior life in some semblance of order"). Like "Queen Esther," whom I told about in the beginning of this chapter, they seem to have

been joyfully, existentially, and positively influenced in their personal growth. One is probably not wrong to suggest that some of that good inner growth has come from the individual's involvement with others in faith community life and learning.

Lifestyle Outcomes

"Lifestyle" includes both cognitive and affective dimensions. Insofar as it does, we have been considering evaluation of "lifestyle" outcomes already. Lifestyle, though, is more than just what one thinks or what one feels. It moves over into *what one does with one's body.* It is the overall pattern of one's life and activities. It is all-inclusive, holistic, having to do with what James Michael Lee calls *"homo integer."*

Being such a totality and having to do with how a person organizes his or her self-system and lives out life, lifestyle outcomes also resist facile evaluative analysis. How would educators know if influence on a person's lifestyle has been made through IGRE? Again, we are almost forced to go to some of the earlier "praise of programs" evaluative statements where people reported things like, "Everyone is saying that the experiences were worth the time and effort and that they resulted in growth for themselves and as a family."[30] With such statements, though, the reader is again thrown against the problem of "attribution" versus "behavior" in social-scientific evaluation. People may claim (that is, "attribute") growth for themselves or for others. They may say they have changed or are become more loving *but,* in fact, has such really happened in behavior which can be seen and verified?

It would be wonderful if some IGRE-related longitudinal studies could be to consulted on lifestyle outcomes. Alas, we can only be episodic: For example, I can point to people involved with IG programs at All Saints Church who indicate over time and by their behavior that they have become more whole. I am thinking of children who participated in the IG programs . . . grew up . . . and became "the youth" in the church. Many were/are still involved in the church's life. The "Steve" and "Nancy," lead singers of the Music Machine program in Year IX, eight years previous to that had been barefoot nomads in the Year I Universe Man program. Eight years later, these two persons were observed by this writer taking part in an intergenerational production of "Godspell." How much of their holistic behavior can be credited to IGRE programs is, of course, an open question. One likes to believe, though, that part of "Steve" and "Nancy's" faith lifestyle was formed in those IGRE programs.

What religious educators always hope for is that their church/synagogue efforts make an impact "at home." Sometimes we can believe it happens. A parent reported that, following the Zaccheus-in-the-Tree

Sunday at All Saints—which program had emphasized "loving the un-likable"—a family council was held. It concluded with a visit by all to an "unlikable" older neighbor, someone whom everyone in their family had previously avoided. That is lifestyle affect.

Church leaders—especially clergy—talk periodically of how growth and change are taking place in their congregation. They *say* it is occur-ring, but seldom is much evidence provided. In this regard churches are akin to institutions of higher learning which regularly claim influence on student values but almost never check to see if/what/how/where change, if any, has occurred.[31]

In recent years some researchers have moved to redress this lack of verification. Jackson Carroll and colleagues at Hartford Seminary devel-oped an instrument which enables congregations to evaluate them-selves. The researchers have a "Parish Profile Inventory" which has been field tested with several hundred churches. The instrument is especially valuable for use by pastoral search committees wanting a closer look at their congregation. The survey queries members in such a way as to help church leaders understand "where the congregation is" on a variety of topics, such as worship needs, mission orientation, organizational characteristics, personal beliefs, style of ministry pre-ferred, and so on.[32] Parts of this instrument could be adapted for fore- and aft-evaluation of intergenerational programing.

Similarly, Jim Davidson and Al Monk at Purdue University with Lincoln Johnson at the University of Notre Dame have been working together on an "Expressions of Faith" project, funded by the Lilly Foundation. They have developed an assessment instrument which taps congregational views on mission and purpose. Sections 2 through 9 of the instrument's thirty-seven sections identify individual "religious be-haviors" such as worship attendance, Bible reading, private prayer, reli-gious education participation, retreat attendance, involvement in church leadership, doing social outreach, and financial giving.[33] Mean-while, Kenneth Pargament and colleagues at Bowling Green State Uni-versity developed a "Congregational Development Program Question-naire" (CDPQ). They have field tested it with churches in the Mid-west. What the instrument is especially designed to do is tap "congregational climate." They now speak of "Congregation Climate Scales" which, among other things, measure "religiosity" on five items: 1) religious service attendance, 2) participation in social activities, 3) number of hours spent in the church/synagogue, 4) number of activities the mem-ber is involved in, and 5) number of members known by first name.[34] Yet another assessment instrument for prospective use has come from Catholic sources. Advertised as "a pastoral tool for conversion and spiritual growth based on Christian teaching, sound theology, empirical research, and proven pastoral practice," *The Catholic Faith Inventory* has been created to assist parishes in getting a "picture" of spirituality in terms of nine categories. The 108-item questionnaire provides congregational and personal profiles helpful to both church leaders and individual members.[35]

These several instruments could be of notable assistance in assessing faith lifestyle.

A pastor doing some holistic evaluation of/for *individual* members (rather than of a congregation compositely) is Alfred Krass in Philadelphia. Using the biblical text of Colossians 1:9-14, Krass worked up a fifteen-item individual assessment instrument. He asks parishioners to complete the form and then come in and talk about it with him. On a seven-point scoring scale, members respond to statements, such as, "I believe I have grown as a Christian in the past several years" or "The Christian education I've had and my own study of the Bible have made it an open book for me." Krass writes, "I decided that since I had been called by this congregation to 'exercise pastoral leadership,' I had a right—like a medical doctor in his field—to make it known I would like to assist every member in having an 'annual spiritual check-up.' "[36] This form or a revised version could be used to assess how/where/whether individuals, and, in turn, the congregation are growing in faith.

Though leaders in faith communities have always had some idea as to which members were "babes in the faith" and which were "the saints—real and phony"—the specification of religious lifestyle for evaluative purpose is still the turning of new ground. Still, if we are to be informed on where we or others may be in faith pilgrimage, then some guiding evaluative instruments are needed. I offer the questionnaire shown in Table 6 as a start on a holistic lifestyle evaluation piece. This document is primarily a byproduct of a behaviorally based confirmation education curriculum which I have been developing in recent years. In that education effort, confirmands are asked "to *do* what Christians do" as much as *"know* and *feel* what Christians know and feel."* Emphasis is on trying to "act our way into new ways of thinking."

There are, of course, many dimensions to religious lifestyle. One, just one, of these is *the ability to talk religious talk.* Attentiveness to or simply an osmotic assumption of "the language of faith" is part of living in any tradition. Learnings which occur from preaching, Bible-lesson giving, mealtime invocations, reading denominational journals, and so forth give familiarity and facility with the sacred words of the community. The faith-words are used over and over until they begin to make some connection with and in people's behavior. At All Saints Church we became especially sensitive to this in the IG program "Saints 'n' Seasons" (Year IV). In dealing with historic people and liturgical topics, the

TABLE 6

SELF-SURVEY ON HOLISTIC FAITH LIFESTYLE PILGRIMAGE

The "items" listed below on the left side of the page are some common practices of the faith. On a scale of 1 to 5 (five being the highest), how would you rate yourself on each? For each item, you may indicate in column two the direction you feel you are going with that item. In the third column, please check 3 or so faith lifestyle items on which you like to work in the next six months. You are welcome to comment on any item with your suggestions or ideas.

Faith Lifestyle Item	Self-Appraisal (Scale 1-5)	Represents + increase 0 sameness − decrease	Areas in which I'd like to grow	Additional Comments and Suggestions
Sunday/Sabbath Observance				
High Holy-day Observance				
$upport of Institution				
Serving/Working Here				
Bible Reading				
Prayer/Meditation				
Family Devotions				
Growing in Knowledge				
Music/Art Enrichment				
Faith Witnessing				
Community Service				
Social Action				
Helping Others				
Ethical Conduct				
Forgiving				
Accepting Forgiveness				
Rejoicing				
Showing Love				
Giving Thanks				
Being at Peace				
Other				

In my overall personal faith pilgrimage generally, I feel that _____ I am advancing _____ am about the same place _____ am slipping.

_____ I would like to talk with someone about this pilgrimage.

Name _____ (optional) Date _____ Age _____
Sex _____ Member since _____ Number in Household _____

leadership suddenly realized how peculiar is the language used inside the Christian community. To talk of saints, the liturgical calendar, paraments, Lent, abbots, martyrdom, translating the canon, and one-hundred-and-one other "cultic/mystery religion" things is no ordinary talk. Faith enculturation happens in great part by putting the sacred words through the ears, on the tongues, and *in* the lives of the people. Assessing how well people talk religious talk is part of the faith lifestyle evaluation. Do the words in the Table 6 self-survey, for example, communicate? Could you use each word in a sentence? How about in life? So it is that believing and behaving are joined.

Intergenerational Outcomes (Goal 1)

In an ideal controlled experiment, it would be interesting to compare two faith communities' "intergenerational development" in a longitudinal study. To be controlled, one institution would embark upon a program of intergenerational life and learning, and the other would simply go about its life in the traditional way. Over time would there be a qualitative difference in both "intergenerational development" and in "religious lifestyle"? Unfortunately there is no such study. For the present, evaluative measure of IG outcomes will come from studies that are more limited and projective.

In this last section the focus is on assessing outcomes of intergenerational relationship. As noted in the earlier sections of this chapter, we have episodic and impressionistic testimony which says that good interage action and affirmation are happening because of IG programs. By way of illustration of how/why this might be so, let me recount an incident—and expand on it—from the All Saints Church experience. In the Music Machine/Fruits of the Spirit program on "JOY SUNDAY," the IGRE of the day was for older and younger participants to jointly compose a message of joy and put it in a helium balloon. Hundreds of balloon messages were sent up. On Friday next, I received a letter for "The Children and Adults of All Saints Church." It was postmarked Hinton, Oklahoma:

Dear Ones,
On Monday morning my husband saw some balloons in a wheat field where he was working. He got off the motorgrader and found messages from:
DOROTHY SMITH and PAUL THOMAS LEWIS.
We were excited to find your balloons and can imagine the thrill all of you had when you sent God's word flying off to everywhere.
God be with you in your work.
(signed) Irbie and Ellen Findlay
P.S. We are about 60 miles west of Oklahoma City, if you want to find Hinton on a map.

I received the letter on a Friday. It was a treat the next Sunday in worship to tell Dorothy (several years retired) and Paul (age eight) that their mutually penned balloon-lift "Message of Joy" sent up the previous Sunday had traveled over 500 air miles to reach the Findlays! Dorothy and Paul were also pleased about the outcome of their collaborative intergenerational conversation and action.

Similar anecdotes of IG relationships could be told hundreds of times by persons doing IGRE. By this one I only want to suggest that some very good things can be observed to happen when a church/synagogue sets out to enable its members to interact across the generations. The history of All Saints involvement in IGRE as told in the Appendix is but one example. In it I recount how the first programs integrated children in grades one through six into a single learning cohort. According to the "Definition of Terms" offered in chapter 2, the intergrade grouping was "intergenerational" even then. Next, we began to bring teenagers into the learning environment. Finally large numbers of parents became active participants in the program. Starting off the Sunday A.M. activities in the sanctuary gave us opportunity to increase the sharing of experiences with nonparent others. In the program of subsequent years, features were structurally designed to bring young and old into more occasions of interactive sharing. Meanwhile, the adult leaders who received IGRE experience and training went on to influence other arenas of the church's life toward greater intergenerational sensitivity.[37]

Some of the "devices" which succeeded in bringing the generations together in the All Saints program included: letters to parents for family activities, cryptograms to be decoded intergenerationally, composing of a newspaper, sharing "Gospels According to My Recollection," going to the Shrine Circus with nonfamily others, delivering flowers to rest homes and children's homes, the provision of backs to be rubbed, and on and on. In myraid ways at All Saints there was work and success improving the quantity and quality of multi-age relationships. The "A.S. Barnum Ethical Show on Earth" program is both illustrative and exemplary for quality IG relations. It had four memorable IGRE features. *One* was the "Intergenerational Marching Band (and Kazoo Society)" which brought people of age seventy to seven into a fun, worthwhile, contributive musical effort. The *second* was the "Talking with Neighbors Time" built into the sanctuary for interage exchange on a mutually interesting topic. The *third* was the relationship of teenagers in significant numbers with grade-school-age children, working on questions of moral choice. *Fourth,* the relationship between teenagers and adult planners was especially good.

There was something about this that felt like "quality intergenerational relationships" (Goal 1) and could be evaluated as such.

In questionnaires submitted to adults for completion, we asked what they thought about intergenerational activities generally and "children in worship," in particular. The overwhelming majority of respondents spoke favorably of the idea and the practice they knew. We asked them, further, to provide illustration of IG interaction from their involvement in the program. Some said they could not recall anything. That was possible. They may not have had any, as involvement is not—and should not be—forced on people. Happily, though, others recalled things and remembered them on paper. In the evaluation of the Music Machine/Fruits of the Spirit program, for example, adults mentioned such things as the carnations given to all men by the children on Father's Day. There was mention of the just-described balloon lift message-writing and sending. A few recalled the matching-the-number-with-the-seed-packet IG garden planting project. Others recalled dancing the Havah Nagila or just talking with different-age others in the coffee/ punch hour.

During the Good News Time program, one mother wrote that "On Tuesday, following John the Baptist's 'appearance' last Sunday, my son wanted to know if 'that guy really ate locusts.' We got into a good discussion of 'olden times' and ended up calling the grandparents in Minneapolis to finish the discussion."[38]

With the group of IG educators at All Saints, whom I called together for a ten-year evaluation, there was a strong sense among these people that *the church had indeed become more of a community with wholeness.* Several felt the IG programs over the years had "shot the magic bullet" which made us one across the ages.

Again, these stories are simply illustrative of what appear to be good outcomes for IG life from IG programing. What we need, of course, are substantive studies measuring the effect IGRE would have on a people over time. Would studies show that IGRE "acquaints" more people? That IGRE creates a sense of connectedness? Generates significant cross-age activities beyond planned programs? Moves the church to become more of an "extended family"? Would/could evaluation show that IGRE helps people overcome feelings of isolation and insulation? Might we know if it infuses the world with love, more so than we experience now? And so on?

A simple way to test part of the above can be devised and administered. Please consult Table 7 for a sample "Intergenerational Congregational Connectedness Questionnaire." This questionnaire might be administered in a faith community semiannually to find out just how extensive—if extensive at all—are the interrelations in a congregation. This could be a total population, select or random sample survey, depending on circumstance. Please see Table 7.

TABLE 7

INTERGENERATIONAL CONNECTEDNESS QUESTIONNAIRE

Our church/synagogue is engaged in ongoing efforts to "edify" (build up) both our faith-community-as-a-whole and each individual member of it. We do so in many ways, including programs which involve persons of several ages together. We want to know how we're doing. Please help us and yourself by completing this questionnaire on congregational connectedness.

In what intergenerational activities of the congregation have you been most involved during the last six months?

_____ _____

                              Please say:
WHAT I LIKED BEST   _____ _____
WHAT I LEARNED   _____ _____
WHAT I WOULD CHANGE   _____ _____

If you are acquainted with persons in our faith community of various ages, please indicate by name those you know best.

Pre-Schooler?   _____ _____ _____
Grade-School?   _____ _____ _____
Teen-Age?   _____ _____ _____
Young Adult?   _____ _____ _____
Early Mid-Age?   _____ _____ _____
40-50's?   _____ _____ _____
Active Retired?   _____ _____ _____
Most Elderly?   _____ _____ _____

Would you say the *"number* of different age acquaintances" for you is greater than _____ about the same as _____ or less than _____ it was six months ago?

Would you say the *"level* or frequency of relationship" with multi-age others is greater than _____ about the same as _____ or less than _____ it was six months ago?

If you remember a personal experience of an intergenerational engagement from the last six months, please share it.

On the basis of such a survey, among other things, it would be possible to do a *congregational sociogram,* showing the connections between and among families and individuals, identifying "isolates," "dyads," and so on, so that a graphic on the faith community could be drawn. Subsequent testing might suggest if the number of cross-age associations had increased because of IG programs. At a minimum, the administration of such a questionnaire would make people *think* about things intergenerational. While serving a year in a church in New Jersey as interim minister, I administered just such a IG connectedness questionnaire. It was done in October and the following May. In between those months, there was very little new introduced as IG programs. The retesting in May, however, indicated considerably improved IG relations. People simply could write more names for others in more age categories. They could and did record more personal IG experiences in church and elsewhere. I attribute the gains primarily to "a heightened awareness of the concept of and need for IGRE aroused by the first questionnaire."[39]

(For social-scientific validity, there should be that "control" congregation not "treated" with the IG variable. My hypothesis is that the congregation undergoing IG programming and testing would develop a sociogram with much stronger lines of connectedness and, likely, would have a stronger sense of being a congregational extended family.)

Concluding Evaluation

Obviously there is much work to be done to test and evaluate what happens in intergenerational life and learning programs and in religious "building up" efforts generally. We have seen some of the evaluation which has been done and is going on now. Much of it is highly subjective, impressionistic, episodic, and/or anecdotal—which is all right for a beginning. It is illustrative of things good and whole which seem to be happening. Some of the evaluative efforts are more rigorous, showing harder evidence of positive things happening through various educational programs. The years to come will likely bring with them more and better assessment of IGRE, generally, and the Total Parish IGRE Paradigm. That will be good for what is a good thing already—so people seem to say.

Notes

1. Marc J. Rosenberg, "The ABC's of ISD" (*Instructional Systems Design), *Training and Development Journal* (September, 1982), p. 45.
2. Iris Cully, *Planning and Selecting Curriculum for Christian Education* (Valley Forge, Pa.: Judson, 1983), p. 71.
3. Personal conversation with Maria Harris, then Professor of Christian Education, Andover-Newton Theological Seminary, at the Annual Meeting of the Association of Professors and Researchers in Religious Education, Toronto, Canada, November, 1979. James Michael Lee says much the same thing about religion textbooks and other curriculum materials used in religious schools, Sunday schools, and CCD programs. Most have not been field tested or evaluated. So Lee calls for "research-based testing, rewriting, and retesting"—which may take five to seven years—before any religion textbook is issued. See James Michael Lee, "Blueprint for Action," in *The Religious Education We Need: Toward the Renewal of Christian Education,* ed. James Michael Lee, (Birmingham, Ala.: Religious Education Press, 1977), p. 129.
4. Mel Williams and Mary Ann Brittain, *Christian Education in Family Clusters: 38 Sessions for the Church Year* (Valley Forge, Pa.: Judson, 1982), p.

72; Jeannette Benson and Jack L. Hilyard, *Becoming Family* (Winona, Minn.: St. Mary's College Press, 1978), p. 28; Joseph and Mercedes Iannone, "Family Learning Teams Approach to Total Parish Education," *Pace II* (September, 1980), p.5; Susan S. Bingham, "A Family Cluster Experience," *Baptist Leader* (February, 1977), p. 15.

5. David and Shirley Chaney, "I. G. Models for Summer," *The Church Leader* (July, 1976), p. 37; Jeffry D. Jones, "Adults and Kids in Church School Together," *Baptist Leader* (January, 1976), p. 7; Robert P. Shire, "Last September Our Sunday School Died," *New Forms Exchange* (1978), p. 3; Carolyn Engelhardt, "Church School for All Ages," *Spectrum* 46:4 (July-August, 1970), p.6.

6. Mary Heath, "An Intergenerational Program," *New Forms Exchange* (December, 1978), p. 2; Nancy E. Schroeder, "A Summer Intergenerational Program," *The Church School* (August, 1974), p. 52; Patricia Robbennolt, "Teddy Bear Night," *The Family Connection* (1983, mimeographed); Shirley Coll, "A Puppet Pageant for Christmas Eve," *The Family Connection* (1983, mimeographed), p. 2; Arlene Marks, "Family Dinner Theater," *The Family Connection* (1983, mimeographed), p. 2.

7. Joseph A. Iannone, "Family Learning Teams, Part 3," *Religion Teacher's Journal* (April, 1980), p. 9; Jane S. Carter, "Christian Initiation," *Aware* 8:5, p. 3; Personal note made following an intergenerational cross-country ski weekend worship service, February, 1985; John H. Westerhoff III, *Bringing Up Children in the Christian Faith* (Minneapolis: Winston, 1980), p. 43.

8. Bob Stowe, "All-Age Church Programming," *New Forms Exchange,* (December, 1978), p. 13; Laurie and Hank Lauridsen, personal letter regarding the All Saints Church IG program on world religions, 1978; Undated note from a parent in my personal files, re. 1981; William Beaven Abernethy, *A New Look for Sunday Morning* (Nashville: Abingdon, 1975), pp. 172-3.

9. Bonnie Clemow, "IG Lab School," *The Church School* (March, 1976), p. 41; Katharine Reeves Knudson, "An Intergenerational Camp," *Intergenerational Learning Experiences,* ed. Ruth McDowell (Nashville: Graded Press, 1980), p. 44; Gary Hackenberg, "Annual Congregational Retreats," *New Forms Exchange* (1978), p. 3; Herb Yeager, "All-Church Winter Weekend," *The Family Connection* (1983), p. 2; Charles and Carol McCullough, "The Lifestyles Theme," *Pilgrim Call* 15:1 (February, 1987), p. 4

10. M. Franklin Dotts, "Intergenerational Education: A Summary of Research," A Report of the Project Exploring and Developing Intergenerational Education (EDIE), Board of Discipleship, The United Methodist Church (September, 1979), p. 14.

11. Dotts, "A Summary of Research," p. 14.

12. Charles R. Foster, "Intergenerational Religious Education," in *Changing Patterns of Religious Education,* ed. Marvin Taylor (Nashville: Abingdon, 1984), pp. 279, 282, and 284-5.

13. James W. White, "THE GOOD NEWS TIMES: A Summary Report on the Ten Week Church and Church School Program of First Plymouth Congregational Church (UCC), Englewood, Colorado, 1977" (March, 1978), p. 14 (mimeographed).

14. Barbara Kortney, *To All Generations: Sunday Church School Intergenerational Events and Classes* (Philadelphia: Parish Life Press, 1983), p. 39-40.

15. R. Ted Nutting, *Family Cluster Programs: Resources for Intergenerational Bible Study* (Valley Forge: Judson, 1977), p. 16.

16. Howard P. Colson and Raymond M. Rigdon, *Understanding Your Church's*

Curriculum (Nashville: Broadman, 1981), p. 103.

17. George Koehler, *Learning Together: A Guide to Intergenerational Education in the Church* (Nashville: Abingdon, 1976), p. 68.

18. William McKinney, "Community and Congregational Factors in Membership Growth and Decline in Local Churches," a paper presented at the Annual Meeting of the Association of Professors and Researchers in Religious Education, Cincinnati, Ohio (October 31, 1980), p. 4 (mimeographed).

19. Genie Williams, "Minnesota Church Tries *Belonging,*" *Families* 2:4 (Summer-Autumn, 1981), p. 6.

20. Report by the author on some comments by parishioners. First Congregational Church (UCC), Moline, Illinois, 1986-87.

21. Cooperative Curriculum Project, *The Church's Educational Ministry: A Curriculum Plan* (St. Louis: Bethany, 1965), p. 34.

22. James Michael Lee, *The Flow of Religious Instruction: A Social Science Approach* (Birmingham: Ala.: Religious Education Press, 1973), p. 275.

23. Robert J. Havighurst, *Human Development and Education,* quoted in D. Campbell Wyckoff, *Theory and Design of Christian Education Curriculum* (Philadelphia: Westminster, 1961), p. 199.

24. James H. Block, ed., *Mastery Learning: Theory and Practice* (New York: Holt, Rinehart, and Winston, 1971), p. 199.

25. James Michael Lee, *The Shape of Religious Instruction: A Social Science Approach* (Birmingham, Ala.: Religious Education Press, 1971), p. 205.

26. Dennis Milburn, "A Study of Multi-Age or Family-Group Classrooms," *Phi Delta Kappan* (March, 1978), p. 514.

27. Kaye Parnell, "Young and Old Together: A Literature Review," *Childhood Education* 56:3 (January, 1980), pp. 185-186.

28. Cynthia Kramer, Anita Dubey, and Sally Newman, "Generations Together, Senior Citizen School Volunteer Program, Evaluation 1983-1984," pp. 9-10 (mimeographed); and, for the quotation, "The Experience of Senior Citizen School Volunteers in Intergenerational Programs and the Relationship to Life Situation" (Pittsburgh: Generations Together, 1983), as reported in a Publications Catalogue, p. 5.

29. See Virginia Satir, *Conjoint Family Therapy: A Guide to Theory and Technique* (Palo Alto, Calif.: Science and Behavior Books, 1964) p. 141; and William G. Perry Jr., *Forms of Intellectual and Ethical Development in the College Years: A Scheme* (New York: Holt, Rinehart and Winston, 1970), pp. 24-27.

30. Benson and Hilyard, *Becoming Family,* p. 28.

31. See Nevitt Sanford, ed., *The American College: A Psychological and Social Interpretation of the Higher Learning* (New York: Wiley, 1966), pp. 71 and 805 ff.; also see Kenneth A. Feldman and Theodore M. Newcombe, *The Impact of College on Students* (San Francisco: Jossey-Bass, 1969), p. 3.

32. Jackson W. Carroll, Carl S. Dudley, and William McKinney, eds. *Handbook for Congregational Studies* (Nashville: Abingdon, 1986), pp. 181-190.

33. James D. Davidson, Alan K. Monk, and C. Lincoln Johnson, "Expressions of Faith: A Study of Parish Beliefs and Practices," (West Lafayette, Ind.: Department of Sociology, Purdue University, 1987), pp. 3-4.

34. Kenneth I. Pargament, William Silverman et al., "The Psychosocial Climate of Religious Congregations," *American Journal of Community Psychology* 2:4 (1983), p. 360.

35. Kenneth Boyack, Robert D. Duggan and Paul D. Huessing, *Catholic Faith*

Inventory (New York: Paulist, 1987), with inventory, answer sheet, scoring keys, and other forms and guides.

36. Alfred C. Krass, "Growing Together in Spirituality: Pastor and Parish Have a Check-Up," *Christian Century* 104:10 (April 1, 1987), p. 311.

37. See Appendix I for more detail.

38. Personal correspondence, 1977.

39. James W. White, "Write Up of Findings from Administration of Questionnaires on Intergenerational Connectedness," First Congregational Church, Westfield, N.J., p. 1 (mimeograph).

Chapter 12

Concluding Perspective

"And may there be, somewhere, a community of men, women, old people, children and nursing babies who may be a first fruit, an aperitif, a caress of the future. Amen."[1]

The most disturbing movie scene I know of is the opening fifteen minutes of Ingmar Bergman's *Winter Light* (originally entitled, in Swedish, *The Communicants)*. There is a country church. It is a late November Sunday, cold and bleak. Inside the church the pastor is serving communion at the altar rail to nine persons, "all of whom are representative specimens."[2] In each face, as he serves them, Pastor Tomas seems to be asking, "Is there faith here? Is there faith here?" Each person, in turn, seems to ask the same question of him. There is none . . . anywhere. Each communicant is cut off and alone, separated, perhaps even from God. It is a soul-saddening scene.

By contrast, one of the most heart-warming images I have about the church and the people in and around it comes from Madeleine L'Engle's *Summer of the Great-Grandmother*. She describes an earlier-age setting.

> Mother wrote, "When I was a little girl, I loved Louisa May Alcott's books: *Little Women, Little Men, Eight Cousins*. As I look back now I can see the similarity in my life and *Eight Cousins*. There were always plenty of children to play with, aunts and uncles to run to for comfort. Life more or less revolved around St. John's Church, and at the four corners of the church lived four great uncles and their large, multigenerational families."[3]

It is a more pleasing picture.

We moderns are not likely to get back to L'Engle's mother's nine-teenth-century, Jacksonville, Florida, church, but I hope we do *not* find ourselves at Pastor Tomas' communion rail. The L'Engle idea of the church with its corners in neighborhoods of extended families offering comfort, play, and faith is a better setting from which to operate. The Total Parish IGRE Paradigm with various models for interage life and learning and the theory and the counsel for the same contained in this volume may provide help in a needed resetting.

Our journey into IGRE began with a recognition that in contemporary society there is increasing separation/isolation/insulation of persons. I said that the one institution most available to help reconnect people across the generations is the church/synagogue. In the first section of this book, then, we reviewed what religious communities were doing in the way of multigenerational life and learning. Their diverse activities were categorized in terms of six "Models of IGRE."

Part II of the book was an undergirding of the many forms of IGRE with theory coming from work being done in various disciplines by a number of contributors in religious studies (biblical, historical, theological fields), social-scientific research, developmental-stage thinking, and religious education per se. This attempt at providing a theoretical underpinning for IGRE is best understood as a prolegomena to a comprehensive treatment waiting to be done. Nevertheless, it is a start.

Finally, in the last four chapters we turned to a spelling out of what a Total Parish Paradigm for IGRE might be. I talked about establishing goals and creating curriculum for IGRE, as well as evaluating what is done. All has been offered that the whole process of implementing IG life and learning may move forward.

A Troubling Question

As this decade-long writing project came to an end for me, a most disquieting issue began to arise: Taking so long to complete this book, have I ended up heralding a passing phenomena? Is IGRE something which was here yesterday but fast-fading today? Something big in the seventies and diminishing to an historical blip by the eighties?

The urgency of this question came up in the concluding months of writing as I contacted publishers and denominational officials regarding recent developments and publications in the field. Some publishers (especially Roman Catholic contractors) indicated that "The Decade of the Family" which the 1980s were to be for Catholics turned out to be a poor-sales time for them with their Family-Life and IG-like offerings. Then too, from some of my contacts, I sensed that denominational officials who had been quite interested in IGRE were now turning their attention to other things, such as "education for spirituality." Furthermore, my former parish, All Saints Church, had dropped its longstanding IGRE summer program.

So . . . yes, I have to conclude, there is evidence that the highwater mark of interest in IGRE was earlier.

And yet . . . and yet, several other perspectives need to be taken. The first is just to say that very, very much in the way of IG life and learning is going on. There always has been a great deal, as IGRE is a way of being together naturally for many religious communities. And that which has long been goes on, whether "fussed over" or not. Said another way, just because things are not in the spotlight does not mean they are offstage.

Indeed, IGRE has not left the theater. Churches and synagogues across the land continue with the programs started. Or, quite often, they expand existing activities or develop new ones to fit changing situations. Two books, Donald Miller's *Story and Context* and Janice Alper's *Learning Together,* indicate that the IGRE beat goes on strongly in Christian and Jewish congregations.[4] Religious education magazine publishers now carry "regular" feature stories on IGRE happenings. Denominational leaders also say congregations often ask how to do things intergenerationally as it seems "a more excellent way." And so on. Second, there has been quiet building of IGRE in places that might have trumpeted its development more loudly because it was then new. What seems to be happening is that people, instead of starting de novo, put their hands on accessible implementation material and use this to recapitulate IG programs in their institutions. And, third/always there are the faith communities that start up IG efforts on their own without prior consultation. These communities find that what they self-discover and do makes sense.

What one has to conclude is that IGRE is being done quite widely but more quietly. It is doubtless evolving and changing emphases as it goes on, but it goes on. Because of ongoing cross-age associations, people are increasingly grateful for what has occurred and still view IGRE as a "better way" to be in faith community life and learning.

Moreover (lest I forget), there is still a sense that what has been described and prescribed in these pages is for many people and religious agencies a "new" item. "Intergenerational Religious Education" is still a phrase that furrows the brows of people—even of folk one might have thought knew all about it. Instead, they ask for an explanation. In phone calls with and letters from some publishers I heard, "It (IGRE) sounds like an interesting concept. Tell me about it. Is it new?" Or words to that effect. In one sense, then, IGRE is still aborning.

Perhaps this volume will provide additional impetus to the movement.

In these concluding pages I want to talk motivationally about why IGRE is worth promoting in both theory and action. I believe that

1) the need for it is ongoing, 2) its development will help religious institutions do better what they characteristically are already doing best, and 3) IGRE will bless us quite broadly.

THE ONGOING NEED COMPOUNDED

It has been contended in these pages and elsewhere widely that we are in a "societal drift" pattern. This drift is in increasing distance between and among people. Our drift is toward atomization of individuals. To go against this drift is no easy thing.

One of the reasons there could be resistance to IGRE in various faith communities is because this social pattern is in effect. Trying to sail with IGRE may feel like going against the current of the times. Among other things, promotion of IGRE runs counter to the idea of the "self-made man" (or, "woman," increasingly). Moderns want to think, "I am autonomous, not dependent on others—or, at least, I'm self-sufficient." This idea and ideal of individual independence as an ultimate good is deeply imbedded in our cultural/societal value system. Most significantly, it is imbedded deep in our psyches. We do, after all, embody the values of the milieu in which we live.

So . . . then . . . along comes a proposal to increase interage contact and programs in a faith community. For some persons IGRE becomes, in effect, a critique of the notion of their self-sufficient, autonomous individuality. The idea of the *interdependence* of the human family does not set well with persons who take the Pledge of Allegiance to say "one naked individual under God." Said another way, lots of folk cherish anonymity. They are in our churches and synagogues. They are well known to us, as "We have met the enemy, and they is us" (Pogo). They/we are people reluctant to get involved—sometimes even with people the same age—much less with those who are younger or older. They/we have a privatistic "Me and God" or "Me and the Televangelist" orientation to faith. It is the "triumph of the therapeutic" in society and in our conception of religion.

This is a major aspect to the problem of isolation: We think we like being so.

THE BEST VISIBLE SOLUTION

All of the above is said just to underscore the problem for which IGRE in the church/synagogue is presented as the most appropriate response in our times. We need something very like what is proposed in these pages to help overcome disconnectedness between and among people and generations—and to overcome the thinking that we like it this way. We need multigenerational life and learning in the *present* both for the *past* and especially for the *future*.

IGRE protagonists, of which I am one, say that the church/synagogue is the only contemporary institution—other than the struggling family itself—which has people of all ages in its natural constituency. Faith communities include the whole age spectrum, and everything that can happen for weal or woe in the life-span of people intersects the faith community daily. Happily, many folk do get support "in joy and in sorrow" from these communities. It comes from religious leaders, from friends-in-the-faith, and from other people—sometimes of multiple ages. This sort of support happens in the course of normal congregational life. The holding together of "all ages, tongues, and races," however imperfect, helps break down atomizing tendencies and gives people a sense of being made one for another.

With a modicum of further thought and action we can do and be much more along these lines. Since the faith community is the most viable institution within which cross-age life and learning can be facilitated, we should go with it. The foundation (to use a building metaphor) for IGRE is already laid. In many places solid framing is up. I contend that it is possible to build from-strength-to-strength until a strong house for all is standing.

What seems to be called for is a sensible implementation process which can direct and shape things. Such a process was described in chapter 8 on the Total Parish Paradigm. Another way to suggest this is to review "the learning process" which Jack Seymour and Donald Miller outline for individual learners. It is applicable to larger collectivities. They say that learning involves *awareness, intentionality, coherence,* and *mutuality.*[5] These are also needed for a successful incorporation of significant IGRE. People would need to be *aware* of "the problem" of our times and the possibilities for addressing the same by building bonds among the generations. They would then need to be *intentional* in planning for IGRE development, thinking through where they want to go and how to get there. Complementing that intentionality would be the work of pulling things together in a *coherent* structure of understanding and action. And, finally, there is that *sense of mutuality* among people which grows in the learning/building process. As we talk to one another, grow to trust one another, such mutuality will develop to advance the whole cause.

AND, FINALLY, THE BLESSINGS

The results of following the process of implementing the Total Parish IGRE Paradigm may be very good. There are many likely positive outcomes of improved intergenerational life together in faith communities. The "blessings"—the bene-fits—are for 1) the society, 2) the faith institutions themselves, 3) those who take leadership in IGRE development, 4) God (if we may be so presumptuous), and 5) both families and individual persons. We shall consider each.

Society Blessings. If the church/synagogue lives out its mandate to heal and unite in a broken world, then IGRE is such a living out. It is a creative response in the faith community to a needful situation of our time. It is a propitious living model of a more excellent way. It is a being with one another that others may join. In the long run, it is a training/inspirational activity which can propel motivated persons into reenactments of the same in the wider world.

In this latter facing, let me say that the movement outward into the wider world might include support for various secular proposals to facilitate IG developments in the larger society. One such proposal is that of Congressman Edward Roybal of California, called the "Intergenerational Volunteer Act." Among other features, if enacted, it would enhance programs for senior citizen involvement in the public schools. That has to be seen as desirable for those seniors, the young, their parents, the schools, and society generally. Such programs coming from the government will be a positive expansion of IG activity, a boon to the *polis.*

In our day and time people live more nearly in what Philip Slater calls networks. "A network is an address book—a list of people who may have little in common besides oneself."[6] Our roll-o-dex directories and Christmas/Hanukah card lists are full of names. But most associations signified there are just that: paper relationships. We do, though, have some better lists of folks, those contained on a smudged, well-used page of "frequently called numbers" near the kitchen phone. It is a more meaningful list though, unfortunately, indicative of part of our problem too: The list is of *out-of-town* family and/or *peer-age* others.

By contrast to networks and peer-lists is "community," something infinitely more desirable. "Community" in the neighborhood and in the world is, I am convinced, a great need of our time.

Dr. Strangelove, in the movie of the same name, was informed that the Soviet Union was ahead of the United States in the development of underground bomb shelters in abandoned mines. He reported angrily, "Ve haf gut un *gah min shaft* gap!" What a marvelous play on words! *Gemeinschaft* in German means something like "face-to-face loving community." Indeed, we have a *Gemeinschaft* (community) gap—internationally, locally, everywhere.

Speaking to the point, David Steward says, "There is widespread need to get beyond networks; to build corporate contexts which encourage persons to relate to limited and therefore wholesome ways. This is the concern which impels many of us in our professional work in churches and synagogues."[7] That impelling might be with IGRE. Were IG life to prosper in church and synagogue, we would have a better handle for narrowing the gaps in neighborhoods, anyway. Establishment of community—or, at least, establishment of better "communal relations" (Moran)—close-to-hand even can be a positive springboard experience toward broader societal realization. So, IGRE could be a blessing enabling individuals to get beyond networks and our world to get into something closer to *Gemeinschaft.*

Church/Synagogue Blessings. The lack of community which pervades the wider society is, regretfully, all too often reflected in faith collectivities. Persons join the church/synagogue as individuals or as families with little assurance that sustaining "ties that bind" will be tied. Significant relationships are not guaranteed merely because one's name is on the membership roll. One of the positive things about IGRE is that it can address this problem, bringing people together and enhancing not only the "believing" and "behaving" aspects of religious affiliation but also the "belonging." All three Bs are important.

While it is the faith-community-as-institution which acts to establish and maintain IGRE, it is the same body which also benefits from the work. *The church/synagogue becomes more nearly what it was intended to be and what it vows to be, namely, a living/learning/faithing people of God.*

Effective IGRE is likely to have several add-on benefits. People invested in religious institutions as institutions, especially clergy, are interested in "success" for that group. "Success" for many is measured in terms of the other three B's: Bodies, Budgets, and Buildings. IGRE may help on all three fronts. The lively and satisfying participation of people of all ages in the IG activities of the congregation is likely to produce enthusiasm for the institution (hence, spirited "telling others about" and resultant membership growth), increased financial generosity toward the church/synagogue, and even expansion-mindedness regarding the facilities. Part of the benefit of IGRE, in other words, can be support of the nuts and bolts of the organization itself.

Another positive, though secondary, good forthcoming is leadership development. IGRE programs call forth the creative best in people, providing training and experience for people in leadership of programs and people. Such development of persons has good immediate outcomes and good "fall out" later in the life of the institution. Those who have written up descriptions of IGRE programs regularly report the people who worked on IGRE continued working and contributing to the good of the church/synagogue.

Blessing of the Leaders. Though the religious institution and the wider society may be beneficiaries from IGRE programing, it is invariably the leadership core who will proclaim "showers of blessings" received most loudly as the result of their participation. They will perceive of themselves making the most gains on a variety of fronts. These instigators and laborers in the IGRE vineyard will point out: "Truly, there is joy found in working along with other people of similar and different ages. We spark one another. Friendships have been built. The faith comes alive. I've grown. Others are growing too. In short, we bless one another." Every single evaluation ever made of the programs at All Saints Church by the planner-doers concluded excitedly, "WE LEARNED THE MOST!" That is a promise and a plus.

In addition, let it be said for the adults who are likely to take the lead in IGRE programing, this endeavor is an excellent life-investment channel. If "acquiring a sense of GENERATIVITY and avoiding a sense of self-absorption—(thus, developing) a realization of care"[8] is the middle-aged adult's main developmental task, this effort is one of the best places in which to work on it. We who have received much by this endeavor may put back into the world some good things for future generations. In our own exercise room we can accept Jane Fonda's video and cassette tape accolade given to home workout pupils: "You did a *great* job. You should feel *real good* about yourself."

Blessing God. For persons of faith, the last question is not whether we feel good or even whether the society or church is healthier because of our efforts. No. Our ultimate concern is one about whether our IGRE efforts are aligned with the aims of God.

Are they?

Answer: It is possible. Surely it seems that God wills us to be together, generation with generation. If we grant that "the initial aim of God" is for the human family to live in love and grow by significant becomings . . . and, if, in process terms, this desire is part of "God's primordial nature" . . . then perhaps IGRE's successful work serves strong holy purpose. Insofar as living/learning/growing is God's intention and insofar as we help realize it, then we return to God that which is a blessing. God's own becoming (in process terms, God's "consequent nature") is advanced.

In biblical times a blessing was often accompanied by the laying on of hands.[9] The thought was that the power of the spirit of one person flowed out to another through the fingers and palm, by touch. Certainly in IGRE with lifestyle goals there is the joining of hands. "Pressing the flesh," pleases the Eternal One. (Christians especially should affirm this as we have a doctrine about that Eternal One who "became flesh.") God in God's self is fulfilled when persons touch. As we learn to relate across the generations in the faith and bless one another, then, we give to God a new becoming that all the generations of heaven enjoy too. So we say in IGRE with the Psalmist, "Bless the Lord, O my soul"—and God is.

Family/People Blessing. Though it may be the leadership cadre who are most cognizant of receiving blessings from their work, finally it is families and persons in the congregation for whom this emphasis is intended who are blessed. They too go to graceland.

Consider *the family.* Though this institution in our time has been attenuated, it is still important. It seems now to exist as a "modified extended" entity. If the faith communities do their job in bringing family members into closer, more meaningful contact with each other and with older and younger non-kin persons, the possibility is there that a "larger and significant extended family" will develop. With that, young and old alike will not feel so alone in the world. They will know that they are well-accompanied on their pilgrimage. That is to the good.

Consider *individual persons.* Each person in the family and any person "single" in the community may come to know and appreciate what the inclusion with others in that circle means. They will sense the benefit. They will be, in other words, the beneficiaries.

What I want to do is conclude this book with a "Pretend Trip" story about "A Day in the IGRE Life" of two persons. The Trip illustrates both the workings of a good IGRE program and what its impact on a young boy and an older woman might be.

A DAY IN THE LIFE—A PRETEND TRIP

Were a church (in this case)—say, one named All Saints[10]—to become intentional about interage life and learning, there likely would be impact on the lives of persons. Consider what might be seen, heard, felt, and *thought* by two different-aged people as they went through an IGRE Sunday at All Saints Church. The program described is built on an actual IGRE event in an actual church, here expanded and "perfected" to meet illustrative needs. The stream-of-consciousness suggested, of course, is strictly projection. The dialogue from internal reflections indicates how an IGRE program might make a holistically positive impact on people. So pretend . . .

PRETEND

pretend   pretend

YOU ARE SEVEN	YOU ARE SEVENTY

[Start here.]
It is Sunday morning. Your mother drives into the church parking lot.

It is Sunday morning. It's your first trip to church in several months. Nan, your driver and younger friend, picks you up outside the apartment. As you ride she tells you about her children. You talk about a letter from your daughter.

You see a girl on the church steps selling newspapers. "What have I missed?" you wonder. You've been away in California with your dad most of the month. Mom parks the car and gives you a nickel to buy a paper from the newsgirl. It's called *The Good News Times.*

Nan lets you out before the church doors and goes to find a parking place. As you move toward the building a grade-school-age-girl wearing a T-shirt saying "Good News Times—5¢" offers to sell you a mimeographed "newspaper." "What is this?" you ask her. "It's about a fight—a fight in the kitchen last week between Martha and Mary," she replies. "My, my!" you say.

You enter the church. Once inside the building a lady greets your family and asks you to sign a paper. You do. She then pins a nametag on your shirt. It's yellow and in the shape of a walking crutch—like the one you used last ski season!
"Weird!" you think.
And weirder still are two of your friends sitting by the door of the sanctuary. Their eyes are shut. They are dressed in rags. And they're supposedly begging! You put your used chewing gun in Jimmy's tin cup.

Nan joins the churchstep conversation and purchases two copies. A story from the back page of the paper reads: "We were singing and all of a sudden we heard pots and pans so we went and saw Mary and Martha having a war. They told stories. But after, we acted them out. —by John K." "That must have been something!" you think, wondering what to anticipate for this day. "Church was never like this back in Nebraska!" you say out loud.

Nan smiles, knowingly.

A young couple greets you "Welcome" inside the building, and an usher gives out a bulletin as you enter the sanctuary. You pass a teenager dressed in a bathrobe and leaning on a crutch in the center aisle. Your wonderment increases.

Once in church, you, your mom, and your brother (age 14) take a seat near the front. Your mom whispers to your brother, "The minister is away today but the worship leaders are the parents of your friend, Chris."

"Far out," he whispers back.

As the service begins, Chris's father reads something about "all generations" (whatever they are) shall praise God." He invites everyone to sing from the hymnbook. You share the book with a lady sitting next to you. She smells very nice. You notice that the man in front of her has almost no hair. "Strange," you think, checking your own scalp. The song is "For All the Saints." You know it, sang it in church school last year.

Next comes a "litany"—a back and forth reading. You can read the words marked for "children" easily. There are parts for adults to read too.

In the sanctuary your eyes move to the chancel area where a large wooden newsstand is built. Across the top of the stand are the words, "GOOD NEWS TIMES." Hanging beneath the title is an enlarged newspaper reading, "SOLDIER TELLS OF JESUS' HEALING POWER." A crutch symbol is also visible on the page. Similar mock-up newspapers hang on the side walls of the nave, suggesting what the programs of previous weeks must have been, namely about New Testament events. You take a pew seat near the inside of the center aisle in front of a girl . . . No, it's a boy "with rather long hair!"

After the lay liturgist gives the call to worship, you join in the hymn. The responsive "Litany of Confession" and "Words of Forgiveness" are different, you think, but nevertheless meaningful. "Long Hair" in front reads well.

Soon a man named "Dr. Luke" comes out. He's wearing a white robe and has a deep voice.

"Far out!" your brother whispers.

The friendly Doctor invites the children to come and sit on the steps with him. You scramble out past the nice-smelling lady. Your brother leaves the pew too, but goes to the back of the room with a bunch of other teenagers. You sit down next to some "little kids."

Then a lady in the choir loft right above you sings a song. The words sound funny. When the song is finished, Dr. Luke introduces a Roman soldier, a "centurion." Boy is he big! The centurion tells about how he once had a servant who was sick but was heaied by Jesus.

Dr. Luke says, "We need to learn more about Jesus the healer. Let's go down to the fellowship hall. (Later you recount: "Dr. Luke took *my* hand—and some girl's too. His hand was rougher than yours, Mom.") You fairly skip out of church, wondering as you go if Jesus was as big as the centurion or as nice as Dr. Luke.

As a costumed "Dr. Luke" is presented, "Long Hair" scoots out to the chancel area. You smile as you see a younger child timidly come down the aisle.

A lovely alto version of "De Blin' Man

Stood at De Road and Cried" is sung, and then the story of Jesus healing a sick servant is told by a Roman centurion.

Seeing the Roman, you whisper to your friend, *"Gallis est omni diviso in partes tres."*

Nan replies, "What?"

You smile.

Then the music starts. It's a lively song about "We've got Good News . . . Good News . . . Let's help spread the News around here." You watch with interest as the children leave down the center aisle with Dr. Luke.

As you enter the fellowship hall, the "Good News" song which was played on the organ is here being played on the piano. Dr. Luke invites everyone to sit on the carpet by his well. The piano player comes and sits beside you. You ask her, "Which one's your kid?"

She whispers, "None. I'm single."

"Oh."

Dr. Luke then begins by saying that you and the other children are newspaper reporters for *The Good News Times* paper. "This summer," he adds, "we are writing stories and drawing pictures of people who knew Jesus." He reminds the children of previous newspaper stories which had been "covered"—such as that of Mary and Martha last week. He tells about future assignments, such as an upcoming visit by Jesus' friend, Mary Magdalene.

With the children gone and you still standing, the liturgist encourages everyone to get acquainted with other worshipers. "Try to find something in common with your neighbor," she suggests. You meet the parents of "Long Hair" and discover that the wife was originally from Omaha—as are you.

"Well, Go, Big Red!" the woman's husband says to the two of you.

Following the choir anthem, the guest minister reads the scripture from Luke's Gospel, the seventh chapter. It's a repeat of the centurion's story, personified earlier. You reflect this time more on what tremendous faith that Roman must have had.

Dr. Luke next reintroduces the big Roman who was in the church. The soldier leads your whole group outside to the portico area. He retells his story and answers questions asked him by your fellow reporters.

Just as he is finishing, some sand falls on your head. You look up. From the portico roof there is a man being lowered right into the circle of kids. He's in costume and made up, but he looks familiar. You think to yourself, "I've seen that guy before. He looks like Debbie's dad."

From his stretcher the man tells his story: how he once couldn't walk, how he had to be lowered into a room where Jesus was and how Jesus healed him from his "paralysis."

You ask him, "Can you walk now?"

And he stands up.

"Yeh," you think, "that's Debbie's dad, all right."

You wonder what the minister will say about the centurion's story. His sermon title is "Notes from a Modern Healer." He begins by retelling how this Roman "Lieutenant Colonel," who sought help from "the prophet from the hills," had his servant healed without Jesus ever going to the centurion's home. The minister asserts his belief in healing energy which transcends distance. He then gives some personal examples of "long-distance healing." You whisper to Nan, "I wonder if our regular minister takes much stock in such an notion?"

"Probably not," she whispers back. "He's awfully straight."

The clergyman continues, saying Jesus had the spiritual energy to heal and that the healings were not self-induced.

Then Dr. Luke says, "Maybe we can be healers too, bringing happiness to those who are ill or can't come to church." He leads all the group back inside where tables have been set up. You notice bright-colored tissue paper, newspapers, sticks, and tape on each table. Across the room you see your brother at one of the tables. You consider going to his table but decide, instead, to go to a different one. A pony-tailed high-school girl shows you how to make a big tissue paper flower. You make one and start on another.

Continuing with his sermon, the preacher says, "You and I can heal people with our energy." He makes quite a point of the power of human touch to positively help people. He gives some examples from his experience again. You reflect on the fact that America really is a "no touch" culture. There was precious little touching while you were in the hospital.

Unexpectedly, Nan squeezes your hand . . . knowingly . . . and you feel goosebumps. Your look says, "Thanks. I needed that." You get a little lost when the sermon moves into a discussion of inner psychological states and external health conditions. But you agree: Humans really are one piece. "In addition to having a healing effect on others," the minister concludes, "we also can heal ourselves; but we have to identify our pain and hates and be willing to let them go. We need to love ourselves." "Ah," you think, "that can be hard."

Suddenly Dr. Luke shouts, "PRESS TIME! PRESS TIME!" You finish your flower and report to the Press Room behind the partition. You decide to draw a picture of the man being lowered from the roof for your "story." Soon it is done.

Seeing your fifth-grade friend, Andy, at the writing table, you ask, "What did ya write?" He shows you: "We make flowers to make people feel better when they are sick. It won't heal people, but it will make them feel better. You can smell the flowers but they don't have a scent of smell."

You say, "Pretty good," and he says the same about your drawing. You both hand in your work at the editor's desk and go back to Dr. Luke's well.

During the liturgist's prayer, which follows the sermon, you are aware of needing to pray for a friend. You also resolve to write her. During the offertory prayer, you are particularly taken by the printed words about "rearranging our lives in more open and honest ways." The service concludes with the singing of "God of Grace and God of Glory" and the Benediction.

The group recites another "litany" (they call it). It's written on a chart and is about "marveling about the future." Some lady gives you some refreshment of *"Dr. Pepper."*

"Oh, my!" you can almost hear your mother say, "Soda pop in the morning—and at church?!"

Soon your mom is there to pick you up. As she comes in, one of the teachers gives her two of the tissue paper flowers and a card with some names on it. The names are from a "Shut-Ins" list, the teacher says.

Before you can leave you have to find your brother. He's in the refreshments-hour crowd, talking to Debbie's mother. You hear him say,

"Your husband got sick."

"Really?" she asks.

"Yeh, but Jesus healed him."

"Yes," she smiles. "Every day."

After the service—upon Nan's insistence— you go to the refreshments hour. You feel a little uneasy because it has been such a long time since you were last in church. Still you stay. Then you notice someone standing quite alone. You go over and introduce yourself to a young man. Instead of just shaking his hand, though, you add your left hand to the clasp. There seems to be a glimpse of appreciation and meaning in his returned look. He tells you he has moved to the city with the Air Force. The two of you talk about the worship service. He suggests that the centurion cared so much about the servant because "They were both from the same hometown."

Very shortly, the children start entering the room. You direct a little one to the punch table. Soon Nan says, "We better go."

Later that afternoon, your mom takes you to visit the people whose names were on the card she'd gotten at church. The first stop is a home just for very old people. You give a man in a wheelchair a flower. He nods and smiles and nods and smiles but says nothing.

Leaving the nursing home, you say to your mom, "I've never seen anyone so old. But," you add, "he sure could smile—and his teeth were perfect."

Early that afternoon you get a call from a lady at the church saying to expect a visitor later on.

You get out some cookies and your favorite tea. At three-thirty a sevenish looking boy and his mother show up with a present. It's a paper flower, big and bright.

"What a nice surprise!" you say, secretly wanting to give the boy a hug.

You ask the boy about the morning program, and he tells about a drawing he did.

The second stop is at an apartment building. The lady invites you in for some tea and cookies. Even with extra sugar you let the tea get cold, but you take doubles on the cookies. The lady says she was at church this morning too. Your mom and she talk

about the sermon. "Pretty boring talk," you
think. You mostly play with the lady's dog
and look at some pictures on the table.

In talking with the boy's mother, you learn
how she especially liked the sermon thought
on letting pain go. You understand.

"I understand," you say to her.

Tears seem about to well up in her eyes for a
second. You turn to talk with the boy about
family pictures he's found on the coffee table.

One picture is of a girl on a swing. "What a
big hat she's got!" you exclaim.

"That's my daughter, my daughter when she
was seventeen," she says. "Now she's grown
and lives in Seattle."

"Yeah?" you say, "I've been there—and
went up the Space Needle."

She says she's been up it too. "It was scary."

"Well," you say, "You shoulda had me
along."

Reviewing the pictures provides an opportunity to talk about your married daughter in
Seattle and your trip there the previous
summer. They say it is time to go. You put a
few extra cookies in the boy's shirt pocket,
and—lo and behold—he gives you a hug!

Driving home, your mom talks about "the
spirit of healing."

"You have some of that, Roger. So does the
lady."

But you're thinking about next Sunday,
wondering if your picture will be printed in
The Good News Times.

Later that evening your are reminiscing
about the day's experiences and learnings
when your daughter calls long distance. You
tell her about Nan, about church, the program, your visitors, and the flower. You say,
"And the little boy loved the pictures of you
when you were little."

It was a full day. That night   Upon retiring you are grateful
you think about the day . . .   for everything and say/pray . . .

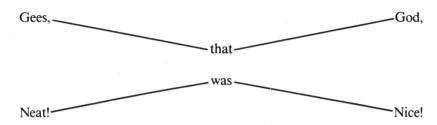

Thus, an intergenerational worship/education/community "pretend" exercise from two age perspectives. In our faith communities we need more of this to overcome our separations.

Notes

1. Rubem Alves, *I Believe in the Resurrection of the Body* (Philadelphia: Fortress, 1984), p. 78.
2. John Simon, *Ingmar Berman Directs* (New York: Harcourt Brace Jovanovich, 1972), p. 146.
3. Madeleine L'Engle, *The Summer of the Great-Grandmother* (New York: Seabury, 1979), p. 198.
4. Donald E. Miller, *Story and Context: An Introduction to Christian Education* (Nashville: Abingdon, 1987), pp. 92-95, for example; and Janice P. Alper, ed. *Learning Together: A Sourcebook on Jewish Family Education* (Denver, Colo.: Alternatives in Religious Education, 1987), pp. 41-54, for another example.
5. Jack L. Seymour and Donald E. Miller with others, *Contemporary Approaches to Christian Education* (Nashville: Abingdon, 1982), pp. 89-90.
6. Philip Slater, *Earthwalk* (Garden City, N.J.: Anchor, 1974), p. 15.
7. David S. Steward, "Beyond Networks: Professional Conversation for the 1980's," a paper delivered at the Annual Meeting of the Association of Professors and Researchers in Religious Education, Cincinnati, Ohio, October 30, 1980, p. 11.
8. Henry W. Maier, *Three Theories on Child Development: The Contributions of Erik H. Erikson, Jean Piaget, and Robert R. Sears* (New York: Harper & Row, 1969), p. 71.
9. Reference: "Bless, Blessed, Blessing" in *A Theological Word Book of the Bible*, ed. Alan Richardson (New York: Macmillan, 1964), p. 33.
10. All Saints, as previously indicated, is a fictional name but for a real church. Much of the forthcoming description is based on a real program of that real church.

Appendix

All Saints Church and IGRE

The theory and practice of intergenerational religious education discussed in this book have their experiential beginnings for the author in some age-inclusive programing at All Saints Church.[1] The start of IGRE programing at All Saints was the development of a summer church school program for children of several ages. In short years, consciousness of multigenerational possibilities expanded to affect other parts of the congregation's life. It also led the author to a long-term research and comprehensive study of intergenerational religious education, both in macro-theory and macro-events.

This Appendix, in the main, describes nine age-inclusive summer programs at All Saints Church. It traces the development of IGRE consciousness to involve additional programs of the church and larger numbers and ages of people. This description indicates how the nine programs evolved, built on each other, expanded, were repeated, lived, and went on to influence the whole life of the church. The learnings from All Saints' IGRE programs were shared with religious educators in other churches but, just as significantly, the learnings had a strong ripple effect on All Saints itself. Those results are described in the final section of this Appendix. The very first section here describes in broad strokes the church in which the IGRE developments occurred.

A Look at All Saints

All Saints Church is a mainline Christian church. The church began in the 1860s and merged with another same-denomination congregation in the late 1920s. For most of its history, All Saints was a downtown church. In 1956 the congregation voted to move from its inner-city location to another site in the growing suburbs. The site selected for the new building was on the corner of a major east-west and north-south intersection for the metropolitan area. In a commanding position the church became for the denomination in the city and in the state something of the "cathedral" church.

There are over 1400 adult members. Church school enrollment exceeds 500, including infants through senior-high youth. The membership is drawn from a forty-mile radius, but the majority now comes from the major nearby suburbs. Quite a few older members still reside in the downtown area. The primary constituents of the church are middle-aged adults. Children in families now tend toward the upper end of the schooling ladder, though a number of younger families regularly enter the church. As a geographically dispersed congregation in a near two million population metro-plex area, the members themselves are seldom involved in day-by-day face-to-face relations on any main street or in one supermarket.

All Saints is a congregation of white professionals mostly, some with economic means and most with significant educational attainment. The vast majority of members have in-migrated to the area from other states, coming from a variety of mainline denominational backgrounds. For the most part All Saints' members wear the name "liberal" without apology—especially so in things "religious," usually so on matters political and social, somewhat so on economic questions, and regularly in terms of toleration for diversity in point of view.

The expectation of and for "community" is not high among members. Some worshipers even seem to desire anonymity. Given these factors and others suggested above, intergenerational programing has to be seen as harder to do in such a congregation than in a congregation which is smaller, geographically concentrated, less uprooted, regularly interacting, and families-connected.

Over its 100-plus year history the church has established a reputation for calling ministers who are strong preachers. Solid biblical exegesis with relevant contemporary social and psychological analysis characterize the pulpit discourse. The worship services tend to be "traditional-formal." For the last decade or so there has been a collegial understanding in the call of the two primary ministers. They share responsibility for the whole church program and "cover" for one another. One minister gives more time to worship and administration, the other to education and parish development. The latter was my own portfolio while serving All Saints.

The religious education program at All Saints is governed by the Religious Education Committee. This committee determines policy, draws up the budget, establishes programs, and reviews the whole. The programs are administered by four paid, but part-time, lay people: an executive coordinator, an early childhood director, a director for the elementary grades, and a youth program coordinator. The religious education program during the academic calendar year is a Sunday church school with fully graded classes. The classes usually are team taught. Children's education is conducted simultaneously with the adult worship services. For many years the church school used curriculum materials published by the denomination. More recently an ecumenically assembled resource curriculum has been in use.

Confirmation-age and high-school youth meet one evening a week with choir/supper/program as part of the Youth Night. Adult education has been programed for two principle times. One is a weekday evening "School of Religion" program. The other is after Sunday worship when an adult forum on current issues is held.

Intergenerational religious education at All Saints developed somewhat outside of and then supplementary to the regular church school. Over the years it has become integral to the life of the church. The church now finds itself significantly involved in a broad range of IGRE programs. The regular Sunday morning schedule, weekday activities, and seasonal events have all been affected. These affected areas are described following the recap of nine programs which brought the church to its present strong intergenerational life posture.

Nine IGRE Programs

IGRE Programs I and II at All Saints were quite experimental. Entitled "Universe Man" and "The Fabulous Church Time Machine," the programs were small in scale compared to what later developed. They were, however, a positive portentous beginning—something solid on which additional intergenerational programs could be built.

* * *

I. Universe Man.[2] Working with conceptual, symbolic, and pedagogical material produced by the Chicago-based Ecumenical Institute, the originating IGRE team designed a ten-week, summer educational experience for children of elementary-school age. The program was seen as supplemental yet complementary to the curriculum and activities of the regular church school year. The program sought "to convey an understanding of and appreciation for the life of people (especially children) of the global village." Two weeks per each were given to consideration of Tan Man, Black Man, Yellow Man, Red Man, and Brown Man.

The most distinctive feature of the Universe Man program was that for the first time children of All Saints between five and twelve years old were learning in a combined ages program. Only occasionally that summer did the sessions fall back and divide into grade-level arrangements. The combined elementary grades approach was no mean undertaking. It meant new kinds of learning activities had to be devised—activities which had wide appeal, neither over the heads of the youngest nor boring to the older children. To meet this need, each Sunday's schedule proceeded to a lively beat—rather than a quiet, study-discussion cadence. Learning came through active doing. In addition, the attempt was made to appeal to the richness of the senses with food, dance, crafts, viewing, chanting, touching, and so on. Universe Man was a learning experience more in the affective and psychomotor domain than in the cognitive domain—which was the usual fare offered All Saints youngsters.

With this initial program, the designers and the church members generally were aware that something special was happening. Parents could see more of what was going on with their children as activities took place in the fellowship hall rather than in an obscure Sunday school basement room. They also saw the artifacts which came home each week. They heard excited talk about how fun it was to "take your shoes off at church." One parent said, "We are glad our *two* girls can have *one* learning experience together." Others were appreciative of the fact that in this very Caucasian church, children could develop some acquaintance with the colorful people of the world.

II. The Fabulous Church Time Machine. In the second year of programing, I joined the planning team. As it happened, I had seen a children's movie about a time machine which transported people back to other historical eras. The sharing of the movie's storyline with the planning group sparked an idea: Why not do similar era and geographical transposition in terms of *religious* history?

Out of a huge freezer-refrigerator box, the IGRE planners built a "history transport machine." An entrance and exit door were cut in the cardboard box. A steeple was placed on top. The whole was painted bright baby blue. Buzzers and flashing Christmas tree lights were added, along with a simulated computer instrument panel, switches, and a large historical time dial. Thus: "The Fabulous Church Time Machine." On a Sunday morning, when a designated child set the dials properly, the entrance door swung open, a buzzer sounded, lights flashed, and music played. Then all the children went into the machine (which was flanked on each side by the room's sliding partitions). They came out the back side into another historical age. They were greeted by an historical character. By changing the historical setting children were transported back to nine different ages of Judaeo-Christian time, such as that of King David, the Early Church, or Frontier America.

The curriculum of the Time Machine program was a composition from the heads of the planning committee. Planners discovered the excitement of coming up with something that was educationally unique and usually effective.

In actually putting the program together, other parents were brought in to help. To the committee's pleasure and surprise, some older youth became involved. During that second summer, minimal separating by grades was done in the program. The schedule was again kept to an active pace. To facilitate post-hour learning, a mimeographed note was composed for parents and sent home with each child. The note explained what went on that day and invited parents to come in anytime and observe the activities. The note encouraged adults to ask their children, "What are some facts or feelings you picked up this morning?" One parent, in checking out the authenticity of her child's report on a historical event, said she discovered the church library!

* * *

With the Universe Man and Time Machine offerings, the program at All Saints were launched. Programs III and IV witnessed considerable expansion and established other basic ingredients which grew to characterize the model. The primary expansion was to move part of the program hour into the sanctuary and to make the learning available to greater numbers of people and of ages. One program was called "The Wonderful Wizard of OT" (meaning, Old Testament) and the next "When the Saints Go Marchin' . . ."

* * *

III. The Wonderful Wizard of OT. Program III turned All Saints church toward a fuller intergenerational character. Sunday mornings began with children and adults together in the sanctuary. For children to be in "Big Church" was then something most unusual. They were accustomed to church school classroom attendance only. Being in worship with "all those people" was new and special. Opening in the sanctuary was special for parents too. For the first time they worshiped formally/regularly with their children.

The intergenerational service was special also for older childless and empty-nest adults. They spoke to the planning committee members animatedly: "It is *so* nice to have a child sitting next to me again" and "For the story time, I just *love* to see one child timidly step out from behind the pew and another boldly race down the center aisle!"

In the service together, young and old sang a simple song from the hymnal. Together they heard the clergyperson read a story-poem from an *Arch Book* about an Old Testament character. Such was an "in common experience" which multiple generations shared. It could be remembered and talked about later.

After about fifteen minutes in the sanctuary, the children left. In the narthex they were greeted by a most exciting character: The Wizard of OT. The Wiz wore a black pulpit robe upon which bright felt symbols were embossed. He had an orange-and-pink cape, wore a chartreuse green hat with silver tinsel, and carried a crooked chartreuse walking stick. He was quite a sight—so it seemed, in the mirror.

The Wiz led the children down a "Yellow Brick Road" (contact paper stuck on the hall floor) to "The Land of OT." There in the fellowship hall the children were retold the story just heard in church. After this and other preliminary exercises, from their location in the center of the room, children were directed to learning centers where the same story was recreated in still other ways. In this manner the program planners sought to fulfill the overall goal of "increasing children's familiarity with important but less-well-known Old Testament personalities."

Meanwhile, back in the sanctuary, the minister read a scripture lesson concerning the Old Testament character-of-the-day and delivered a sermon on the same text. Thus, what is called "parallel learning" was initiated at All Saints. Adults were learning along the same lines as children but in different rooms and at appropriate but different development levels.

Parents were also related to what their children were doing by "Family Packets." Information packets concerning each Sunday's biblical character were sent home with the children. In these there might be a related puzzle to work or a game to play. There would be suggestions for discussion, especially along the lines of "What might the life of X [the Old Testament personality] mean today?" "Interactive sharing" was thus facilitated. To help such sharing along, families were encouraged to buy the *Arch Book* series being used, so that review reading and discussion within families might go on during the week.

IV. "When the Saints Go Marchin' . . ." In a church such as All Saints neither children nor adults are very familiar with Christian saints or saint days, as may be known to believers in other traditions. Neither has this congregation been closely attuned to the liturgical calendar. To help overcome these gaps in educational-ecclesiastical appreciation, the planning committee for Program IV decided to do three things: 1) join Christian saints with 2) specific holy days and seasons and 3) connect both to a better understanding of ourselves. So, for example, Cecilia, the Patron Saint of Music, was tied into the season of Thanksgiving-Advent and a weekly "Mini-Course on Me" focused on how, by music and other ways, we, like Cecilia, might respond to life with thanksgiving.

High-school students were recruited to portray the various saints. As character-actors they proved to be the major innovation for the summer. By their presence one more generation of significantly involved learner-participants was added to the intergenerational whole. On Sunday morning the teenage "saints" stepped out from behind cardboard "Cathedral Doors" installed in the chancel area. They told their saintly story to the whole congregation. Later in fellowship hall they dialogued with children and with an adult teacher. This teacher carried the up-front program leadership and rehearsed the teenagers in their saintly roles.

With a title for Program IV of "When the Saints Go Marchin' . . ." the planners had an obvious program theme song. It was sung by adult voices as children exited the sanctuary and by the children in the fellow-ship hall. As a supplement to the oral presentation by the teenage saints, each Sunday bulletin carried an insert with a brief biography on the saint of the morning. Along with the sermon of the day, the biographical sketch was offered as a post-service conversation starter. On each write-up three basic and interrelated learning points concerning the "saint, season, and ourselves" were specified. Here is an example:

Saint Jerome was a person who knew the Bible and translated it so others could read it too.

Bible Sunday is the day we remember the importance of the scrip-tures for Christians.

We are persons who can know the Bible and "translate" it so that others may understand it too.

In evaluation of the program at the end of the summer, planners concluded that the teaching reach may have exceeded learners' grasp in many instances, but they liked the age-inclusive direction in which the program was going.

* * *

If Programs III and IV established the basic intergenerational and pedagogical features of the program, Programs V and VI secured those main features with successful replications and supplementary features. The programs were called "Plymouth, U. S. A." and "The Good News Times." Attendance in the programs for children had moved steadily upward. The IGRE committee had an average of twenty-nine first through sixth graders per week in the first program and moved to more than sixty per week by Program V. It was about this time that people became aware of the full teaching/learning significance which these programs held. Other churches began trying them out.

* * *

V. Plymouth, U. S. A. In the Bicentennial Year the steering committee wanted to focus on the American religious experience. *How* to put such complex history together for children and adults was the question.

Eventually it was decided to take American history in fifty-year blocks, beginning with Anne Hutchinson in the year 1626 and moving on through to the year 2026 when Captain Kirk and Mr. Spock would appear. Remembering America's Pilgrim heritage from Plymouth Rock, the planning committee took "Plymouth, U. S. A." as the program name. A Plymouth Town was started, and each week at least one new mock building, such as a New England meeting house or a late nineteenth-century factory, was added to the town.

As had been done in an earlier program, Plymouth, U. S. A. used a central figure to provide week-to-week continuity for participants. The central figure was that of "Uncle Sam" who set the stage each Sunday by presentations in the sanctuary.

In the previous Saints program, planners became convinced that children and adults relate to and learn well from live dramatized characters. Actors were again enlisted from among high-school students and also from fathers and mothers. They played key roles in the "summer stock theater." The parent-actors did impressive research into their historical figures, e.g., Harriet Tubman, John Scopes. They enacted the roles with uninhibited enthusiasm and lifted the learning level for all concerned.

By Program V there were a host of participant "graduates," that is, former grade schoolers now in junior high school. They became an interested presence and helpful auxiliary force employed at various times and places. They served, for example, as slave hunters in the Underground Railroad game.

The major take-home communication for the ten weeks was *The Plymouth News,* a two-page mimeographed news sheet. This newspaper was assembled each week by an adult and teenage team. Each issue had suggestions for things families could do, such as visit a particular local museum or discuss "What will the future be like?"

In Plymouth, U. S. A. planners again tried to "hook-up" the historical focus with the existential life of participants. Moving to a new home, for example, *was* Anne Hutchinson's problem and *is* a real concern for people in our mobile society. Children's programing as well as the sermons in adult worship addressed such issues. Later, all ages could share feelings and experiences about moving, race relations, and so on.

As done in several previous programs, children were "inventoried" at the beginning and end of the program. By the inventories teachers sought to discover students' level of familiarity with the historical figures of religion in America. An evaluation by adults was also made.

VI. The Good News Times. In Program VI one goal was sought in dealing with the New Testament Gospels: "To re-present Jesus as a loving, interesting, and real person."

Question: Would the central character be Jesus?

Answer: No one volunteered to play the part!

How then could Jesus be presented without anyone ever seeing him? The solution found was "Dr. Luke." Luke the Evangelist could be the central figure. He would be the surrogate for Jesus. On Sunday morning Dr. Luke greeted the congregation in the sanctuary and introduced New Testament people who knew Jesus. In fellowship hall he led children on a New Testament times investigation into the life of Jesus. All Saints' Dr. Luke was created a la the portrayal of the Third Evangelist in Taylor Caldwell's *Dear and Glorious Physician.* In this program, however, Dr. Luke was also editor-in-chief of a newspaper called *The Good News Times.* Children met and interviewed persons who knew Jesus. They wrote stories, took photographs, and drew sketches of people and scenes from their morning experience. After the children in grades one through six had completed their newspaper drawings and stories, the "copy" was screened by junior- and senior-high youth. They made editorial selections of what to include in the next edition of the paper. The teenagers' selections were then turned over to adults who typed, retraced, and finalized the copy. The church office staff duplicated the papers on a multilith machine, and *The Good News Times* was sold the next Sunday morning by children. The youngsters "hawked" papers to adults entering the church and often found themselves engaged in conversations with their customers. It was a "mutually contributive" effort.[3]

The program planning committee worked hard in Program VI to involve people from multiple generations in the planning process as well as in the program presentations. Some grandparent-age members of the church sat in on the planning meetings, while junior- and senior-high youth, college students, young married, parents, and senior members were involved in other aspects of the program, especially in playing the roles of the New Testament characters. Moreover, the committee was conscious of the need to effect more "interactive sharing," such as the pre-service newspaper selling, or that between and among people in the pews, or that of having children explain their own individual "Good News According to _____ [name]" booklets to non-parent church members.

The newspaper theme prompted the committee to make mock-up newspapers on large posterboards. These were hung in the sanctuary. Each giant-sized newspaper carried a headline, e.g., "JESUS CALLS DISCIPLES," and had a symbol on it, such as boat. The mock-ups were painted by an octogenarian artist. In the sanctuary when Dr. Luke made his weekly presentations, he pointed to these huge newspapers and did a reinforcing review of learnings for both the children and adults. He also tried to preview what subsequent weeks would bring.

Reviewing and previewing (R & P) were done every week.

One of the amazing things which happened in Program VI was that the planning committee became male-dominated. At one planning session there were nine men and only three women present. Such is probably a plus for religious education which traditionally has been a female domain. The suspicion is that such heavy male investment also contributes significantly to intra-family sharing.

* * *

The two programs following the Good News Times continued the basic operational structure which had evolved through the years. The most notable thing regarding Programs VII (FP2C Holy Earth Log) and VIII (A. S. Barnum's Ethical Show on Earth) is the difficulty of the subject matters presented, namely, "world religions" and "ethics." Much greater attention had to be given to developmental differences among the people involved.

* * *

VII. ASC Holy Earth Log. Having completed six years of programing, questions arose in the planning committee: "Have we done a cycle which returns us to Point 0? Should we redo 'Universe Man'? Or 'Folk'?" The program planners decided *not* to go for a duplication. That with which the first committee began did not fit the current situation. Besides, the more veteran members reminded others, "Half the fun of doing these programs is in coming up with something new!"

It was agreed, however, to stick with the world cultures theme of Program I, but to focus specifically on "major religions of the world." "People" and "place" of each world religion would be secondary foci. Though learners were studying religions of the *earth,* an *outer-space* format was adopted to facilitate country- and continent-jumping in the study of religions.

The planning committee took suggestive clues from the year's pop-culture movie phenomenon, *Star Wars.* On the opening Sunday at All Saints, therefore, two space visitors, C-Ker-A and C-Ker-Z (obvious symbolic names), from Raftan Alp (that is, "far planet" spelled backward) showed up in the sanctuary along with their computer-droid, FP2C (a la *Star Wars'* R2D2). The space visitors and all earthlings, young and old, received instructions from Raftan Alp over a large intergalactic communicator placed in the chancel. Raften Alp's instructions were, for example: "YOU ARE TO INVESTIGATE THE RELIGION KNOWN AS 'SHINTO' IN THE LAND OF JAPAN AND

REPORT BACK YOUR FINDINGS." Slides of Japan were then shown on a communicator-scrim to introduce the religion, land, and people of Japan. The instructions and audio-visuals launched the children, as well as the clergy and congregation, into an exploration of Shintoism—or whatever was the religion of the day. The children's activities of the morning were recorded on a Super-8mm movie camera which an older teenage youth operated.

While the exploration was great fun for the children, it was the adults whose interest especially peaked in Program VII. Many began doing serious mid-week reading on world religions. Approximately eighty copies of Huston Smith's *Religions of Man* were sold through the church office. Adults were also curious about what was happening in the children's end of the building, often questioning the youngsters and members of the planning committee.

Another feature of the program which had not been incorporated in previous programs was a woman "central character." Space visitor C-Ker-Z was a female and effective. The committee also enlisted the talents of a young man who was wheel-chair bound by muscular dystrophy. With a specially built box-cover with bubble lights and space sounds he became FP2C, the computer-droid. Everyone loved him!

One effective device used to facilitate intergenerational sharing was the cryptogram. A symbol-scrambled coded message was given the younger children each week. As adults left the sanctuary they received a cipher for translating the symbols, e.g., *-a, #-b, etc. It was fun to watch tow head and bald head comparing notes in the coffee hour after church. Many a parent reported spending good chunks of time on Sunday afternoon trying to decode a message. The content of the message always was the central teaching objective of the day, for example: "Hinduism is the religion of the people of India in which Hindu believers place emphasis on the sacredness of all life."

FP2C Holy Earth Log was a program of depth and spunk.

VIII. A.S. Barnum's Ethical Show on Earth. "Ethical Issues" had been considered in years past as a possible program focus. To "teach morals" or "raise ethical concerns," though, is not an easily programed endeavor. Moreover, children, youth, and adults are at such different stages of moral reasoning that an intergenerational program would be especially difficult to do well. Still, personal and social moral decisions are crucially related to religious faith and are often neglected in church school curricula—for the very reasons given. So, in spite of all misgivings, it was decided to take on the heretofore avoided: "Ethical Issues."

What was needed for this program was a lively vehicle in which to carry serious moral questions. But what? In a Lenten intergenerational worship service that previous winter, clown ministry was used effectively. Clowns could also be used to present ethical issues—clowns in a *circus* format! In many ways the circus is a microcosm of the world and its moral dilemmas. The whole cast of silent *and* speaking circus performers—including animals—could be used to dramatize selected ethical issues. Under the Big Top a juggler, for example, could help people focus on how to handle competing relations between and among family, friends, and self. Thus, the "A. S. (All Saints) Barnum's Ethical Show on Earth" was conceived.

In opening up moral issues the planning committee wanted to avoid making the sessions moralize. Instead the ideal was to focus on live ethical concerns over which people (young and old) have conflicts and have to make decisions. By polarizing options in selected moral issues and by revealing the various value conflicts in them, each individual might be helped to come up with decisions which were more or less appropriate to his or her own ethical situation.

On one Sunday in the Circus' "Center Ring," high-school youth dramatized stereotypic male/female roles, e.g., ironing clothes and playing ice hockey. In the midst of the play-action the dramatization was stopped, frozen, and the children in the grandstands were asked to decide "Could/Should boys/girls do such things too?" Then and there with large flash cards the children voted "YES" or "NO" on the question of male/female roles. They practiced deciding. That was for the children. In the sanctuary adults were exposed to the same moral issue in a sermon this particular Sunday on "Androgynous and Sex-Specific Living."

Three things were done or happened which facilitated interage sharing. One of the things was to regularly and verbally inform adults in the sanctuary what children were doing in fellowship hall. Informed parents could later reflect and interact better on the issues with their children. Another, and one of the brightest aspects of Program VIII, was the heavy investment which a large number of teenagers made in the program. They were planners, actors, group leaders, and participants. If, in fact, they generally represented a stage of moral reasoning which was *above* the stage level where most of the younger children were, then they likely were modeling advanced moral reasoning for the others. Yet a third good feature of the program was that of the "A. S. Barnum's Intergenerational Marching Band (and Kazoo Society)." This instrumentalist group was composed of persons from age seven to seventy who practiced and played the theme song every week. It was a new and valuable way for ages to come together.

* * *

The last program of which I was a part of the planning committee was Number IX, called "The Music Machine." As the reader will discover, it has some special features too, while still operating within the parameters of the basic IGRE model that had evolved over the previous eight years. (Details on programs of subsequent years are not reported, but I observed them to be of continued creativity and significance.)

* * *

IX. *The Music Machine.* The positive experience with the music portion of the A. S. Barnum program promoted an interest among planning committee members in a full musical emphasis in the next season. In looking around for an organizing idea, the planners heard about and then focused upon a curriculum called "The Music Machine." It was adopted hesitantly and adapted forthrightly to the All Saints Church situation. People came to endorse it enthusiastically, as it proved to be singularly effective in getting children and adults singing together. The songs were about "Love," "Joy," "Goodness," and so on— the "Fruit of the Spirit," spoken of by St. Paul in Galatians 5:22, which became the overall text for the program. The songs for each biblical fruit came in a song book that was a part of a total curriculum resource packet. Also included was a ten-week course guide with sample materials, the script to a musical play, an LP record, and paraphernalia such as buttons, decals, and more for use in the program. An adult choir member and two college students carried the dramatic and vocal music portions of the program as "Mr. Conductor," "Stevie," and "Nancy." The visual center of the program was a huge, bright, gadgeted, mobile "Music Machine" which an intergenerational task force built. During the Sunday service Mr. Conductor would put a real fruit into a receptacle on the machine. This caused it to whir and puff, and then from another opening a large card came out with a word on it, such as FAITH or PATIENCE. On the back of the word card was a musical score with lyrics, which one or more of the central characters sang. After the singing, the Music Machine whistled and smoked, signaling time for children and youth to leave the sanctuary. All sang the program theme song as the Music Machine rolled itself down the center aisle and led the procession to Agapeland.

The minister's sermon was on the theme word for the day.

Two things were done consistently every Sunday to facilitate intergenerational exchange. One was simply to have people of all ages introduce themselves one to another in the sanctuary *and* informally communicate something of their lives or opinions on a subject-related topic. The liturgist suggested, for example, "Share with one another something which is especially 'peace-full' to you." The other self-conscious IGRE moment was at the end of the hour. Adults were invited to the fellowship hall for a closing event with the children. There might be a Gentleness backrub exchange, a combined message-writing effort for the Joy balloon lift, or a round dance which all did together.

To get in touch with the "Spirit-Within," both the children's program and the adult worship service incorporated quiet meditative time. Adults had opportunity each Sunday for ten minutes of silent centering prayer. With the children, closed-eye fantasy trips and body relaxation exercises were used effectively. That such quiet times could be created was a pleasant surprise for many.

All people, young and old, received something of the "Spirit" from the *en-thusiasm* of singing, generally, and from the musical production of "The Music Machine" on the final Sunday, specifically.

* * *

Intergenerational Ripples in the Whole Church

In reading this program-by-program account perhaps the reader has a greater understanding of *one* significant intergenerational program model as well as this writer's and All Saints Church's process of discovery and growth in intergenerational education. There was, necessarily, a good deal of trial and error in the efforts, and the journey in some ways was "a practice in search of theory." Coming into intergenerational programing by the back door, it took planners a while to realize what they had done and how valuable it was.

At the end of each program I usually wrote up a summary report on what had occurred for the planning committee.[4] The initial write-ups only described what was attempted. The writing, however, fostered basic reflection on the theory and practice which the program embodied. Specifically, the reflection came to focus on the concept of "intergenerational religious education"—a fourteen syllable construct of which few, if any people at All Saints, had even heard.

The reports on the program eventually ended up in a composite paper which I presented at a meeting of the Association of Professors and Researchers in Religious Education.[5] Prior and subsequent to that paper, examination of other intergenerational education efforts in other churches and synagogues began, as well as an ongoing review of the literature in the field. All this enacting, reading, conversing, reflecting, and writing enabled me, as well as other members of the church, to help other area churches into IGRE programing. This was done through individual consultation, workshops, seminars, camps, and one-shot IGRE events. In effect, the experimental programs proved to be the teaching/learning experience which facilitated the ability to share with others.

The heaviest overall impact of the intergenerational programs, however, was registered in the life of All Saints Church itself. The IGRE programs had a ripple effect on the whole church. One outcome of designing and implementing IGRE curricula, for example, was to train a cadre of church members who were experienced, skilled, and sensitive in intergenerational activities. Intentional and now near-instinctive intergenerational programing characterizes the presence of these folk in different sectors of the church's life.

Worship is one of those influenced sectors. All Saints used to conduct special "Innovative," then called "Family," worship services four or five times a year. No little agony was spent in years past by the clergy and worship committee leaders in figuring out what to do in these services. Having adults/youth/children together in worship for an hour is *not* easy to plan for! Organizing such services is still a struggle, but after the IGRE programs there were people more self-assured in handling informal, experimental, and multi-aged worship. The services began to be designated as "Intergenerational." Invariably they are a combination of worship, education, and fellowship for everyone. People come expecting a relevant-for-all occasion. Usually they get it. Customarily the special intergenerational services are held in the fellowship hall, while at the same hour there is "formal worship" in the sanctuary. Typically there are 200 to 250 people present. When only one service for all people is offered on a Sunday morning—and that service intergenerational—there may be 500 or more people in attendance in the sanctuary. The congregation enjoys the all-ages-together occasions, even as they still value traditional adult-oriented worship. The experience of planning specific intergenerational worship occasions has made the clergy and lay leaders generally more aware of the dynamic variety of people and ages in all services. All Saints people are now simply more age-inclusive in all service planning and worshiping.

The growing sensitivity to age-inclusiveness is reflected in an adopted major Sunday morning format change. There are now two worship services on Sunday morning. One is at 9:30 and the other at 11:00. Before there had been only one. The earlier service begins as the IGRE special programs start, with all ages together in the sanctuary to pray, sing, and learn together. Then those children, youth, *and* adults wishing to attend regular classes are dismissed to do so. All ages are again together in the between-services coffee and punch hour, which is always enjoyably jam-packed. While the 11:00 service is being conducted, there may be an intergenerational class or experience, a music program which combines several grades, a "hot topic" forum open to all (sometimes two of these), a basic Bible class, and/or other special "do" going on elsewhere in the building.

Overall, in the expanded two-service format, attendance of adults at worship went up a documented 12 percent. The percentage of increased participation for children and youth in worship is, of course, 100 percent. Many young people now stay for the entire first worship service. Their staying does not adversely affect the numbers of children attending regular church school classes. Wonder of wonders, some youth who left the first service for a class have been spotted returning to attend the second service! Adult participation in Sunday morning educational offerings has gone up two and three times over years previous. Generally speaking, more people are staying longer on Sunday morning and doing more together than ever before.

Since the 1960s All Saints has had an annual "Family" Camp in July. It involves a week at a denominational retreat center. The number of people attending is usually 150 to 200. The camp has always been intergenerational in age composition, though not always in programing. For the last ten-plus years, however, the Camp's Co-Directors have been intergenerationally self-conscious in their design of activities. Their sensitivity is due in part to the fact that several have served on planning committees of the IGRE special programs. And too, they have been made aware of intergenerational possibilities through ongoing events in the church. The camp committee has more and more programed athletic events, crafts, chapel services, meal time, talent shows, Bible study, cabin activities, and so forth, to be intergenerational. They also have been aware that many families are *not* "momma, poppa, 1.8 kids, a dog and a cat who hang out around a microwave." There are single-parent families, single adults (never married, divorced, widowed), empty-nest couples, and every other description of "family" who belong to the church. They, too, could and should be a part of the congregation's special week together. Wanting them to feel welcome to come, All Saints now designates the six days together as "All-Church Camp."

Out of the good experiences of the all-church summer camp came a call for a wintertime intergenerational event. So was born the February "All-Church Cross Country Ski Weekend." During this weekend there is mixed-age skiing and instruction for skiing. Ability or lack thereof determines the mixing. In addition to IG cross-country skiing, there is square dancing, singing, fireside "s'mores," games, and worship which people of all ages do together. This multi-aged event seems to pull in more single persons and older couples than the summer camp. Most recently it was attended by over 250 persons—all that the camp facility could take. One Sunday morning communion service had a "Generations Tree" on which worshipers hung nametags for deceased, absent, present, *and* future family members. In multigenerational groups, participants shared who their nametagged persons were.

Intergenerational rippling has occurred at still other places in the congregation's life. Certainly the September-to-May Sunday morning church school program has been affected. Much more effort, for example, is expended to involve parents in the learning with their children. "S. T. P." (Student/Teacher/Parent) Breakfasts are held once or twice a year to facilitate sharing. Special adult-child Saturday workshops are held periodically where several ages "do" things together. Near Christmas, for example, there is a decoration-making afternoon. In the graded church school classes, teachers instruct their pupils in making gifts for older people and supervise a personal delivering of the same. The youth plan one or two events which involve them in discussing a topic or doing an activity with their parents. There are special IGRE classes which meet regularly for four or five weeks at a time. In general, there is a permeation of awareness to be more interage-interactive in the formal educational life of the church.

A church-night supper, a special Seder/Passover meal, an after-worship potluck dinner, and even part of the church's Annual Meeting have become intergenerational by design in recent years.

Then too, the working committees of the church are more broadly representative of the wide spectrum of *adult* members (age twenty to ninety) in the church. The Nominating Committee has become sensitized on this score. Occasionally youth will serve for a term on church committees. These church groups likewise come up with programs and projects that are intentionally age-inclusive. Examples of such are the Outreach or Mission Committee's inner-city house painting project and its sponsorship of a refugee family, the Music Committee's "Collected Choirs" program, the Business Committee's church "Building and Grounds Workday," the Parish Life Committee's "Extended Family— Adopt a Grandparent" program, the Visual Arts Committee's "Intergenerational Art Show," and the Dramatic Arts Committee's IG production of "Godspell."

Adult fellowship groups of the church, while still fulfilling basic peer-oriented social and educational needs, do periodic age-inclusive programs too. The older adults group did an IG talent show. The young marrieds group conducted a family tenting weekend. The singles group regularly has children-included functions. And so on.

In summary, the nine IGRE programs significantly influenced All Saints Church in many ways and times beyond an annual ten weeks in June and July. The first-year experiment in joint education for grade-school children led to intergenerational deepening which, in turn, brought about significant interage developments in worship, camping, fellowship, outreach, education, and other areas in the whole life of the church.

All Saints has not yet attained any "highest stage" in inclusive being together. Nevertheless, the church is in a satisfying progression. Along the way clergy and planners have sometimes tried to do more than was possible. Reach exceeded grasp. Sometimes they did not know what to do or how to do it, and so they did nothing. Sometimes they made mistakes and took backward steps.

And yet . . . and yet . . . All Saints has had, in effect, a significant *breakthrough in religious education!* Intergenerational life movements have made its members a much better, stronger, *more inclusive community.* All Saints is a people becoming more responsive to the problems of their times, the needs of community, and to one another.

The things which have been learned can be shared. The hope is that others may benefit from knowing the church's story and that from reading these reflections others will go on to teach, learn, and live more effectively in their own situations with the people of God, of all ages, together.

Notes

1. "All Saints" is not, of course, the actual name of the church, but the programs and developments described are authentic.
2. If people were to "redo" this program, no doubt the title would be changed to "Universe *Folk.*" In the intervening years there has been some growth in sensitivity to sexist language!
3. Detail from one of these Sundays was given in the "Pretend" exercise of chapter 12, the last section.
4. Several of these reports have been reprinted in the *New Forms Exchange* by the Christian Education Division, Board of Homeland Ministries, United Church of Christ.
5. James W. White, "Interage/Intergenerational Education: A Six Summer's Case Study." Paper delivered at the annual meeting of the Association of Professors and Researchers in Religious Education, St. Louis, Mo., November 20, 1977.

Index of Names

(Names shown below are primarily those of persons explicitly quoted in the text, on the page shown. Their references and hundreds of other names and sources not here listed will be found in the endnotes of the chapters.)

Abernethy, 50
Ackerman, 97
Alper, 247
Alves, 183
Aries, 6
Aristotle, 125, 173
Atkinson, 4
Augustine, 76, 133
A-V Resources, 65n.

Basil, 76
Bateson, 102
Beissert, 34
Bengston/Black, 137
Benson/Hilyard, 35
Berryman, 129n.
Berger, 160
Bergman, 245
Bissell, 42
Blake, 9
Block, 148, 225
Bloom, 142
Boulding, 168
Breck, 208
Brown, 144
Brueggemann, 70
Brunner, 115, 144-145, 198
Buber, 93-94, 117, 125ff.
Burns, 87
Bushnell, 131-133

Calhoun, 173
Call, 162
Carroll, 234
Cobb, 86
Coe, 133-134
Colson/Rigdon, 191, 221
Cronon, 83
Cully, 191, 194, 202, 216
Cutler, 13

Dahlin, 17n.
Davidson/Monk/Johnson, 234
Dee, 16n.
Dix, 149
Dotts, 219
Dressel, 192
Duvall, 4
Dykstra, 162

Elkind, 107, 109
Elkins, 59n.
Erikson, 94-97, 105, 125ff.
Eutychus, 69

Fairchild, 156n.
Foster, 19, 32n., 213n., 220
Fowler, J. R., 97
Fowler, J. W., 105, 115-120, 125ff.
Francis of Assisi, 77
Freud, 94-95, 105, 125ff., 182

Index of Subjects